Whitehall Paper 82

Securing Sierra Leone, 1997–2013

Defence, Diplomacy and Development in Action

Peter Albrecht and Paul Jackson

www.rusi.org

Royal United Services Institute for Defence and Security Studies

Securing Sierra Leone, 1997–2013: Defence, Diplomacy and Development in Action
Peter Albrecht and Paul Jackson
First published 2014

Whitehall Papers series

Series Editor: Professor Malcolm Chalmers
Editors: Adrian Johnson, Ashlee Godwin and Cathy Haenlein

RUSI is a Registered Charity (No. 210639)
ISBN 978-1-138-89229-3

Published on behalf of the Royal United Services Institute for Defence and Security Studies
by
Routledge Journals, an imprint of Taylor & Francis, 4 Park Square, Milton Park, Abingdon OX14 4RN

SUBSCRIPTIONS
Please send subscription orders to:

USA/Canada: Taylor & Francis Inc., Journals Department, 530 Walnut Street, Suite 850, Philadelphia, PA 19106, USA

UK/Rest of World: Routledge Journals, T&F Customer Services, T&F Informa UK Ltd, Sheepen Place, Colchester, Essex CO3 3LP, UK

Contents

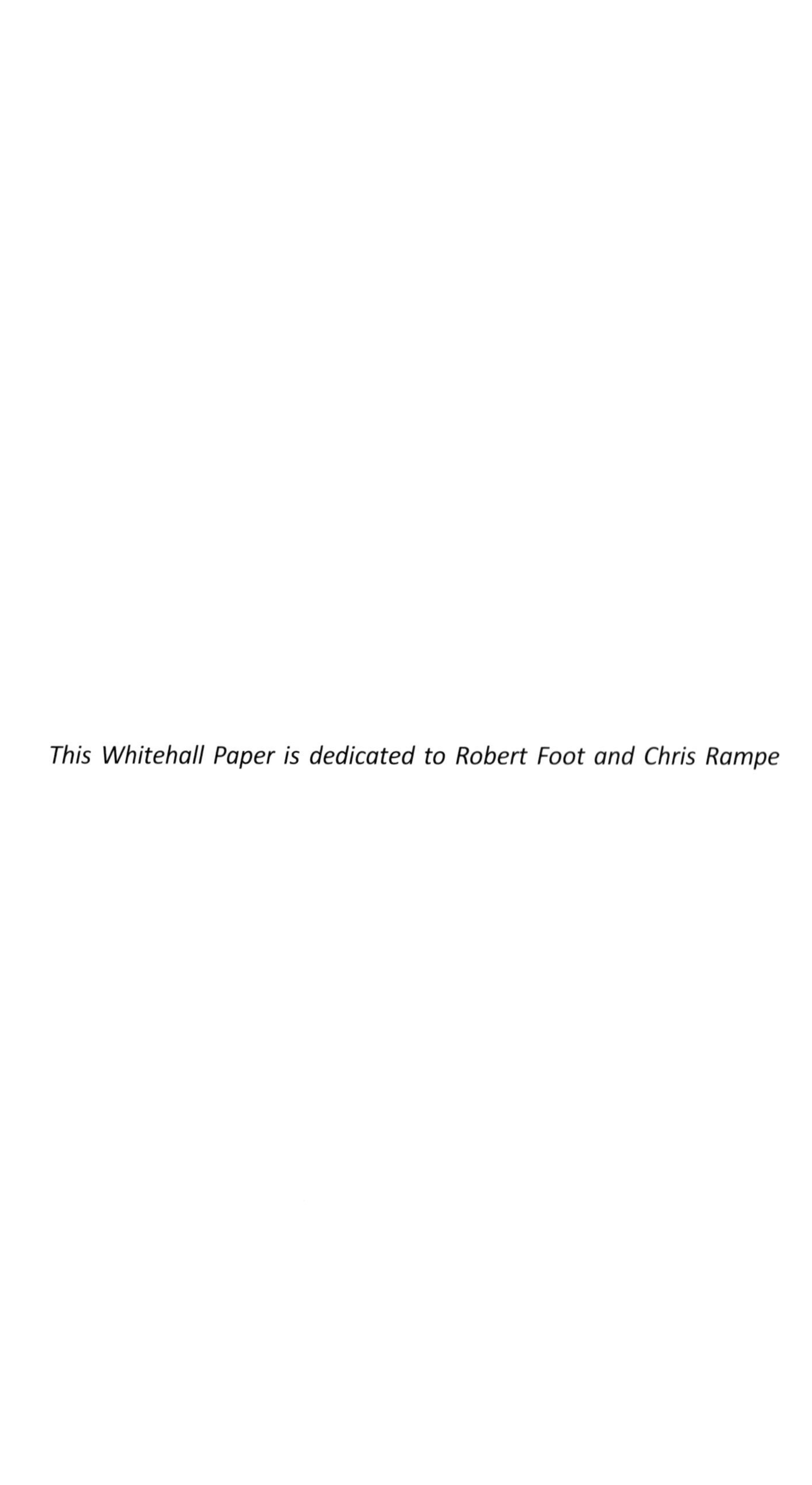

This Whitehall Paper is dedicated to Robert Foot and Chris Rampe

About the Authors

Peter Albrecht is a Security-Sector Development Adviser with the UN in Somalia, seconded by the Danish government from the Danish Institute for International Studies (DIIS), where he is a Senior Analyst. He holds a PhD from Copenhagen Business School (CBS), an MSc from the London School of Economics and Political Science (LSE), and an MA research degree from Aarhus University. Peter has co-authored *Reconstructing Security after Conflict: Security Sector Reform in Sierra Leone* (Palgrave Macmillan, 2011) and co-edited *Policing and the Politics of Order-Making* (Routledge, 2015).

Paul Jackson is Professor of African Politics at the University of Birmingham. He was formerly the Head of the university's School of Government and Society, and Director of both the International Development Department (University of Birmingham) and the Global Facilitation Network for Security Sector Reform (Institute of Development Studies). Paul has worked within the fields of politics and security for several governments, the UN, the EU and the World Bank. He has sat on the Advisory Board of the Geneva Centre for the Democratic Control of Armed Forces, and is a current member of the Folke Bernadotte Institute working group on security-sector reform. He has published extensively on security and development issues.

Acknowledgements

This study is the result of extensive research in Sierra Leone and the UK, and builds on the two authors' practical involvement in the reform process underway in the former. Such a piece always relies on a network of people to bring it to fruition and this study is no exception. First, we would like to thank RUSI – and Malcolm Chalmers, Adrian Johnson and Emma De Angelis in particular – for their encouragement and valuable comments on earlier versions of the study. We would also like to thank Lisa Denney and Erwin van Veen for their detailed observations, and the Danish Institute of International Studies (DIIS) for its support while research for this Whitehall Paper was undertaken.

The authors are both extremely grateful to several key people who over the years have willingly given their time and expertise to this research, sharing their experience of working within or in support of Sierra Leone's security-sector reform process. We would especially like to thank: Mustapha Abdullah; Natasha Aggett; Robert Ashington-Pickett; Jeremy Astill-Brown; Keith Biddle; Piet Biesheuvel; Hugh Blackman; Julian Bower; Iain Cholerton; Emmanuel Coker; Guy Collings; Alfred Paolo Conteh; Kellie Conteh; Olayinka Creighton-Randall; Chris Charley; Andrew Cordery; Mohammed Brima Daboh; Derek Deighton; Mustapha M K Dumbuya; Phil Evans; Aldo Gaeta; Olushegu Garber; Ade Gibson; Ian Hughes; Christopher John; Brima Acha Kamara; Chris Gabelle; Lucy Hayes; Craig Henderson; Anthony Howlett-Bolton; Ansumana Idriss; Mustapha Kamara; S P Kamara; Francis Keilie; Thomas Lahai; Martin Lavahun; Kelvin Lewis; John Magbity; Richard Moigbe; Francis Alieu Munu; Patrick O'Byrne; John Vandy Rogers; Julius Sandy; Eric Scheye; Brima Sesay; Sam Seward; Simeon Nashiru Sheriff; Victor Andrew Sorie; Christian Stolz; Ben Tomkins; Elizabeth Turay; Sophy Thomas; Mark White; and Richard Woodward.

For this specific study, we would like to thank Jamie Martin, Brian Jones and Joe Edkins in particular for their substantial and practical support, and not least for helping to secure funding for the project.

Special thanks go to Ashlee Godwin and Cathy Haenlein for their substantial editorial support on this Whitehall Paper, which has made it a better and more accurate read.

Finally, this project would not have been possible without the support of the UK government and the Government of Sierra Leone. We are grateful to both for allowing us to learn from fifteen years of security-sector reform in Sierra Leone.

Ultimate responsibility for the content of this study lies with the authors, who have added interpretation to the many reports, interviews and meetings held as the project progressed.

Acronyms and Abbreviations

ACOTA	African Contingency Operations Training and Assistance, US State Department
ACPP	Africa Conflict Prevention Pool
AFRC	Armed Forces Revolutionary Council
AMISOM	African Union Mission in Somalia
APC	All People's Congress
ASJP	Access to Security and Justice Programme
AU	African Union
BAST	Brigade Advisory and Support Team
BMATT	British Military Advisory and Training Team
CCSSP	Commonwealth Community Safety and Security Project
CDF	Civil Defence Forces
CGRP	Chiefdom Governance Reform Programme
CHISEC	Chiefdom Security Committee
CISU	Central Intelligence and Security Unit
CPDTF	Commonwealth Police Development Task Force
CSD	Corporate Services Department
CSSF	Conflict, Stability and Security Fund
DAC	Development Assistance Committee
DAI	Development Alternatives, Inc.
DfID	Department for International Development
DISEC	District Security Committee
ECOMOG	Economic Community of West African States Monitoring Group
ECOWAS	Economic Community of West African States
EO	Executive Outcomes
ESF	ECOWAS Standby Force
FISU	Force Intelligence and Security Unit
IDPs	Internally displaced persons
IGP	Inspector-General of Police
IIS	Internal Intelligence Service
IMATT	International Military Advisory and Training Team
IMF	International Monetary Fund
ISAT	International Security Advisory Team
ISU	Internal Security Unit
JDITF	Joint Drug Interdiction Task Force
JFC	Joint Force Command
JIC	Joint Intelligence Committee
JSC	Joint Support Command
JSCO	Justice Sector Coordination Office
JSDP	Justice Sector Development Programme
JSRSIP	Justice Sector Reform Strategy and Investment Plan

LNP	Local Needs Policing
LPPB	Local Policing Partnership Board
LUC	Local unit commander
MACP	Military Aid to the Civil Power
MIA	Ministry of Internal Affairs
MODAT	Ministry of Defence Advisory Team
MoU	Memorandum of Understanding
NEC	National Electoral Commission
NGO	Non-governmental organisation
NPFL	National Patriotic Front of Liberia
NPRC	National Provisional Ruling Council
NSC	National Security Council
NSCCG	National Security Council Coordinating Group
ODA	Official Development Assistance
OECD	Organisation for Economic Co-operation and Development
ONS	Office of National Security
OSD	Operational Support Division
PCRU	Post-Conflict Reconstruction Unit
PMDC	People's Movement for Democratic Change
PROSEC	Provincial Security Committee
PRSP	Poverty Reduction Strategy Paper
PSO	Peace support operation
RSLAF	Republic of Sierra Leone Armed Forces
RUF	Revolutionary United Front
SDSR	Strategic Defence and Security Review
SILSEP	Sierra Leone Security Sector Reform Programme
SLA	Sierra Leone Army
SLPP	Sierra Leone People's Party
SSD	Special Security Division
SSR	Security-sector reform
SSR-IP	Security Sector Review Implementation Plan
TOCU	Transnational Organised Crime Unit
UK	United Kingdom
UN	United Nations
UNAMID	African Union/United Nations Hybrid Operation in Darfur
UNAMSIL	United Nations Mission in Sierra Leone
UNDP	United Nations Development Programme
UNIOSIL	United Nations Integrated Office in Sierra Leone
UNIPSIL	United Nations Integrated Peacebuilding Office in Sierra Leone
UNODC	United Nations Office on Drugs and Crime
UNOMSIL	United Nations Observer Mission in Sierra Leone
US	United States
USAID	United States Agency for International Development

Timeline of Security-Sector Reform in Sierra Leone, 1997–2013

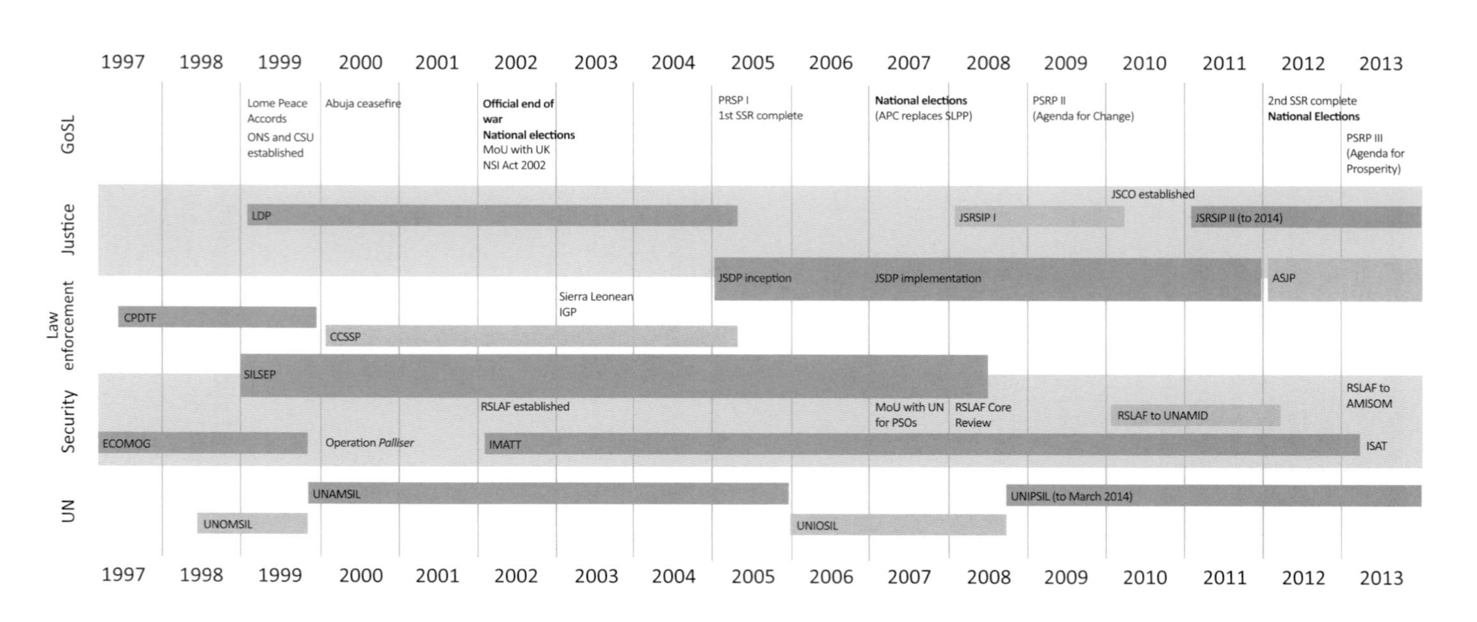

I. INTRODUCTION

The UK's contribution to the post-war reconstruction of Sierra Leone since the late 1990s has been widely held up as an example of successful stabilisation and state-building, particularly in relation to the country's security and justice institutions.[1] Sierra Leone's civil war began in 1991 when the Revolutionary United Front (RUF), led by Foday Sankoh, initiated a campaign of violence along the border with Liberia. The RUF's stated aim was to end state corruption, but in reality this cause intertwined with a desire to assume control over resources, particularly in the diamond-rich areas in the eastern part of the country. The decade of conflict that followed accelerated a breakdown of state institutions that had been fundamentally weakened by the pre-war one-party regime of the All People's Congress (APC) and its leader Siaka Stevens (1968–85).

From the late 1990s, at the request of then-President Ahmad Tejan Kabbah, the UK came to play a central role in stabilising Sierra Leone as well as in the state-building process that was initiated before the conflict officially came to an end in 2002. That same year, the UK government signed a ten-year agreement, pledging £40 million a year for its duration in support of re-establishing peace and stability.[2] At the time, the allocation

[1] The two authors of this Whitehall Paper have contributed to this narrative through a number of publications that blur the line between policy-making and academia; for instance, Peter Albrecht and Paul Jackson, *Security System Transformation in Sierra Leone, 1997–2007* (Birmingham and London: Global Facilitation Network for Security Sector Reform and International Alert, 2009); Paul Jackson and Peter Albrecht, *Reconstructing Security After Conflict: Security Sector Reform in Sierra Leone* (London: Palgrave Macmillan, 2011). For an exploration of how this research has impacted on security-sector reform in Sierra Leone, see Andrea Edoardo Varisco, 'The Influence of Research and Local Knowledge on British-Led Security Sector Reform Policy in Sierra Leone', *Conflict, Security and Development* (Vol. 14, No. 1, 2014), pp. 89–123.

[2] This agreement provided for 'a substantial direct development programme to Sierra Leone over the next ten years' that would incorporate 'a total of at least £120 million of assistance over the next three years.' See HM Government and Government of Sierra Leone, 'Poverty Reduction Framework Arrangement between the Government of the United Kingdom of Great Britain and Northern

was the UK's largest in the world per capita of recipient population. This Whitehall Paper examines how the process of state-building through security-sector reform (SSR) developed in Sierra Leone and the impact of this experience on international conceptualisations of SSR, as well as on international interventions more broadly. The basis of this examination is a detailed analysis of UK engagement in Sierra Leone between 1997 and 2013 to re-establish and support the continued development of security and justice institutions.

International organisations such as the UN played a vital role in supporting Sierra Leone's peace-building process from the late 1990s.[3] However, fundamental to ending the conflict in the country – and to stabilising it in the longer term – was the unilateral decision by the UK to intervene militarily in support of the central government in 2000, and to support the establishment of intelligence and national security agencies, and defence, police and justice institutions. The overarching rationale for these endeavours was that security was a precondition for development, and this was buttressed by what was, at the time, an unusual willingness within the UK's Department for International Development (DfID) to invest in national security programming.[4] Thus, while UK support to Sierra Leone was certainly shaped by undeniably strong ties between the two, first established during the colonial era, it was also shaped by political will in London, especially in the late 1990s, to align and give equal weight to diplomatic, defence and development instruments.[5] This was to prove a

Ireland and the Government of the Republic of Sierra Leone', 2002, section 3.2, <http://siteresources.worldbank.org/SIERRALEONEEXTN/Resources/povertyframework.pdf>, accessed 28 September 2014; Albrecht and Jackson, *Security System Transformation in Sierra Leone*, p. 159. This number covers a broad range of activities, including security-sector reform, governance reform, decentralisation and so forth. It excludes military support through the International Military Advisory and Training Team (IMATT), which in 2005–08, for example, cost approximately £10 million per year.

[3] Mark Malan, Phenyo Rakate and Angela McIntyre, *Peacekeeping in Sierra Leone: UNAMSIL Hits the Home Straight* (Pretoria: Institute for Security Studies, 2002); Funmi Olonisakin, *Peacekeeping in Sierra Leone: The Story of UNAMSIL* (Boulder, CO: Lynne Rienner, 2008).

[4] Robert Egnell and Peter Haldén, 'Laudable, Ahistorical and Overambitious: Security Sector Reform Meets State Formation Theory', *Conflict, Security and Development* (Vol. 9, No. 1, 2009), pp. 27–54; Mark Sedra, 'Introduction: The Future of Security Sector Reform', in Mark Sedra (ed.), *The Future of Security Sector Reform* (Ottawa: Centre for International Governance Innovation, 2010), pp. 16–27; Erlend Grøner Krogstad, 'Security, Development and Force: Revisiting Police Reform in Sierra Leone', *African Affairs* (Vol. 111, No. 443, 2012), pp. 261–80.

[5] Albrecht and Jackson, *Security System Transformation in Sierra Leone*, p. 81; Peter Albrecht, Finn Stepputat and Louise Andersen, 'Security Sector Reform, the European Way', in Sedra (ed.), *The Future of Security Sector Reform*, pp. 74–87, 80–81.

unique period of international intervention that dominated the immediate post-Cold War era, and which came to an abrupt end with the September 2011 terrorist attacks on the US. The interventions in Afghanistan and Iraq that followed were largely driven by military imperatives,[6] and as such disrupted the pattern of applying diplomatic, defence and development instruments on an equal footing.[7]

The analysis within this Whitehall Paper shows why the UK intervention in Sierra Leone has been a relative success. However, it also provides the empirical basis for questioning the sustainability of state-building efforts that are driven by concepts of the liberal state, a form of political organisation that did not exist in Sierra Leone before the conflict.[8] Key challenges remain, not least in the combination of a particular vision of what a state should look like and unrealistic expectations of progress driven by the planning imperatives of international development agencies.[9] The strong focus on rebuilding internal and external security providers – at the expense of other sectors such as justice – may therefore prove to be both the greatest strength and, in the longer term, a considerable weakness of SSR in Sierra Leone. There is no doubt that the process has contributed to a stable country. However, there is also an evident danger that the institutions established through SSR may be exploited by the country's leaders for their own benefit. In this light, the rebuilding of Sierra Leone since the turn of the century has highlighted a number of dilemmas regarding international interventions,

---

[6] Jake Sherman, 'The "Global War on Terrorism" and its Implications for Security Sector Reform', in Sedra (ed.), *The Future of Security Sector Reform*, pp. 59–73; Peter Albrecht and Finn Stepputat, 'The Rise and Fall of Security Sector Reform in Development', in Paul Jackson (ed.), *Handbook of International Security and Development* (Cheltenham: Edward Elgar Publishing, 2015).

[7] Albrecht and Jackson, *Security System Transformation in Sierra Leone*, p. 81. See also Clare Short, 'A Humanitarian Surge and its Demise, 1997 to 2003: A Personal Account', *Peacebuilding* (Vol. 1, No. 1, 2013), pp. 33–37; Mark White, 'The Security-Development Nexus in Sierra Leone', in Peter Albrecht and Paul Jackson (eds), *Security Sector Reform in Sierra Leone 1997–2007: Views from the Front Line* (Zurich: Geneva Centre for the Democratic Control of Armed Forces and LIT Verlag, 2010), pp. 73–94.

[8] Louise Riis Andersen, 'The Liberal Dilemmas of a People-Centred Approach to State-Building', *Conflict, Security and Development* (Vol. 12, No. 2, 2012), pp. 103–21; Francis Fukuyama, *Statebuilding: Governance and World Order in the 21st Century* (New York, NY: Cornell University Press, 2004). For Sierra Leone, see Peter Albrecht and Paul Jackson, 'State-Building through Security Sector Reform: The UK Intervention in Sierra Leone', *Peacebuilding* (Vol. 2, No. 1, 2014), pp. 83–99.

[9] Lisa Denney, *Justice and Security Reform: Development Agencies and Informal Institutions in Sierra Leone* (Oxford and New York, NY: Routledge, 2014).

state-building and the management of international support in post-conflict environments.

Although this study begins in the late 1990s, particular emphasis is placed on the years after 2007 – the year in which the Sierra Leone People's Party (SLPP) lost the national election to the APC. This was the first peaceful change of government in Sierra Leone since the war ended in 2002. As such, the 2007 election provides important insights into the sustainability of those institutions and processes that had been put in place during the decade of state-building efforts that had passed by that point. From the perspective of the APC and the current president of Sierra Leone, Ernest Bai Koroma, the security and justice system had been rebuilt by the opposition, invoking immediate distrust by some within the new government. More positively, it was also the case that when Koroma took over from former SLPP President Kabbah, it was during a considerably more stable period in which the priority was no longer stabilisation and regaining control of the security sector, but economic development. It is in this context that this Whitehall Paper analyses how the period of political transition since the 2007 election has affected Sierra Leone's security and justice system. Inevitably, because of the UK government's involvement in the process, this will also be a study of changing donor priorities, as well as the effects of this on long-running programming and, by extension, on the Sierra Leonean institutions that benefited from support.

The remainder of this introductory chapter briefly sets out the history of Sierra Leone between 1961, when it gained independence, and the late 1990s. It outlines the fundamental breakdown that the country experienced in this period, which was arguably rooted in the structures of governance established by the post-colonial state. Second, it presents the role of the UK in stabilising Sierra Leone in 2000 – the basis on which state-building through SSR moved forward. Third, it explores the impact of the experience gained in Sierra Leone on international definitions of SSR. The UK was central to both, which in turn facilitated the synergy between state-building efforts in Sierra Leone and international policy debates. Finally, the chapter outlines the focus of forthcoming chapters and the main programmes and political dynamics that have characterised the different phases of SSR in Sierra Leone from the late 1990s until the early 2010s.

Politics and Conflict in Sierra Leone

A detailed analysis of the history of conflict in Sierra Leone is beyond the scope of this Whitehall Paper and there are several comprehensive accounts available.[10] However, a brief presentation of Sierra Leone's recent history is required to understand the basis on which stabilisation, state-building and SSR were taken forward. The historical context necessarily influences the direction of future post-conflict reforms, and understanding this conflict may also explain why some post-conflict actions can be perceived as the reconstruction of institutions that contributed to the initial fighting in the early 1990s.

One of the most important elements to consider is the nature of the Sierra Leonean state as it developed in the post-colonial period into a centralised dictatorship that eventually experienced bureaucratic collapse. Before and in the years after Sierra Leone gained its independence from the UK in 1961, the country's political system was centralised and focused on Freetown, with the rest of the country being subject to different governance structures as a legacy of indirect rule.[11] This dualism was reinforced by a continuation of the colonial bifurcation between a Western legal system in Freetown and a form of legal system in the countryside based on a network of district officers and traditional leaders (paramount and section chiefs).[12]

Following the end of the Margai era in 1967, during which time Milton Margai and his brother Albert both ruled as prime minister, the mayor of Freetown, Siaka Stevens, became prime minister. After a period of attempted military coups, Stevens assumed full presidential powers in 1971, which he held until he retired in 1985 and his nominated successor,

---

[10] See Ibraham Abullah, 'Bush Path to Destruction: The Origin and Character of the Revolutionary United Front/Sierra Leone', *Journal of Modern African Studies* (Vol. 36, No. 2, 1998), pp. 203–35; Lansana Gberie, *A Dirty War in West Africa: The RUF and the Destruction of Sierra Leone* (Bloomington, IN: Indiana University Press, 2005); David Harris, *Sierra Leone: A Political History* (Oxford: Oxford University Press, 2014); David Keen, *Conflict and Collusion in Sierra Leone* (Oxford: James Currey, 2005); Krijn Peters and Paul Richards, '"Why We Fight": Voices of Youth Combatants in Sierra Leone', *Africa: Journal of the International African Institute* (Vol. 68, No. 2, 1998), pp. 183–210; Alfred Zack-Williams, 'Sierra Leone: The Political Economy of Civil War', *Third World Quarterly* (Vol. 20, No. 1, 1999), pp. 143–62.

[11] Peter Albrecht, *Foundational Hybridity and its Reproduction: Security Sector Reform in Sierra Leone*, PhD Series, 33.2012 (Copenhagen: Copenhagen Business School, 2012); Richard Fanthorpe, 'Neither Citizen nor Subject? "Lumpen" Agency and the Legacy of Native Administration in Sierra Leone', *African Affairs* (Vol. 100, No. 400, 2001), pp. 363–86; Paul Jackson, 'Chiefs, Money and Politicians: Rebuilding Local Government in Sierra Leone', *Public Administration and Development* (Vol. 25, No. 1, 2005), pp. 49–58.

[12] Richard Fanthorpe, 'Locating the Politics of a Sierra Leonean Chiefdom', *Africa: Journal of the International African Institute* (Vol. 68, No. 4, 1998), pp. 558–84; Mariane C Ferme, 'Deterritorialized Citizenship and Resonances of the Sierra Leonean State', in Veena Das and Deborah Poole (eds), *Anthropology at the Margins of the State* (New Delhi: Oxford University Press, 2004), pp. 81–115.

Major General Joseph Momoh, became president. Throughout this period, Sierra Leone was, in effect, governed as a dictatorship, leading to the increasing alienation of the population – and particularly of young men, some of whom eventually joined the RUF.[13] In October 1990, due to mounting pressure from both within and outside the country to embark on political and economic reform, President Momoh commissioned a constitutional review to assess the 1978 one-party constitution.[14] However, this came too late: Sierra Leone's new constitution was established in 1991 but it was only endorsed after the RUF began its campaign of violence along the Liberian border.

With the RUF revolt taking hold in eastern and southern Sierra Leone, Momoh's government was ousted in a coup in 1992 by a group of young military officers led by Valentine Strasser. However, the National Provisional Ruling Council (NPRC), as the new regime was called, became increasingly ineffective in the face of the progress being made by the RUF: by March 1995, it had advanced to within 20 miles of Freetown and had taken over all mineral-rich areas in the country.[15] This desperate situation led the NPRC to employ a South African private military company, Executive Outcomes (EO), in 1995 at a cost of $1.8 million per month, financed primarily by the International Monetary Fund.[16] Consisting of 500 advisers and 3,000 soldiers, EO was militarily successful, but the NPRC was losing support – and the war – largely because it was neglecting the conditions endured by Sierra Leone Army (SLA) soldiers in the field.[17] The political weakening of Strasser led to his arrest on 16 January 1996 in an internal NPRC coup. In turn, there was an acceptance within the NPRC, now led by Julius Maada Bio (who would later be nominated as the SLPP presidential candidate for the 2012 election), that it would hand over power to a civilian government following an election to be held within the next few months. With significant support from civil-society groups, Ahmad Tejan Kabbah of the SLPP was elected president in March of that year.

Shortly thereafter, discussions began between the SLPP and the RUF and a peace agreement was signed in Abidjan in November 1996.

---

[13] Paul Richards, *Fighting for the Rain Forest: War, Youth and Resources in Sierra Leone* (Oxford: International African Institute/James Currey, 1996). Krijn Peters, *War and the Crisis of Youth* (Cambridge: Cambridge University Press, 2011); Peters and Richards, '"Why We Fight"'.

[14] Alfred Zack-Williams and Stephen Riley, 'Sierra Leone: The Coup and its Consequences', *Review of Political African Economy* (Vol. 20, No. 56, 1993), pp. 91–98.

[15] Ibrahim Abdullah, *Between Democracy and Terror: The Sierra Leone Civil War* (Dakar: Council for the Development of Social Science Research in Africa, 2004).

[16] Malan, Rakate and McIntyre, *Peacekeeping in Sierra Leone*. EO left Sierra Leone in January 1997.

[17] Gberie, *A Dirty War in West Africa*, p. 180.

However, the unwillingness of either party to agree on a process for disarmament or to establish international monitoring arrangements led to a breakdown in the peace in early 1997. In May of that year, another coup in Freetown, this time led by the Armed Forces Revolutionary Council (AFRC), forced Kabbah into exile in Conakry, Guinea. This led to a new cycle of violence that drew in the newly established Economic Community of West African States Monitoring Group (ECOMOG) – a Nigerian-led regional peacekeeping force – culminating in the return and reinstatement of President Kabbah in 1998, backed by ECOMOG and the UN Observer Mission in Sierra Leone (UNOMSIL), established in July 1998.

Enabled by the signing of a new peace deal – the Lomé Peace Agreement – by the Government of Sierra Leone and the RUF on 7 July 1999, the UN Mission in Sierra Leone (UNAMSIL), comprising 6,000 military personnel, was established on 22 October 1999. However, it was plagued by a number of challenges immediately after its deployment. A chronic lack of resources was exacerbated by misplaced faith in the Lomé Agreement, as well as by serious disagreements about strategic direction at a senior level of the UN.[18] A hostage crisis that unfolded in late April 2000, in which several UN units comprising 300 individuals were surrounded by a reanimated RUF, led to a rescue mission by UNAMSIL and UK troops. The key role played by the UK in stabilising Sierra Leone from May 2000 is the main focus of the next section.

Winning the War and Securing the Peace

In early May 2000, the RUF was on the offensive. ECOMOG had left a few weeks earlier. The SLA was weak, having almost completed the process of disarmament and begun disbandment under the terms of the Lomé Agreement. In this context, the UK began a non-combatant evacuation operation, which transformed into a six-week military campaign with all the trappings of a small-to-medium-scale war-fighting operation. The British commander of the operation, then-Brigadier David Richards, who went on to become the UK's Chief of the Defence Staff in 2010, has since observed of Operation *Palliser*: 'We found ourselves de facto closely involved with the direction of a campaign at the operational level'.[19]

These developments were not directed from London. Individuals on the ground transformed the rules of engagement and gained support from their political leaders *post facto*.[20] UK forces co-ordinated and sustained the efforts of the disparate Sierra Leonean armed groups that were loyal to the state, because neither the Government of Sierra Leone nor the UN was

[18] Malan, Rakate and McIntyre, *Peacekeeping in Sierra Leone*.
[19] Albrecht and Jackson, *Security System Transformation in Sierra Leone*, p. 52.
[20] Peter Albrecht interview with David Richards, UK, April 2008.

in a position to do so at the time. This group that formed with UK support after May 2000 came to be known as the 'Unholy Alliance'. It consisted of a loose coalition of SLA personnel (numbering 2,000–3,000, with a further 3,000 being trained by a UK short-term training team), ex-SLA personnel, former members of the AFRC, and Civil Defence Forces (CDF) combatants,[21] as well as elements of the West Side Boys (a splinter faction of the AFRC).

These different force units were directed by a committee chaired by British officers. As Lord Richards recalled in retrospect:[22]

> Unholy they may have been but, guided as they were at every level by British officers over the next few weeks, they succeeded in securing much of the inland road route between Freetown and Lungi, relieving the military and, of course, political pressure on Freetown and its beleaguered government.

The UK's intervention was a catalyst for the RUF's acceptance of defeat, leading to a ceasefire that was signed in Abuja on 10 November 2000. In January 2002, the war was officially declared over. Over the course of the preceding eleven years, some 50,000 people – of a total population of 6 million – were estimated to have been killed, around 500,000 had become refugees and around 500,000 were classified as internally displaced persons (IDPs).[23] The bureaucratic infrastructure of the state had more or less ceased to exist, a process of disintegration exacerbated by the RUF's deliberate targeting of government infrastructure in the countryside.

With regard to internal security, the Sierra Leone Police (SLP) presence was essentially limited to major urban areas until the war was declared over in January 2002 – and the force was still tarnished by its close association with state repression prior to the conflict. Indeed, corruption, violence, and abuse of position had been common amongst SLP officers and the majority of the population remained extremely wary of them, while the institutionalisation of corruption also mitigated against the recruitment and retention of good-quality, younger and less-corrupt officers.[24] In terms of logistics, meanwhile, the SLP was also hampered by

---

[21] The CDF was a group of local militias based mainly in the southern part of Sierra Leone, comprised of Kamajors, Donsos, Gbethis, Kapras, Tamaboros and – from the Freetown peninsula – the Organized Body of Hunting Societies.

[22] Richards quoted in Albrecht and Jackson, *Security System Transformation in Sierra Leone*, p. 53.

[23] Adrian Horn, Funmi Olonisakin and Gordon Peake, 'United Kingdom-Led Security Sector Reform in Sierra Leone', *Civil Wars* (Vol. 8, No. 2, 2006), pp. 109–23.

[24] Simon Robins, 'Addressing the Challenges of Law Enforcement in Africa – Policing in Sierra Leone, Tanzania and Zambia', Policy Brief No. 16, Institute for Security Studies, Pretoria, October 2009; International Crisis Group, 'Sierra Leone

a lack of equipment and infrastructure, including stations, vehicles and radios.

The SLA had experienced similar levels of collapse as the war progressed. Unable to fight the RUF effectively, during the 1990s it had fragmented into various factions; mounted coups; and elements had fought on more than one side of the conflict. The resultant lack of trust in the SLA had prompted the Mende politician Samuel Hinga Norman to establish the CDF in southern Sierra Leone, which merged locally recruited fighters into a national force to protect civilians. Better organised than the army, the CDF was in many areas the only security force on which President Kabbah could rely in the late 1990s.[25]

This was the context in which the establishment of security and justice institutions began, the early intervention tackling a situation in which there was no clear security control across the country. In short, it was a matter of re-establishing state sovereignty. As a result, the ability to exercise a monopoly of violence was a key driver of the approach taken by the UK and others in their early post-war involvement.[26] Given the poor condition of the core state – and particularly its inability to provide basic security – as well as the centrality of state-building to the peace-building process, it became imperative to create stability for the population. Without this, it would be difficult for development activities to be taken forward. There was no doubt in the mind of Clare Short (then the UK's secretary of state for international development) that, as events in Sierra Leone unfolded, 'We could not – we, being the British – let this fragile, but democratically-elected government collapse'.[27]

The Development of a Comprehensive Concept of SSR

The general state of emergency in Sierra Leone in the late 1990s and early 2000s left no space or time to sit back and develop a strategy, and the country was considered in urgent need of support by London. Prior to the end of the war – and its accompanying disarmament and demobilisation processes – security-related programming was very much shaped in response to the situation on the ground. For instance, the lack of any capacity to oversee the armed forces, which had successfully staged two coups since 1992, was addressed – as was the inability to co-ordinate appropriate responses to the security situation or to collect intelligence that formed a coherent picture. Police primacy, which had been a priority

after Elections: Politics as Usual?', Africa Report No. 49, Freetown/Brussels, July 2002.

[25] Horn, Olonisakin and Peake, 'United Kingdom-Led Security Sector Reform'; Keen, *Conflict and Collusion in Sierra Leone*, p. 90.

[26] Albrecht and Jackson, *Security System Transformation in Sierra Leone*.

[27] Quoted in *ibid.*, p. 174.

for President Kabbah since he was first elected in 1996,[28] received considerable and consistent funding from the UK government, particularly from DfID.[29]

The term 'security-sector reform' existed and was referred to both in Sierra Leone and UK government documentation in the late 1990s. However, there was limited clarity regarding which institutions should be included in its definition – and thus in its activities. According to one definition circulating in Sierra Leone during this period, SSR only encompassed the armed forces and the institutions overseeing and managing their actions.[30] Another definition included the intelligence services and specifically the institutions with a mandate to co-ordinate the work of security-sector institutions such as the National Security Advisor's Office – the predecessor to the Office of National Security (ONS) which was set up to co-ordinate the security sector (see Chapter II for in-depth discussion and analysis).[31] Neither of these definitions encompassed the police or the judiciary. In the early years of SSR in Sierra Leone, this lack of clarity over the concept exacerbated turf wars between advisers within different programmes, including, for instance, those who dealt with national security at the strategic level and those who dealt with policing.

Nor was this confusion over the scope of, and best approach to, SSR limited to discrepancies at the international and national levels. Within DfID, there was a split of responsibilities beween various offices, which had direct implications for how funding was channelled into Sierra Leone and thus how SSR was conceptualised. As Keith Biddle, Sierra Leone's first post-war inspector-general of police and a retired British assistant chief constable, recalls:[32]

> CHAD [DfID's Conflict and Humanitarian Affairs Department] was running the show regarding security in the military, and came out on visits. On the other hand, you had [DfID's] Government and Institutions Department, which said that they would retain all policing aspects throughout the world under all circumstances, because it was about governments and communities, and not military solutions to conflict. There was a lot of turf war involved in this. Logically, the police should have been part of the security sector reform part, and DFID, in 1998, in fact issued a book [*sic*] that stated that the police are actually dealt with

[28] Geoff Bredemear, roundtable, UK, December 2007.

[29] Peter Alexander Albrecht, 'Transforming Internal Security in Sierra Leone: Sierra Leone Police and Broader Justice Sector Reform', *DIIS Report* 2010:07, Copenhagen, 2010.

[30] Albrecht and Jackson, *Security System Transformation in Sierra Leone*, pp. 26–27.

[31] *Ibid.*

[32] Biddle quoted in Albrecht, *Foundational Hybridity and its Reproduction*, p. 96.

> on their own provisions [as separate from SSR]. So security sector reform was not part and parcel of what we [as UK advisers in Sierra Leone] were doing and never formally became part and parcel of what we were doing. There was clearly a lack of integration of thought in London.

The fact that police and defence programming was not directed from, or co-ordinated within, the same office in DfID had severe consequences for the implementation of SSR in Sierra Leone, and led to rivalry between programmes and advisers. Robert Ashington-Pickett – adviser to Sierra Leone's ONS from 2000 to 2003 – explained the interdepartmental rivalry that he experienced in relation to Sierra Leone, making the general point that:[33]

> It is a regrettable fact that many government departments, especially in the security sector, create unproductive rivalries, petty jealousies and prejudices towards other security agencies. Inappropriate exaggerated identification with one's own programme can also arise, leading to isolation among SSR advisers and overprotectiveness of one's agency or department. At times, this behaviour is imported into post-conflict arenas, where it creates a new arena for rivalries to be played out, thus undermining key SSR principles and setting a bad example.

Due to these turf wars and personality clashes, but more importantly to the context of ongoing conflict in which SSR efforts began, integration of the various security-related programmes initiated by the UK government did not take place. This incoherence in the early years was compounded by the lack of a comprehensive conceptualisation of the security sector that could guide the process and clearly articulate the breadth of institutions to be reformed and how they interlink. However, such a conceptualisation slowly emerged for Sierra Leone, particularly during the period from 2003 until 2005, when the country's first security-sector review was produced by the newly established ONS.

The security-sector review's primary aim was to assess potential and actual threats to the country; identify the institutions that could counter these threats; and make recommendations as to how they could do so. For this reason, it became vital to clearly articulate a working definition of the security sector. This was the case not only because of sensitivities around making authoritative claims on threats to Sierra Leone,[34] but also because of the related political consequences of including some actors in the reform process and excluding others. Thus, a broad spectrum of

---

[33] Robert Ashington-Pickett, 'Intelligence and Security Service Reconstruction', in Albrecht and Jackson (eds), *Security Sector Reform in Sierra Leone 1997–2007*, p. 31.

[34] Deciding what constitutes a security threat is politically powerful, because it becomes the basis for prioritising the allocation of funding to agencies.

organisations were involved in the security-sector review process, cutting across parliament, government departments (including the ONS), and the military, police, prison services, judicial services and civil-society groups. In short, a comprehensive and detailed understanding of the actors that play a role in providing security was established, driven by an explicit understanding that human rather than state security was at the centre of the process.[35]

This process in Sierra Leone overlapped with international policy developments, which the UK also played a central role in moulding. In this regard, international policies and emerging best practices of SSR shaped peace-building through state-building in Sierra Leone, just as the Sierra Leone process shaped SSR – as a concept, a set of policies and an integrated set of programme approaches.[36]

One of the first and defining statements within the international debate about SSR came in 1999, when then-UK Secretary of State for International Development Clare Short gave a speech at King's College London. In the context of SSR being an important basis for long-term, sustainable development, and with reference to Sierra Leone, Short specifically outlined the role of a development agency in working with 'military, paramilitary and intelligence services'.[37]

In development terms, Short's speech was revolutionary because, as noted by Garth Glentworth, a key adviser in DfID during the early years of the SSR process, 'conflict did not mean anything for development at the time'.[38] It established links between development and security, which was futher elaborated through UK – and particularly DfID – work with the Organisation for Economic Co-operation and Development (OECD) on SSR-related policy developments. The SSR community in DfID was – and remains – relatively small, but it has been the most persistent in conceptualising and operationalising policy connections between security,

---

[35] The human security agenda is based on two key principles: first, that the protection of individuals is critical to both national and international security; second, that the security conditions required by people for their development are not limited to traditional matters such as national defence and law and order, but incorporate broader political, economic, and social issues and concerns. Gavin Cawthra, *Securing South Africa's Democracy: Defence, Development and Security in Transition* (London: Palgrave Macmillan, 1997).

[36] Albrecht and Jackson, 'State-Building through Security Sector Reform', p. 96; Albrecht, Stepputat and Andersen, 'Security Sector Reform, the European Way'; Albrecht and Stepputat, 'The Rise and Fall of Security Sector Reform in Development'.

[37] Clare Short, 'Security Sector Reform and the Elimination of Poverty', speech to the Centre for Defence Studies, King's College London, 9 March 1999, <http://www.epolitix.com/Resources/epolitix/MPWebsites/Images/c-d/9%20March%201999.doc>, accessed 1 October 2014.

[38] Peter Albrecht interview with Garth Glentworth, UK, February 2008.

development, justice and democracy. Broadly speaking, in the mid-2000s, as Sugden notes, there was 'an overwhelming [international] agreement that the UK is the leader in the field of SSR',[39] the 'godfather' of the comprehensive approach to SSR.

One of the most comprehensive definitions of SSR was elaborated by the OECD's Development Assistance Committee (DAC) in 2005. In parallel to Sierra Leone's security-sector review, the DAC produced the reference document *Security System Reform and Governance.*[40] The process which led to the publication of this key document, and the *Handbook on Security System Reform*, published two years later in 2007,[41] was not only given substantial support by the UK, but it was also informed by experiences of implementation in Sierra Leone. According to the DAC's definition, the security sector is composed of four clusters of actors, including:

- Core security actors: armed forces, police, gendarmeries, paramilitary forces, presidential guards, intelligence and security services, coast guards, border guards, custom authorities, and reserve and local security units
- Security management and oversight bodies: legislatures, including committees, Ministries of Internal Affairs, Foreign Affairs and Defence, national security advisory bodies, customary and traditional authorities, financial-management bodies, and civil-society actors, including the media, academia and non-governmental organisations (NGOs)
- Justice and rule-of-law institutions: Ministry of Justice, correction services, criminal investigation and prosecution services, the judiciary (courts), other customary and traditional justice systems, human-rights commissions and ombudspersons
- Non-statutory security forces: liberation armies, guerrilla armies, private bodyguard units, private security companies, private military companies and political-party militias.[42]

This broad-based and inclusive definition of the institutions that are to be encompassed by SSR has become widely accepted internationally. However, it also throws up significant dilemmas regarding sequencing and

---

[39] Jennifer Sugden, 'Security Sector Reform: The Role of Epistemic Communities in the UK', *Journal of Security Sector Management* (Vol. 4, No. 4, November 2006), pp. 1–19.

[40] Organisation for Economic Co-operation and Development (OECD), *Security System Reform and Governance: Policy and Good Practice. A DAC Reference Document*, DAC Guidelines and Reference Series (Paris: OECD, 2005).

[41] OECD, *The OECD DAC Handbook on Security System Reform: Supporting Security and Justice* (Paris: OECD, 2007).

[42] OECD, *Security System Reform and Governance*, pp. 20–21.

prioritisation in implementation – issues that are returned to throughout this Whitehall Paper.[43]

About this Paper

This Whitehall Paper analyses how SSR unfolded in Sierra Leone between 1997 and 2013. It explores how the process shaped international conceptualisations of SSR and international interventions more broadly, and vice versa. This is done through a detailed account of the establishment of security and justice institutions – many of which had collapsed during the civil war of the 1990s, but some of which had to be built from scratch – and the direct role of the UK government in shaping that process. Indeed, as noted by Garth Glentworth, 'Sierra Leone was a scale of involvement [on the part of the UK government] that had not been seen before'.[44]

The development of SSR in Sierra Leone provides rare insight into a process in which the three foreign-policy instruments of development, politics and defence were utilised simultaneously – and on an equal footing – before the general militarisation of international interventions that followed the 9/11 terrorist attacks. By extension, the study also provides insight into a rapidly changing global security environment and how it impacted on the UK's ability to deploy these three foreign-policy instruments with equal weight. Above all, however, this Whitehall Paper is an account of how Sierra Leone's security sector was built up from a point of collapse, and it tells the story of some of the key individuals involved in that process, in both Sierra Leone and the UK.

Chapter II explores the period 1997–2007, when external support was provided in order to win the war, stabilise Sierra Leone and begin the process of re-establishing state institutions that had been destroyed during a decade of conflict. Given the bureaucratic collapse that Sierra Leone had experienced during the 1990s, external support and internal developments were shaped as responses to consecutive crises. The UK played a crucial role at every step of this process, having been invited to do so by the Sierra Leone government.

Related to the need to bring the army under some level of control was President Kabbah's priority, in the early years of this period, of establishing police primacy.[45] The SLP was given a new ethos, that of Local Needs Policing, and – in a concrete state-building exercise – vehicles, communications equipment and uniforms were procured under

---

[43] European Commission, 'A Concept for European Community Support for Security Sector Reform', Communication from the Commission to the Council, COM (2006) 253, May 2006; Sedra (ed.), *The Future of Security Sector Reform*.
[44] Albrecht interview with Garth Glentworth.
[45] Albrecht and Jackson, *Security System Transformation in Sierra Leone*, p. 29.

the DfID-funded Commonwealth Community Safety and Security Project (CCSSP). Similarly, in the chaotic years of the late 1990s, a variety of high-level national security institutions were supported by DfID, with activity including a fundamental reorganisation of the Ministry of Defence (MoD) and intelligence services and the establishment of the ONS to strengthen co-ordination of the security sector as a whole.

During 2000–01, following the success of the UK's military intervention in the civil war, the International Military Advisory and Training Team (IMATT) began its deployment in support of the armed forces and Sierra Leone's new MoD. IMATT emerged in parallel to, and partly as an extension of, the UK's Operation *Silkman*, which deployed in November 2000 as it became clear that a more permanent military presence was required in Sierra Leone. By 2001, sixty-five personnel were on the ground, operating in parallel with short-term training teams, and filling key appointments in both the MoD and the rank and file of the army.[46]

If the late 1990s and early 2000s were reactive – about winning a war, stabilising Sierra Leone and laying the foundations for institution-building – 2002–05 became years of transition from 'emergency mode' to peace-building and a longer-term view. An SLP presence was building up outside the Western Area, the district containing Freetown. The first post-conflict elections were held in 2002, bringing victory again for Kabbah and the SLPP. Within the security sector, a primary focus was on producing and linking a security strategy for Sierra Leone with the country's development objectives. This reflected a significant stride forward across the security sector, where the political space for new organisations, such as the ONS, and fundamentally transformed ones, such as the MoD, was opening up. The security sector was coming into its own and when elections were held again in 2007, it was Sierra Leone – and not the international community – that took the lead in co-ordinating security.

2007, the starting point for Chapter III, was a watershed year politically and, by extension, also for Sierra Leone's security-sector institutions. With the APC now in power, following its victory over the SLPP, the new political context that emerged had different implications for different security institutions. SSR had been initiated in a context of war by the SLPP, which fully aligned its objectives to those of its closest international partner, the UK. Inevitably, an APC-led government, which had not been part of the post-conflict reconstruction process, was going to approach the security sector differently. Indeed, with the change of government, many within the security sector experienced increased political pressure. In particular, newly established organisations such as the ONS and the Central Intelligence and Security Unit (CISU) found

46 *Ibid.*, p. 54.

themselves having to prove their relevance to an executive that did not fully understand or trust them.

By this point, the armed forces – renamed the Republic of Sierra Leone Armed Forces (RSLAF) by Kabbah in 2002 – had a dedicated minister of defence, who had taken over what had, until then, been the constitutionally designated role of the president, and the implementation of a core review had led to a downsizing of the army from 10,500 to 8,500. This warranted a defence review, which was never produced. As contributions to peace support operations (PSOs) became the RSLAF's top priority, this was therefore more about seizing an opportunity than about following a planned strategic direction. It was also evident that besides bringing organisational pride to the RSLAF, contributing to PSOs had a stabilising effect: it provided the force with a purpose.

With the new government in place, however, it became evident that the police and the court system, in particular, were experiencing political pressure on a day-to-day basis. Unlike the army, ONS and CISU, the SLP's role in providing security as a basic service is continuous, and organisational change can have major consequences for how that service is delivered. Indeed, external support to the SLP had been reduced considerably in 2005 when the DfID-funded Commonwealth policing project was terminated. While its successor, the Justice Sector Development Programme (JSDP), which was implemented by the British Council, continued supporting the SLP, it placed much less emphasis on logistics and infrastructure than had previously been the case. It was also becoming increasingly clear that a stronger link was required between the SLP and the Ministry of Internal Affairs, which historically had only a loose affiliation. The RSLAF's dedicated minister was able to withstand external pressure to recruit outside due process – yet the SLP, CISU and ONS, with no dedicated ministerial support at the top political level, were not able to do so to the same extent. The third chapter thus analyses in detail how politicisation of the security sector had – and continues to have – the potential to undermine the integrity of these institutions.

The period between 2010 and the present, which is covered in Chapter IV, witnessed significant change, in terms of both UK support and the leadership of key institutions within the sector. March 2013 saw the termination of IMATT, the longest and most consistent programme of support to a security-sector institution in Sierra Leone. By then, the RSLAF's role as a security force was well understood and accepted within the rank and file of the army. There have been plenty of obstacles, such as that of replacing soldiers lost through downsizing with force multipliers and consolidating the position of civil servants within the MoD – efforts which so far have proven largely unsuccessful. The Achilles' heel of 'Pebu' and 'Pumas' – the failed programmes to build barracks for the RSLAF and to re-establish the air wing, respectively – was still fresh in the minds of the RSLAF leadership as the mission drew to a close. IMATT was, rightly or wrongly, held to account for these failures.

However, what IMATT left behind was a stable armed force that stayed out of politics and was increasingly built around the intention of contributing troops to PSOs overseas. By fiscal year 2013/14, this focus took up an estimated 75 per cent of the RSLAF's resources. The dominance of the PSO agenda may be considered too one-dimensional, but it has given the RSLAF a purpose and provides an external check in terms of maintaining the professionalism of the RSLAF.

The ONS has experienced considerable challenges since 2010, including a change of the national security co-ordinator in early 2012 and limited receptiveness from the executive. As early as 2005, when the SLPP was still in power, the possibility of renewed conflict was seen as unrealistic, and the attention of the executive was shifting to economic development. The 'Agenda for Prosperity', formulated by the APC government in 2013 as the vision for Sierra Leone's path to middle-income status over the following five years, cemented this focus, and inevitably had consequences for the attention that the executive was prepared to give the security sector as a whole, in both political and financial terms. In response to this, the security-sector review produced by the ONS in 2011–12 emphasised the role of the sector in support of the country's long-term development. Sierra Leonean-led, the review was also the manifestation of an organisation that had become consolidated and adapted to new roles and functions.

During this period, however, the greatest changes occurred within CISU. The combined shock of a new government coming to power in 2007, the termination of external funding in 2010, and relative international isolation put significant pressure on the organisation. However, this did not lead to institutional collapse; instead, CISU was increasingly able to show itself as an apolitical body that could play a useful role in preparing intelligence for relevant ministries, departments and agencies to act on. In the run-up to the elections in 2012, CISU had some success in showcasing its capabilities, even if ongoing doubts in the executive meant that parallel systems of politically motivated information-gathering persisted. In 2013, the president pledged to make CISU's budgets independent from the ONS. In sum, CISU's reorientation provides insight into how an institution can adjust when external funding is withdrawn and political pressure changes.

Within the police, meanwhile, a split was emerging. On the one hand, there was a continued rhetorical emphasis on Local Needs Policing and the need to engage communities in service provision through community policing. On the other hand, the poorly managed and rapid expansion of the armed wing of the police, the Operational Support Division (OSD), meant that this division now accounted for a third of the SLP, at more than 4,000 officers. From 2011, increasing numbers of shooting incidents involving OSD officers exposed their insufficient training and consequent tendency to panic when under pressure. Both Local Needs Policing and armed policing remain strong characteristics of policing in Sierra Leone, but it is evident that the inherent contradiction between them may yet come to undermine the SLP.

Chapter V explores the past fifteen years of SSR in Sierra Leone from the perspective of upstream conflict prevention. 'Investing in upstream prevention', the UK government's 2011 Building Stability Overseas Strategy notes, means 'helping to build strong, legitimate institutions and robust societies in fragile countries that are capable of managing tensions and shocks so there is a lower likelihood of instability and conflict'.[47] The shift to upstream conflict prevention may represent an important change following a decade of international interventions that have relied heavily on military strength.

Indeed, upstream conflict prevention is emerging as the UK's vision for international interventions and as the core of a comprehensive strategy to maintain stability in fragile situations. When exploring the principles that underpin this concept, it becomes clear that it is not fundamentally new. It articulates the key outcome of a decade-long process of learning within UK policy-making, including from the country's experiences in Sierra Leone: that effective international interventions must go beyond military engagement and involve diplomatic efforts and development expertise. This combination, this Whitehall Paper will argue, was the underlying rationale for the UK's initial involvement in Sierra Leone in the late 1990s.

[47] Department for International Development, Foreign Office and Ministry of Defence, 'Building Stability Overseas Strategy', London, July 2011, p. 5.

II. 1997–2007: THE EVOLUTION OF SECURITY-SECTOR REFORM IN SIERRA LEONE

Since the very beginning of the process of security-sector reform (SSR) in Sierra Leone, prior to the end of the country's civil war, the UK has played a disproportionate role in efforts to transform Sierra Leonean security institutions. This has extended from assistance while war was ongoing to support for post-conflict stabilisation in a context of peace: the lead role assumed by the UK in military intervention through Operation *Palliser*, in May 2000, translated into an equally prominent role in the post-conflict environment as one of the leading donors within efforts to stabilise and rebuild the country. The UN peacekeeping mission, UNAMSIL, which at one point comprised 17,500 peacekeepers,[1] remained in Sierra Leone until 31 December 2005 and, together with various UN agencies and the World Bank, played a central role in the country's reconstruction. However, there was broad acceptance of the UK's position of leadership – not least in security-sector development – given its long-term commitment to the country, enshrined in the 2002 Memorandum of Understanding (MoU) between the UK and Sierra Leone governments,[2] and its military support.

[1] Peter Albrecht and Mark Malan, 'Post-Conflict Peacebuilding and National Ownership: Lessons from the Sierra Leone Peace Process', Center for International Peace Operations, Berlin, 2006, pp. 35–36.

[2] Forming the basis of the Memorandum of Understanding was the 2002 Poverty Reduction Framework between HM Government and the Government of the Republic of Sierra Leone; see sections 1, 3.2 and 3.3, <http://siteresources.worldbank.org/SIERRALEONEEXTN/Resources/povertyframework.pdf>, accessed 1 October 2014. The document states that 'the UK Government will commit itself to maintaining a substantial direct development programme to Sierra Leone over the next ten years' – that is, between 2002 and 2012 – and 'will continue to build on the work it has already engaged on with the Office of the President[,] … the Ministry of Justice[,] … the Ministry of Defence and Republic of Sierra Leone Armed Forces (RSLAF), the Office of National Security, the Sierra Leone Police,

UK involvement in Sierra Leone began at a low level, primarily through the Department for International Development (DfID), in 1997 after President Kabbah requested support to re-establish the Sierra Leone Police (SLP) in 1996.[3] It was bolstered in 1999 during the ceasefire surrounding the negotiation of the Lomé Peace Agreement, which was eventually signed by the Government of Sierra Leone and the Revolutionary United Front (RUF) on 7 July of that year. It was around this time that two of the main pillars of the UK's involvement in Sierra Leonean security-sector reform were established: the DfID-funded Sierra Leone Security Sector Reform Programme (SILSEP) and the International Military Advisory and Training Team (IMATT), the latter not only initiated, but also largely funded by the UK.

SILSEP was the first to be established, in June 1999, constituting a 'governance approach' to national security co-ordination, intelligence-gathering, and the rebuilding of the Ministry of Defence (MoD).[4] It was the MoD Advisory Team within SILSEP – Colonel Mike Dent and Robert Foot, a UK civil servant – that identified the need for a British Military Advisory and Training Team (BMATT) to be deployed. Indeed, it was considered 'key to the sustainable implementation of SILSEP reforms'.[5] As such, the BMATT was viewed as the 'logical extension of the SILSEP MoD Project',[6] with integration of programming from the very outset between SILSEP and BMATT.

---

the Anti-Corruption Commission, the National Commission for Disarmament, Demobilisation and Reintegration … and other Government Institutions'.

[3] Peter Albrecht and Paul Jackson, *Security System Transformation in Sierra Leone, 1997–2007* (Birmingham and London: Global Facilitation Network for Security Sector Reform and International Alert, 2009), p. 29.

[4] The governance approach has been one of the key innovations in SSR thinking. As Mark Sedra, a leading scholar on the topic, notes, in contrast to security assistance during the Cold War, 'the professionalism and effectiveness of the security sector is not just measured by the capacity of the security forces, but how well they are managed, monitored and held accountable'. It is also necessary to conceive of 'the security sector as more than its blunt, hard security instruments, recognizing that the security forces cannot perform their duties effectively in the absence of competent legal frameworks and judicial bodies as well as correctional institutions and government oversight bodies.' Mark Sedra (ed.), *The Future of Security Sector Reform* (Ottawa: Centre for International Governance Innovation, 2010), pp. 16–27, 16. See also Peter Albrecht and Finn Stepputat, 'The Rise and Fall of Security Sector Reform in Development', in Paul Jackson (ed.), *Handbook of International Security and Development* (Cheltenham: Edward Elgar Publishing, 2015).

[5] Sierra Leone Security Sector Reform Programme (SILSEP) and Ministry of Defence Advisory Team (MODAT), 'Project Report for Period 11–24 October 1999 (weeks 18–19)', unpublished.

[6] MODAT, 'Future UK Military Commitment in Support of the Department for International Development's Security Sector Reform Programme (SILSEP)', November 1999, unpublished.

It was the integration of hard-security, public-administration and civil-service reform that broke new ground by bringing together DfID, the Foreign Office and the UK MoD – and thus closely combining development, politics and defence. Funding for a conventional BMATT would come from the Foreign Office and UK MoD. However, given that the BMATT's purpose was not only to advise and train the Sierra Leonean armed forces, but also to implement SILSEP-designed reforms in the Sierra Leonean MoD, the BMATT would also effectively become engaged in institution-building. This more elaborate and politically sensitive role led to the internationalisation of the BMATT, into an international MATT (IMATT). This broadening of participants also reflected the UK's conclusion that the involvement in Sierra Leonean state-building of the ex-colonial power alone was morally contestable.

To implement this internationalisation, the UK MoD arranged a conference in London in January 2000 to brief Commonwealth and overseas defence attachés and advisers on the IMATT project, and to invite them to provide personnel to fill command and staff appointments.[7] Commonwealth countries, including Canada and Australia, contributed staff, as did the US. At the core of the internationalised MATT was, in the words of one of its commanders, Barry Le Grys, 'very much a "we are now stable, let's think longer-term" initiative'.[8]

IMATT deployed in parallel to and partly grew out of Operation *Silkman*, which deployed in November 2000, as it had become clear that a more permanent military presence was required in Sierra Leone.[9] By early 2001, IMATT was staffed by sixty-five personnel, operating in parallel with short-term training teams and filling key civilian and command appointments within the Sierra Leonean MoD and armed forces, respectively.

Those deployed to Sierra Leone under these initiatives were greeted with chaos on the ground. As Colonel Mike Dent, who deployed as part of SILSEP's MoD Advisory Team, commented:[10]

> On our arrival ... We were taken by car to the MoD in Freetown to meet the Deputy Minister of Defence. On the journey from our accommodation we passed through seven checkpoints manned by various groups of armed persons. From their dress it was difficult to ascertain if they

[7] E-mail exchange, Mike Dent, 2008.

[8] E-mail exchange, Barry Le Grys, 2008.

[9] Operation *Silkman* saw the introduction of command, executive and advisory posts across the Sierra Leonean MoD and the army. It was mainly focused on the military reintegration programme and the subsequent delivery of RSLAF training. See IMATT, 'Future Delivery of RSLAF Transformation by IMATT', Freetown, February 2006, unpublished.

[10] Dent quoted in Albrecht and Jackson, *Security System Transformation in Sierra Leone*, p. 45.

> were military, civilian or police. The rule of law and order appeared to have broken down completely.

The initial deployment of SILSEP had been derailed in 1999 by a resurgence of the RUF, with both the UN's peacekeeping troops and the Sierra Leone Army (SLA) unable to contain it. This RUF assault led directly to the launching of Operation *Palliser* in May 2000 by the UK armed forces (see Chapter I), which had a profound effect on the form of the country's subsequent involvement in Sierra Leone's security sector. In the context of genuine fears that the Government of Sierra Leone and the UN mission, UNAMSIL, would collapse in the face of the RUF's onslaught, UK forces co-ordinated and sustained the efforts of disparate groupings of loyal Sierra Leoneans.[11]

This so-called 'Unholy Alliance' was a loose coalition of pro-government troops that included remnants of the SLA (which, at this time, officially numbered 2,000–3,000 personnel organised into three brigades, each of three battalions), as well as ex-SLA personnel and Armed Forces Revolutionary Council (AFRC) troops, Civil Defence Forces (CDF) combatants and elements of the West Side Boys.[12] Many of these groups had recently fought each other but were now directed by a Government Joint Force Operations and Support Committee, chaired by British officers and comprising representatives of the various factions.

Despite these less than auspicious beginnings, the makeshift military force made significant gains against the RUF and, with UK support, pushed it back into its heartlands in eastern Sierra Leone, where it had initiated its campaign. The RUF's leader, Foday Sankoh, was isolated in custody and, in his absence, Liberia's President Charles Taylor attempted to exert increasing political influence over the RUF.[13] Militarily, the group was on the back foot, with numerous reports of low morale and desertion, and an ever-widening split between its Eastern and Northern Commands.

By mid-June 2000, the security situation had stabilised sufficiently for Operation *Palliser* to be terminated. Following visits by the UK Chief of Defence Staff, General Sir Charles Guthrie, and then-Foreign Secretary

---

[11] *Ibid.*, p. 25.

[12] Peter Albrecht interview with David Richards, UK, April 2008. The West Side Boys were a group of combatants claiming loyalty to the former AFRC regime and its leader Major Johnny Paul Koroma, living on the outskirts of Freetown. Their primary area of operations was on the Okra Hills close to the primary Freetown-to-Masiaka highway. They predominately relied upon robbery, the looting of local villages and other criminal activities for funding.

[13] From the outset of the RUF's campaign, it was backed by Liberia's President Charles Taylor and his National Patriotic Front of Liberia (NPFL). Taylor authorised nearly 2,000 combatants from the NPFL to serve as 'special forces' within the rank and file of the RUF. Apart from gaining access to the diamonds harvested from areas controlled by the RUF, Taylor's support was also in retaliation for Sierra Leone's support for ECOMOG's intervention in Liberia in 1990.

Robin Cook, the UK agreed with the nominal government of Sierra Leone, led by President Kabbah, to provide additional support to the SLA, in the form of financial and training assistance, committing a total of £21.27 million for the re-equipment of the SLA and deploying an infantry battalion to implement a retraining programme that became known as the short-term training team package.[14]

This chapter provides an overview of the reform process from 1997, the point at which the UK's involvement with security-sector reform began in Sierra Leone. It continues through the early work on police reform up until the election of 2007, when the Sierra Leone People's Party (SLPP) handed over State House to the All People's Congress (APC).[15] Starting with the overarching government department responsible for national security, the Office of National Security (ONS), and the country's security architecture, the chapter outlines the role of the reconstructed MoD and the Republic of Sierra Leone Armed Forces (RSLAF) – as the SLA was renamed in 2002. It then goes on to look at the tensions within the law and justice elements of SSR, and the post-conflict evolution of the SLP within this period. Finally, it analyses some of the core issues arising from these developments as the election took place in 2007, including national ownership and programme co-ordination.

Intelligence and the Overarching Security-Sector Architecture

With the establishment of SILSEP in June 1999, the UK led on the development of the ONS – the secretariat of the National Security Council (NSC) – and the Central Intelligence and Security Unit (CISU). These efforts were initiated in a period of uncertainty: not only was war ongoing at this point (although peace negotiations were underway), but there was also a lack of clarity among Sierra Leonean officials and international donors and advisers as to what SSR would and should entail. According to one definition circulating in Sierra Leone in the late 1990s, SSR would deal with security and defence management, specifically institutions such as the ONS. An alternative definition discussed at the time included the intelligence services.[16] In sum, it was unclear which institutions to include in activities that were labelled as SSR and, more importantly, how they

---

[14] Albrecht and Jackson, *Security System Transformation in Sierra Leone*, p. 53.

[15] This has been explored in detail elsewhere. See, for example, Albrecht and Jackson, *Security System Transformation in Sierra Leone*; Lisa Denney, *Justice and Security Reform: Development Agencies and Informal Institutions in Sierra Leone* (Oxford and New York, NY: Routledge, 2014); Paul Jackson and Peter Albrecht, *Reconstructing Security After Conflict: Security Sector Reform in Sierra Leone* (London: Palgrave Macmillan, 2010).

[16] Albrecht and Jackson, *Security System Transformation in Sierra Leone*, pp. 26–27.

were to become effective and legitimate organisations. The establishment of a clear working definition became increasingly important as Sierra Leone developed a functioning security sector because this process would include some national actors and exclude others in defining the meaning of security. In turn, these processes would help to inform international debates on SSR that the UK, and particularly DfID, was instrumental in pushing forward (see Chapter I).[17]

Funded by DfID, the ONS eventually played a key role – alongside CISU – in the final defeat of the RUF. Led by the aptly named 'national security coordinator', who became the president's principal adviser on national security, the organisation was set up in part due to pressure from international partners because it had been clear not only that *advice* intended for the president and the NSC was improperly co-ordinated and addressed, but also that *intelligence* reaching the president and NSC was unco-ordinated, unverified and piecemeal. This meant, for instance, that the chiefs of the army and police would feed conflicting information into the Office of the President, leading to paralysis of a bureaucratic system that had become increasingly dysfunctional by the late 1980s and early 1990s.

The ONS became a prime example of what the UK considered to be best practice, which defined the SSR process during this period: the separation of organisations that collect intelligence from those that assess it, and the creation of an organisation aimed at establishing an autonomous space of operation for the state, protected from political interests. Establishing the ONS constituted an attempt to ensure that the security sector was properly overseen and held to account, and that the different security actors involved were properly co-ordinated in the face of the ongoing crisis.

Integral to establishing the ONS and its ability to produce sound analysis was the collection of accurate intelligence. An effective CISU was therefore crucial. Under the terms and conditions of official development assistance, DfID was not allowed to engage in the operational activities of the security sector.[18] It was therefore agreed that the UK intelligence community would step in and work in parallel with SILSEP, whose focus was on 'non-operational' matters. With war still ongoing, this meant, in effect, that intelligence – and the analysis of that intelligence – had to be delivered to the National Security Council while the ONS and CISU were

---

17 Jennifer Sugden, 'Security Sector Reform: The Role of Epistemic Communities in the UK', *Journal of Security Sector Management* (Vol. 4, No. 4, November 2006), pp. 1–19.

18 For an in-depth discussion of what official development assistance (ODA) is, see Organisation for Economic Co-operation and Development (OECD), 'Is it ODA?', factsheet, Paris, November 2008.

still being constructed.[19] In reality this also meant that international advisers became intimately involved in operations against the RUF.

One critical factor in the success of the ONS and CISU was the presence of able staff, both Sierra Leonean and British. Specifically, the ONS had a dedicated, full-time intelligence adviser from the UK, which facilitated trust between the newly established institutions and the Sierra Leonean leadership and also allowed the development of key skills among local staff within the organisations, most of whom had no experience in intelligence or security co-ordination. In addition, the UK adviser supporting the ONS was able to play a critical role in preventing the re-politicisation of the security architecture. As then-National Security Coordinator Kellie Conteh explained in 2008:[20]

> I was in London in 2002–2003 and was asked a question about how long we would need advisers in the ONS. I said that we would need them for an extensive period of time – far beyond 2007. They were thinking about withdrawing in 2002. Our adviser had been fighting wars in the sense that much of their job was to protect the institution [from political interference] and allow it to grow. Election time [in 2007] showed security was still an issue and the entire system could have been thrown down.

The critical role of the UK adviser in opening political space within which the ONS could develop at its own speed is likely the single most important contribution an external actor could have made in such a context (something also reflected in the appointment of a Briton to the position of Sierra Leonean inspector-general of police in 1999). Indeed, in late 2002, elements within the Government of Sierra Leone continued to try to undermine the newly established ONS by convening a parallel group of national security advisers.[21] In sum, there was political pressure on these institutions from the very outset. As Kellie Conteh recalls:[22]

> I will talk to one important, but elusive point of the SSR process in Sierra Leone: creating the political space. As I saw it, if that space is not created, it is not going to work. I was the National Security Adviser for two days, and then on the third day I became the Coordinator. People

[19] For an elaborate discussion of these distinctions, and the difficulty of maintaining them in practice, see Robert Ashington-Pickett, 'Intelligence and Security Service Reconstruction', in Peter Albrecht and Paul Jackson (eds), *Security Sector Reform in Sierra Leone 1997–2007: Views from the Front Line* (Zurich: Geneva Centre for the Democratic Control of Armed Forces and LIT Verlag, 2010), pp. 19–37, 31.

[20] Kellie Conteh, working-group meeting, London, 2008.

[21] Albrecht and Jackson, *Security System Transformation in Sierra Leone*, pp. 112, 116–17.

[22] Conteh quoted in *ibid.*, pp. 112–13.

> came in with their own views, five people who picked up stories here and there. I wasn't going to work with all of them, since some of them were clearly political and I had a problem with that. If interventions are going to be made by external actors, then there has to be a structure in place – advisers, and so forth – to provide the space so actors within the country can perform. We didn't know how to do it, but Kabbah knew what he wanted to happen. The structures that are being put in place should be answerable to the president alone, but through committees, not through ministries. It should be apolitical … Gradually, people who could do sound assessments emerged. In 2003 it started to make sense.

Post-War Consolidation: Legislation and Threat Reassessments

When the conflict was officially declared over in January 2002, the process of consolidating the ONS came to the fore. Two key stages are worth mentioning here: first, the formulation and passing of the 2002 National Security and Intelligence Act (hereafter referred to as the National Security Act) and second, the production of the security-sector review between 2003 and 2005.

The 2002 National Security Act is an exemplary piece of legislation for intelligence collection and handling, providing direction for reporting to the political leadership and Parliament.[23] At its core, the Act was designed to lead to a decrease in political pressure on the collection, handling and use of intelligence. It was also designed to delineate the relationship between the ONS and CISU, and to boost the confidence of staff in the permanence of these organisations, as clearly stated in the legislation passed by the Sierra Leonean Parliament. As a result, and with the support of advisers to the ONS, a national requirement-setting system was gradually created.

The security-sector review that was produced between 2003 and 2005 was similarly crucial for a number of reasons. Importantly, it forced through the process of clearly defining those institutions that should contribute to SSR in the country. Its primary aim was to assess potential and actual threats to the implementation of Sierra Leone's 'Vision 2025', which was published in 2003 as the Government of Sierra Leone's 'national vision for long-term development'.[24] To do this, the security-sector review was to identify the institutions that should counter those threats, and make recommendations on how they could do so. For this reason, it became vital also to have a clearly outlined working definition of the security sector. This was not only because of sensitivities around making an authoritative claim on threats to Sierra Leone, but also because

---

[23] Ashington-Pickett, 'Intelligence and Security Service Reconstruction', p. 29.

[24] Government of Sierra Leone, 'Sierra Leone Vision 2025: "Sweet Salone"', Freetown, 2003, p. xi.

of the political consequences of including some actors in the process and excluding others.

In the second half of 2003, a definition of the security sector was proposed as a precursor to the review process in one of the preparatory documents drawn up by UK advisers. Under the heading 'What is the Security Sector?', the following institutions were mentioned:[25]

- Governance and oversight mechanisms, including parliamentary committees
- The ONS and CISU
- Government departments, including interior, justice, defence, foreign affairs and finance
- Uniformed services: the military, police, prisons service, customs and immigration
- The judicial system, including the Anti-Corruption Commission
- The Truth and Reconciliation Commission
- Private security companies
- Non-state paramilitary forces
- Civil-society stakeholders and non-governmental organisations (NGOs).

This was a very broad definition of security stakeholders but one that was accepted at the time. Indeed, as noted by Desmond Buck, who was seconded to the ONS from the SLP during this period: '2003 sort of harnessed all the other transformations that were taking place [with the onset of the security-sector review]. From then on it became clear that all institutions should be involved. It also became clear that there were other security institutions than just the police and armed forces.'[26] As such, the 'SSR', as the review is commonly referred to within the ONS, clarified what a linked-up security

[25] SILSEP Defence Advisory Team, 'Draft Terms of Reference for the Sierra Leone Security Sector Review', Briefing Paper on the Security Sector Review, 2003, unpublished. The involvement of the Anti-Corruption Commission and the Truth and Reconciliation Commission in the security-sector review reflected the broad and inclusive concept of security that informed the process. As noted in Government of Sierra Leone, 'Sierra Leone Vision 2025', p. 43, the Anti-Corruption Commission was set up to assist in the 'war against corruption', which was considered to be one of the principal causes of instability. Indeed, the private exploitation of public resources was considered one of the primary reasons that war broke out in the country; see Krijn Peters, *War and the Crisis of Youth in Sierra Leone* (Cambridge: Cambridge University Press, 2011). In the same vein, the research involved in implementing the Truth and Reconciliation Commission's mandate meant that it had comprehensive insight into the causes of the conflict; see Sierra Leone Truth and Reconciliation Commission, <http://www.sierraleonetrc.org/>, accessed 7 September 2014.

[26] Desmond Buck, working-group meeting, Freetown, 2008.

system might look like, and clearly articulated the many actors involved in ensuring human security – the guiding concept of the ONS at the time.

Beyond assessing threats to Sierra Leone's national 'Vision 2025', the review also aimed to facilitate the making of difficult choices about the distribution of scarce resources – as required by the World Bank-led Poverty Reduction Strategy Paper (PRSP) process.[27] As the key document governing Sierra Leone's development strategy, the PRSP, published in 2005, was wide-ranging and critically important for setting both the agenda and planning targets. Linking the security-sector review with the PRSP in this way reflected the fact that many of the threats to Sierra Leone came from a lack of economic opportunity, rather than potential military interventions or rebel insurrections. Through this process, Sierra Leone became the first country in which the central function of security in facilitating economic development was explicitly recognised in a PRSP. As noted under the heading 'Strengthening National Security': 'It is obvious from various consultations, development and security reviews that meaningful reduction of poverty and overall development in Sierra Leone is predicated on a strong and effective system that is capable of defending the state and protecting its people'.[28]

By 2006, the ONS had emerged as one of the most effective organisations in Sierra Leone's security architecture, reflected in the wide range of issues that the organisation had dealt with as it gradually matured. However, there was also a tendency to overstep its original mandate; for example, the ONS had been involved in co-ordinating rubbish collection from the streets and in responding to the water crisis that occurred in the summer of 2006. Similarly, the responsibility for the security-sector implementation plan that followed the 2003–05 review fell to the ONS, instead of the different departments of government contributing their specific expertise. So whilst the ONS became effective, this may have had a detrimental effect on other delivery mechanisms across government, as they were 'crowded out'.

The Ministry of Defence and the Armed Forces

Parts of the armed forces of Sierra Leone had staged coups in 1992 (the National Provisional Ruling Council – NPRC) and 1997 (the Armed Forces Revolutionary Council – AFRC), and the SLA had all but collapsed during the country's civil war. In fact, the military had become so distrusted that then-President Kabbah considered completely disbanding it in 1999.[29]

---

[27] International Monetary Fund (IMF), 'Sierra Leone: Poverty Reduction Strategy Paper', IMF Country Report No. 05/191, Washington, DC, 2005.
[28] *Ibid.*, p. 86.
[29] Albrecht and Jackson, *Security System Transformation in Sierra Leone*, p. 23.

Table 1: Military Reintegration Programme.[30]

	Successful Candidates				
Faction	**Sergeant**	**Corporal**	**Lance Corporal**	**Private**	**Total Intake**
RUF	13	83	140	1,173	1,409
CDF	1	46	55	535	637
AFRC	0	3	7	35	45
Total	14	132	202	1,743	2,091

However, based on planning within SILSEP,[31] in 2002 the military was officially renamed the Republic of Sierra Leone Armed Forces (RSLAF), incorporating 2,091 fighters from various factions outside the SLA, into an overall establishment of 12,000 (see Table 1). Cutting numbers further was considered at the time unnecessarily disruptive to the fragile peace process (even though the number of army personnel had grown disproportionately to around 17,000 during the war as a consequence of irregular recruitment).[32] The last basic intake through the Military Reintegration Programme graduated on 17 May 2002, and soldiers were subsequently mixed up so that membership of units and sub-units was not exclusively ex-SLA, ex-RUF or ex-CDF.[33]

From 2000, military support was provided by IMATT. Paid for and led by the UK, it took up, integrated with and expanded the work undertaken by the short-term training team that had been deployed following Operation *Palliser* as part of Operation *Silkman*. In addition to setting up and consolidating training facilities, IMATT started a comprehensive mentoring scheme for the army, including for those personnel working within the Sierra Leonean MoD. Support to the MoD, as an exercise of institution-building, was prioritised in an attempt to concentrate the control and management of national security in an organisation that was tied into the state system.

---

[30] Albrecht and Malan, 'Post-Conflict Peacebuilding and National Ownership', p. 126.

[31] Albrecht and Jackson, *Security System Transformation in Sierra Leone*, p. 48.

[32] Of the 67,309 public-sector employees estimated in 2006, some 22,322 were employed to provide services to the security sector. Of these, 11,077 (16.5 per cent) of employees were MoD/RSLAF; 9,576 (14.2 per cent) were SLP/Ministry of Internal Affairs; 352 (0.5 per cent) were employed by the justice sector; and 1,317 (2 per cent) were 'other' security staffing. Peter Middlebrook and Sharon Miller, 'Sierra Leone Security Sector Expenditure Review (SS-ER)', prepared for the DfID Sierra Leone Country Office, September 2006, <http://www.gsdrc.org/go/display&type=Document&id=4472>, accessed 15 September 2014, p. iii.

[33] Albrecht and Malan, 'Post-Conflict Peacebuilding and National Ownership', p. 127.

In January 2002, President Kabbah opened the new MoD on Tower Hill, across the street from State House. It was inaugurated as 'a joint civilian/military institution',[34] headed up by a director general and a Chief of the Defence Staff. (As per the 1991 constitution, the president remained the minister of defence and day-to-day affairs were run by a deputy minister, a situation that changed in 2007 under the new APC government.) The president also officially renamed of the armed forces at the opening ceremony in recognition of a new beginning for a new force. On the same day, the Defence Headquarters were restructured and split into two new organisations: the Joint Force Command (JFC) and the Joint Support Command (JSC).

Although the JSC was later disbanded (a development that is returned to below), it was evident from the start that the defence sector was being structured according to, and would remain aligned with, the British model. Wing Commander Richard Woodward, who was the UK personnel adviser in Sierra Leone's MoD between February 2010 and January 2013, observed:[35]

> I didn't know what to expect … the only thing that was helpful was that the organisation and the structure [of Sierra Leone's defence sector] was similar to the UK armed forces, in terms of having a MoD, a Joint Force Command – rank structures, organisation from section, to platoon to companies to platoons. It was very much a British structure.

Both the JFC and JSC were subordinated to the MoD and Chief of the Defence Staff and both were under the command of IMATT, whose objective was to steer initial development and help to build capacity. The aim of this twin force structure was to reduce the chances of a coup by dividing command responsibility. It was based on the premise that it would be much more difficult for a single 'force commander' to exert control over combat troops and support personnel, particularly in terms of access to equipment, supplies and administration. At the same time, there was a considerable practical and financial need to concentrate the geographical location of the military and withdraw from over fifty small-scale sites (some at platoon level) to nine battalion-based sites and three brigade headquarters that reflected the command-and-control structure. Budgetary constraints also meant that the RSLAF was retained as an essentially infantry army at this stage, despite ongoing discussions about a proposed maritime wing and increased air support.

---

[34] Emmanuel B Osho Coker, 'Governance and Security Sector Reform', in Albrecht and Jackson (eds), *Security Sector Reform in Sierra Leone 1997–2007*, pp. 109–18, 109, 114.

[35] Peter Albrecht interview with Richard Woodward, UK, August 2013.

The October 2003 defence White Paper defined roles within the RSLAF, between the MoD and JFC, and also between civilian and military personnel. Its production ultimately provided a good example of Sierra Leonean-owned policy-making and was evidence of a MoD that was no longer a 'clearing house' for the military. UK advisers, particularly the civil servants, supported their Sierra Leonean counterparts in the process through mentoring and partnering. In particular, the director of policy in Sierra Leone's MoD, Al-Hassan Kondeh, became focused on policy-design analysis, whilst the deputy minister and other senior staff in the ministry were encouraged to co-operate, support and participate in the process of collating information for the White Paper. In parallel, the UK provided opportunities for overseas study trips to research the production of comparative country case studies in South Africa and the UK. However, the most crucial contribution made by the UK's advisers was in supporting the editing of the final version of the White Paper for publication.

From the outset of the process, although Kondeh recognised the vital input of UK advisers,[36] he was determined to ensure that production of the White Paper was fully managed by Sierra Leoneans. However, Kondeh was faced with the challenge of making UK advisers understand the Sierra Leonean context and the impact this would have on the content and, more importantly, the process of development and delivery of the White Paper. What was not clearly understood, according to Kondeh, was that the population had not been involved in or informed about reforms of Sierra Leone's military structures. Hence, any attempt to undertake a defence review would require, in the first instance, information to be made publicly available on developments so far. The process of putting together a defence White Paper was seen as a good opportunity to do so.[37] Given the differences between this and the conventional British approach to conducting a defence review, it was not surprising that one London-based adviser observed at the time: 'the paper appeared to us to contain the kind of detail and direction that we would expect to see in a

---

[36] Indeed, Kondeh noted in an interview in 2008: 'Robert Foot [civil adviser] gave hope, mentoring [me/us] on an individual basis. He was central to early reforms'. Peter Albrecht interview with Al-Hassan Kharamoh Kondeh, Sierra Leone, 2008.

[37] Al-Hassan Kharamoh Kondeh, 'Formulating Sierra Leone's Defence White Paper', in Peter Albrecht and Paul Jackson (eds), *Security System Transformation Working Paper Series*, No. 6 (Birmingham and London: Global Facilitation Network for Security Sector Reform and International Alert, October 2008). See also Al-Hassan Kharamoh Kondeh, 'Formulating Sierra Leone's Defence White Paper', in Albrecht and Jackson (eds), *Security Sector Reform in Sierra Leone 1997–2007*, pp. 149–59.

completed White Paper, written after a Defence Review and full country-wide consultation'.[38]

Focused purely on 'defence', the White Paper was not linked into wider discussions of SSR, nor did it incorporate substantial civil-society views at this time, instead presenting a very conventional approach to reconstructing the military. Within this process, also in 2003, then-Deputy Minister of Defence Joe C Blell and some international advisers concluded that the structure of the MoD was far too complex. In alignment with the findings of the defence White Paper, a Command Structure Review Committee, also led by Sierra Leoneans, was consequently established in late 2003 to review the structure of the MoD and the RSLAF. It aimed to set out an organisation that Sierra Leonean staff could work with, understand and run, and to move away from the pattern of advisers substituting rather than building capacity. One of the main outcomes of the review, produced in January 2004, was to disband the Joint Support Command, leaving RSLAF management in the hands of a revised MoD and Joint Force Command.

This review process did not fundamentally alter internal MoD structures, but it did help to simplify the organisation. The UK blueprint that had been its original point of departure had never been fully implemented; it was also inappropriate in terms of the historical and cultural context in Sierra Leone, an understanding of which would prove essential in gaining Sierra Leonean support for the transformation process and ensuring national ownership. For example, in Sierra Leone there was no established culture of military and civilians working together, particularly given the historical attitude of the military towards civilians and the documented history of human-rights abuses.[39] For a civilian even to sit next to an officer required a degree of 'cultural adjustment', let alone for a civilian to disagree with or give instructions to military personnel.

Following the publication of the defence White Paper in 2004, then-Commander of IMATT Brigadier Simon Porter developed Plan 2010,[40] the aim of which was to deliver a smaller, better RSLAF with capable maritime and air wings. He also envisioned handing over training responsibility to

---

[38] Kondeh, 'Formulating Sierra Leone's Defence White Paper', in Albrecht and Jackson (eds), *Security Sector Reform in Sierra Leone 1997–2007*, p. 156.

[39] See, for instance, Truth and Reconciliation Commission, 'Witness to Truth: Report of the Sierra Leone Truth and Reconciliation Commission', Freetown, 2004.

[40] Broadly speaking, Plan 2010 focused its assistance in four strands: first, developing effective security-sector structures; second, enabling the RSLAF to run itself; third, supporting the RSLAF in developing the structures, logistics base, material and policy framework that underpin the functioning of a disciplined force; and finally, building the capacity of the force, individually, collectively, intellectually and physically, to allow it to fulfil the missions and tasks asked of it by the government. See IMATT, 'Plan 2010', 17 July 2004, unpublished.

the RSLAF 'in all but the most specialist areas', instead of relying on external – and costly – short-term training teams.[41] The plan noted a common theme expressed by actors involved with and affected by the security-system transformation process during this period:[42]

> Hitherto, driven by the security situation, IMATT (SL) has been largely reactive. Greater stability has allowed the development of the IMATT (SL) staff effort. Failure to act [that is, to adapt appropriately to the new context] will have negative implications for the development of the RSLAF and IMATT (SL)'s credibility.

Indeed, external threats to stability were deemed to be low; existing challenges were regarded as largely internal – a fact also reflected in the security-sector review co-ordinated by the ONS and published in 2005 (both reflecting a human-security concept). This was fully recognised within IMATT: as simply stated in Plan 2010, 'the situation in Sierra Leone is generally stable. The primary threat to stability is internal'.[43] In sum, it was recognised that Sierra Leone did not need an externally facing defence force at this stage; what was needed was internal development.

In 2004, structured training had begun at platoon and company level in some units, 'despite the constraints of resource shortages and the distraction of Op PEBU', the programme to build new barracks.[44] Similarly, substantial training, including at the senior level, was provided to RSLAF officers at the IMATT-sponsored Horton Academy. With Plan 2010, however, a more structured approach to the training of the RSLAF – and a path toward self-sustaining development – emerged, along with a clearer picture of IMATT's role and eventual drawdown. The plan was an important step in the direction of a more joined-up approach by IMATT. In the words of Brigadier David Santa-Olalla, who took up the position of commander of IMATT the following year: 'it shaped a lot of what I did. I tried to give IMATT plans some shape. Before [Plan 2010] there was a plan, but it hadn't been written down, and was basically tied to immediate

---

41 *Ibid.*

42 *Ibid.*

43 *Ibid.*

44 Operation *Pebu* was initiated in 2003 with the primary aim of building barracks for the RSLAF. As part of the restructuring exercise, the RSLAF was to be concentrated in nine battalion barracks and three brigade HQs (rather than fifty HQ/company/platoon sites). The project was marred with problems. See Albrecht and Jackson, *Security System Transformation in Sierra Leone*, pp. 106–07; Aldo Gaeta, 'Operation Pebu', in Albrecht and Jackson (eds), *Security System Transformation Working Paper Series*. By the end of 2005, 70 per cent of the project had been cancelled and in 2007, project management had been transferred from DfID to IMATT, with the commander of IMATT then overseeing its closure.

goals.'[45] As such, Plan 2010 helped to provide continuity of planning as new IMATT commanders assumed control of the long-term project of rebuilding the RSLAF.

As a final point in this section, a permanent fixture of the context in which the defence sector evolved was a lack of allocated funding from the Government of Sierra Leone. The defence budget for fiscal year 2006/07 was $13.3 million, leaving 49.5 per cent of programmed defence expenditure during that period unfunded.[46] This in turn reflected the spurious nature of national budget forecast mechanisms and resource allocation. The preceding financial year – 2005/06 – had similarly seen the anticipated defence budget cut by 50 per cent.[47] This partly reflected poor working practices within the Ministry of Finance, which had assumed centralised control of RSLAF salaries.[48] According to Barry Le Grys – commander of IMATT in 2005/06 – this centralisation negated 'a sense of ownership and responsibility on the part of the RSLAF when undertaking restructuring and redundancy programmes'.[49] In sum, this emphasises the obvious point that reforms cannot take place in isolation, but depend on systemic change that spreads beyond the sector in which targeted reforms are taking place.

Delineating the Roles of the RSLAF and the Police

Before and during the war, the SLA had in effect lost (or deliberately relegated) its main role of protecting Sierra Leonean citizens. It had collapsed and rebelled at the same time, having become an integral part of political life.[50] The task following the war was therefore to construct an

---

[45] Santa-Olalla quoted in Albrecht and Jackson, *Security System Transformation in Sierra Leone*, p. 104.

[46] IMATT, 'Future Delivery of RSLAF Transformation by IMATT'.

[47] Total government spending in 2006 was $344 million. Once projected off-budget security spending (incorporating gifts, donated equipment and so forth) was included, spending across the entire security sector in 2006 was $99 million – 29 per cent of total on-budget spending. These numbers are consultants' projections only, and are drawn from a security-sector expenditure review carried out in 2006 (clear and coherent figures are difficult to obtain). Due to a backlog in the Ministry of Finance, the latest available reconciled actual budgetary numbers for the report were for 2003. The Office of the Accountant-General, in co-operation with the Ministry of Finance budget department, was at the time in the process of reconciling the accounts for 2004/05. See Middlebrook and Miller, 'Sierra Leone Security Sector Expenditure Review (SS-ER)', p. 15.

[48] An average of 78 per cent of public spending in 2003–05 was allocated to cover wage and non-wage recurrent costs, as well as interest payments on both domestic and external borrowing from a high of 80 per cent in 2003 to a low of 75 per cent in 2005. *Ibid.*, p. 19.

[49] IMATT, 'Future Delivery of RSLAF Transformation by IMATT'.

[50] It is worth keeping in mind that the APC government under Siaka Stevens appointed the force commander and the IGP as members of parliament.

army that could be effective against any future rebellion, protect the territorial integrity of Sierra Leone and also, perhaps, act as peacekeepers elsewhere. Above all, however, the aim was to ensure that the RSLAF stayed out of the political arena.

One of the contentious issues that affected the RSLAF as it emerged from conflict and collapse was rivalry with the police, particularly over the issue of domestic security primacy. A meaningful distinction between internal and external security threats as the responsibility of the police and the army, respectively, had weakened under Major General Joseph Momoh from 1985, and had collapsed with the 1992 NPRC coup. The ten years of conflict that followed led to a fundamental disintegration of boundaries between the country's two primary security agencies, with the distinction between those forces identified with the collapsed bureaucratic state and rebel groups (such as the RUF and the West Side Boys) and local militias (such as the CDF) also disappearing. By the late 1990s, re-establishing roles and responsibilities of both the police and army was therefore crucial, and part of the broader vision of establishing a democratic state.

Until 2004–05, the two organisations had received fundamentally different types of external assistance through IMATT and the Commonwealth Community Safety and Security Project (CCSSP), respectively. By 2005, the view had developed within the SLP that the RSLAF's achievements thus far had been delivered or driven by IMATT, ultimately making reform efforts less sustainable in the long term. Nonetheless, a qualitative perception survey among RSLAF officers conducted in 2006 also showed that since 2004, relations between the police and the army had 'become, if not stronger, then more accepting'.[51]

A sense of vagueness in roles and responsibilities also appeared less pronounced by 2006. As the same perception survey noted, 'In 2004, it was suggested that although aware of the message of police primacy, participants perceived RSLAF and police roles to be unclear and overlapping'.[52] However, by 2006, RSLAF members had begun 'perceiving their role in relation to the police more clearly with less need to make direct comparisons between themselves and the police'.[53]

One reason for this shift in perception no doubt related to the ONS's formulation in 2005 of the policy defining Military Aid to the Civil Power (MACP), which clearly asserted police primacy within domestic security and outlined when and how the SLP could call on RSLAF assistance, should the security situation demand it. Given historical tensions, MACP was an important first step in giving much-needed clarity to relations

[51] Defence Intelligence Report, 'Sierra Leone: Assessment of the Effectiveness of EX GREEN EAGLE in Managing Perception in Sierra Leone', 2006, unpublished.
[52] *Ibid.*
[53] *Ibid.*

between the SLP and the RSLAF, and by defining precisely when and how the armed forces could play a role in internal security it had the effect of reducing rivalry between the two groups,[54] with a further revision of the policy initiated during 2013.

Another means of further clarifying the RSLAF's role, as well as investing the force with a stronger identity, emerged through the possibility of contributing troops to the ECOWAS Standby Force (ESF), as well as UN and African Union (AU) peacekeeping missions. By 2006, as noted by then-Commander of IMATT Barry Le Grys in his end-of-tour report, RSLAF contributions to international military operations were seen as an important mechanism for reinforcing national pride and developing operational capability.[55] However, while it was one of the RSLAF's stated priorities, at this stage it lacked several capabilities that would be essential to a successful contribution in this regard. As noted in a 2006 report discussing IMATT's ongoing support to the RSLAF:[56]

> Rather like the difficulty of conveying the concept of community policing to the SLP, a shift from conventional to PSO [peace support operation] activities will need much close involvement at the tactical level. The subject has been introduced but there is far too much still to do, if the first PSO deployment is to be one that starts a reputation to be proud of.

In this report, IMATT stated its willingness to support the development of some of these capabilities, but this assistance was to be conditional on what was referred to as a 'comprehensive and sustainable plan' for an appropriately sized and trained force.[57] This could in turn pave the way for an in-depth defence review after the 2007 elections,[58] which, along with a formalised and inclusive preparatory process, would have been critical as the strategic foundation of downsizing the RSLAF (the defence review did not, ultimately, take place).

However, downsizing the armed forces to an affordable and sustainable size continued to be hotly debated in Sierra Leone. In 2006, there was persistent tension between the need to produce a defence review and resistance from the RSLAF leadership to doing so, partly because it knew that it would lead to significant further reductions in personnel numbers. 'If you reduced the numbers, you reduced the

---

54 Albrecht and Malan, 'Post-Conflict Peacebuilding and National Ownership', pp. 127–29.

55 Barry Le Grys quoted in Albrecht and Jackson, *Security System Transformation in Sierra Leone*, p. 153.

56 IMATT, 'Future Delivery of RSLAF Transformation by IMATT'.

57 Albrecht and Jackson, *Security System Transformation in Sierra Leone*, p. 153.

58 IMATT, 'Future Delivery of RSLAF Transformation by IMATT'.

influence of the senior forces', recalls Iain Cholerton, the commander of IMATT in 2007, because there would be fewer people under their command.[59] Furthermore, there was resistance from the soldiers themselves, because of the identity, sense of belonging and, not least, the income inherent to being part of the RSLAF. The bottom line, as noted by Jonathan Powe, who followed Cholerton as commander of IMATT in 2008, was that '[it was a] difficult thing to do in a country with little employment opportunity'.[60]

Despite the ongoing discussions about downsizing the RSLAF, ambitions to contribute to PSOs persisted. In 2006, the RSLAF had already contributed a staff officer to the ESF headquarters in Nigeria. Whilst not yet deployable, a force structure was designed based on the potential contribution by Sierra Leone of at least an infantry company, and possibly a battalion, to the ESF. The debate in 2006 revolved around whether to select the company or battalion as a whole, which would be based on the best operational evaluation reports, or whether selection should be carried out by picking the best individuals to make up the company or battalion that would be sent. Either way, there was an obvious incentive in the possibility of being employed on UN subsistence rates through ESF contributions: as noted in 2005, long-term income generation could emanate from RSLAF contributions to peacekeeping missions.[61] Yet up until 2006, these were theoretical discussions based on a genuine need to formulate a role that the RSLAF would find meaningful.

The maritime sphere was not mentioned in the main body of Plan 2010, but financial gains from operations in support of fisheries protection became one of IMATT's key priorities.[62] It was generally believed that if an effective maritime authority was established, Sierra Leone could access a significant source of revenue, with the RSLAF's maritime wing policing the country's territorial waters and Exclusive Economic Zone.[63] As then-Deputy Commander of IMATT Colonel Hugh Blackman observed in December 2008: 'The development of a coherent and capable Maritime Wing (MW) remains fundamental to the long-term economic success of GoSL [Government of Sierra Leone]'.[64]

---

59 Peter Albrecht interview with Iain Cholerton, over Skype, August 2013.

60 Peter Albrecht interview with Jonathan Powe, over Skype, August 2013.

61 Albrecht and Malan, 'Post-Conflict Peacebuilding and National Ownership', p. 138.

62 In one of the annexes to Plan 2010, it was noted that the one remaining patrol boat of the maritime wing was damaged in May 2004 and beyond economic repair. IMATT, 'Progress of the RSLAF in 2003/04', 17 July 2004, unpublished.

63 It was estimated that effective maritime control could result in an additional $10 million per year for the government. *Ibid.*

64 IMATT, 'IMATT Reorientation Phases 3 and 4 – Initial Thoughts', 2008, unpublished.

Indeed, 2007 and 2008 were the years when capacity of the maritime wing peaked.[65] As noted by Patrick O'Byrne, UK adviser to the maritime wing in 2013–14: 'During this period [2007–08], they were quite a capable force on paper, and they were able to go out, and were able to patrol'.[66] A Joint Maritime Authority was developed, the maritime wing received considerable support from UK and Canadian IMATT advisers, and was donated new vessels by China and the US.[67] However, the bottom line was that maritime security was more of an IMATT than an RSLAF priority, showing that while in theory it may have been a good idea, success is predicated on local political will to translate an idea into practice.

Operation *Phoenix*: Resurrecting a Police Force

The necessity of building order and moving beyond war-fighting was prioritised through the re-establishment of the SLP, which began in the late 1990s and dominated reform efforts up until 2005. As early as 1996, President Kabbah had requested support from the UK to resurrect the central government's ability to enforce order within the country's borders. This exercise became known as Operation *Phoenix*, and was approached on the assumption that the SLP was recovering from crisis. As noted in an internal Commonwealth Police Development Task Force (CPDTF) document, it would now have to 'reclaim its rightful primacy in the maintenance of public tranquillity and law enforcement ... There is a need for visible targeted policing to be introduced on a twenty-four hour basis every day of the year'.[68]

Operation *Phoenix* was initiated by the UK-dominated CPDTF,[69] and taken over by the Commonwealth Community Safety Security Project in 2000. In parallel to the CCSSP – which focused exclusively on the police in the period of its implementation, between 2000 and 2005 – the smaller, DfID-funded Law Development Programme worked on the state-sanctioned court system following its establishment in 2001.[70] From the outset, there was a separation at the level of policy and programming between access to legal services (the judiciary) and the provision of security (policing). The prioritisation of the latter was also reflected in funding.

---

[65] Peter Albrecht interview with Patrick O'Byrne, Sierra Leone, February 2014.
[66] *Ibid*.
[67] One Chinese patrol boat and three US cutters.
[68] Commonwealth Police Development Task Force (CPDTF), 'Sierra Leone Police – Re-introduction of Effective Operational Policing', 1999, unpublished.
[69] The CPDTF was initiated in 1997 but was delayed because of the AFRC coup. Albrecht and Jackson, *Security System Transformation in Sierra Leone*, p. 36.
[70] Denney, *Justice and Security Reform*, p. 104.

Whereas the CCSSP had a budget of £27 million, the Law Development Programme had just £3–4 million at its disposal.[71]

How the re-establishment of justice and security in Sierra Leone was envisioned and pursued cannot be analysed separately from how considerable investments were channelled by the CCSSP into equipment, infrastructure, logistics and human capacity in support of the SLP. The CCSSP constituted the 'heyday' of police reform in Sierra Leone. During the life of the programme, investments were made with the sole purpose of establishing a state-centred police organisation that could enforce 'internal security' and replace the chaos of war and military coups with the rule of law. Central to the CCSSP was the purchase of new vehicles, uniforms and radios by the UK on the part of the SLP, which became an essential component of the post-war state-building effort.[72]

Given the extent to which the Sierra Leonean state bureaucracy had collapsed in the late 1990s, the two British police advisers, Keith Biddle and Adrian Horn, who led the international contribution from 1997 until 2003, believed that they were working from a clean slate. It was also commonly assumed that if the state did not fill the 'power vacuum' created by war, criminal groups and warring factions would. Horn, who managed the CCSSP, believed that 'a complete re-structuring of the police service in Sierra Leone' was necessary.[73] As he recalls: 'I had the luxury of free thinking … my previous involvements in developing change were usually constrained by systems and procedures, which only allowed tinkering and not "blue sky" thinking. This was different.'[74]

Apart from the work of the CCSSP, Keith Biddle, a retired assistant chief constable from the UK, was appointed by President Kabbah as Sierra Leone's inspector-general of police (IGP) in 1999.[75] This was a remarkable move, which was taken because Kabbah did not trust a Sierra Leonean in that role. Not since W G Syer had led the country's police force during the final years of colonial rule, before handing over command to L W Leigh in 1963, had a non-Sierra Leonean been the executive head of the SLP.[76] Yet forty years later, in 2003, a UK police officer would yet again hand executive powers over the police to a Sierra Leonean successor, Brima Acha Kamara.

---

[71] Peter Alexander Albrecht, 'Transforming Internal Security in Sierra Leone: Sierra Leone Police and Broader Justice Sector Reform', *DIIS Report* 2010:07, Copenhagen, 2010, p. 69.
[72] *Ibid.*, p. 33.
[73] Horn quoted in Albrecht and Jackson, *Security System Transformation in Sierra Leone*, p. 32.
[74] *Ibid.*
[75] *Ibid.*, p. 33.
[76] Erlend Grøner Krogstad, 'Security, Development and Force: Revisiting Police Reform in Sierra Leone', *African Affairs* (Vol. 111, No. 443, 2012), pp. 261–80.

Relations between Biddle and the president were personal and close, with regular one-on-one meetings between the two.[77] According to Garth Glentworth, a senior civil servant in DfID who was closely involved in the development of both SILSEP and the CCSSP, this relationship was partly shaped by Biddle's insistence on having direct access to the president, instead of communicating via the Ministry of Internal Affairs (MIA). Otherwise, Glentworth recalled, Biddle said that he would not take up the position.

This, in combination with the fact that there has been limited political will within the Government of Sierra Leone to strengthen the MIA since the end of the civil war, has had a profoundly negative impact – not only in terms of the ministry's continued limited capacity, but also on policy development relating to the police. As Biddle noted in retrospect:[78]

> [Y]ou can only do what the climate allows you to do. The Ministry of Internal Affairs was not seen as [part of] SSR. The development of the MIA was included in the CCSSP with the Permanent Secretary as Project Director. However, due to the political dynamics at the time, work with the MIA wasn't taken forward, it just didn't happen.

The consequence was that since late 2000, the political interface between the SLP and the executive has been through the vice president in his role as chair of the Police Council, the highest decision-making body of the police as per the 1991 constitution.[79] During Kabbah's presidency (1996–97 and 1998–2007), the RSLAF suffered from not having a dedicated minister representing its interests at Cabinet level; however, particularly in

---

[77] While based on observations by others, this uniquely close relationship between a head of state and an adviser also came across clearly in a number of interviews that one of the authors of this paper, Peter Albrecht, conducted with Biddle over the course of two days in France in 2009. Not only did Biddle and Kabbah regularly meet one-on-one, but Biddle also knew Kabbah's private thoughts on a number of issues, including Sankoh's imprisonment, his own appointment and so forth. The closeness of this relationship is not surprising. Kabbah was, as noted earlier, particularly keen on initiating police reform from the start of his first term, and personally requested that Biddle, who had come to Sierra Leone as part of the Commonwealth Police Development Task Force, become the inspector-general.

[78] Biddle quoted in Albrecht and Jackson, *Security System Transformation in Sierra Leone*, p. 80.

[79] According to Article 157 of Sierra Leone's constitution, the 'Inspector-General shall be appointed by the President acting on the advice of the Police Council, subject to the approval of Parliament'. Similarly, it lies within the powers of the Police Council to appoint officers to the rank of assistant superintendent of police and above (except the IGP) and to dismiss, reduce in rank and exercise disciplinary control over them. Under Article 158, the Police Council also advises the president on all major matters of policy relating to internal security, including budgeting, financing and administration.

the early years of the MoD, significant effort was put into building and sustaining civilian policy-making capacity. As with the RSLAF, the SLP was not sufficiently represented at Cabinet level, but in addition, the police also suffered from the general weakness of policy-making skills within the MIA. As the authors of this Whitehall Paper concluded in 2009: 'Papers prepared to rationalize legislative or institutional changes as well as SLP budget proposal, which, strictly speaking, would have been the task of the Minister of Internal Affairs to take forward, have often stalled or been side-lined'.[80]

Apart from the desire by the executive to maintain political control of the SLP, there are a number of other factors that, together, have prevented the reform of both the MIA and the Police Council – even to the present day. One main stumbling block has been the upper executive's reluctance to hand its powers over the police to a separate ministry (just as the president, until the APC came to power in 2007, maintained his position as minister of defence, with a deputy handling the day-to-day work of the MoD). Second, Keith Biddle established a pattern – in his insistence on direct access to the president and vice president – of bypassing the MIA on issues relating to the SLP. Third, the CCSSP remained narrowly focused on police reform, rather than embracing the full range of justice-sector institutions. This may have been all that was possible at the time, and it was certainly by design, but it had the effect of isolating the SLP from, for example, the RSLAF and ONS, as well as the broader governance system. Finally, and related to the above, the personality of advisers, as well as consecutive ministers of internal affairs, contributed to an atmosphere of confrontation, rather than one of collaboration: Ministers Charles Margai, Prince Harding and Sam Hinga Norman, for example, were largely regarded as corrupt by prominent international advisers.

Generally speaking, the initial phase of police reform between 1997 and 2005 emphasised building capacity at the senior levels of the SLP – including the provision of training at the College of Policing in Bramshill, in the UK – and was characterised by the notion that building a strong police force from the centre (in Freetown) outwards (to the provinces) would eventually allow the police to monopolise the provision of security and provide better services at the local level. This was, very clearly, state-building by police reform. Prior to 2002, reform efforts took place predominantly in Freetown and emphasised strategic issues, in part because of a genuine need to do so, but also because it was not possible to move outside the capital due to continued fighting. The emphasis on

[80] Albrecht and Jackson, *Security System Transformation in Sierra Leone*, p. 132. The point is based on an interview with Biddle's successor as IGP, Brima Acha Kamara, conducted in 2008 in Sierra Leone by Peter Albrecht.

Freetown was also precipitated by the severity of the security situation in the capital at the time, given the high number of internally displaced persons occupying any building available, particularly in the east of the city.

Due to the security situation in the country, Biddle and Horn, supported by Kabbah, considered it crucial that the SLP retain significant armed capability. The Operational Support Division (OSD) – the armed police unit responsible for public-order management – was thus established around the remnants of the Special Security Division (SSD) that had been founded by Siaka Stevens (indeed, in March 2002 the SSD was renamed the OSD).[81] It was believed that without arms the SLP would be unable to assume responsibility for internal security. The proposal was, in effect, to establish a colonial-style police structure with similarities to that of the UK. As an assessment in the late 1990s suggested:[82]

> Even in a more established peaceful environment [in Sierra Leone], there will undoubtedly be considerable violent lawlessness from both 'rehabilitated' and renegade rebels, as well as the criminal population. Despite disarmament, there will be large numbers of illegally held firearms available. Consequently, it will be impossible for the SLP to maintain law and order without a high level of armed response available to them. There is no police service in the world that is not armed to some degree. However, it is not envisaged that the SLP will be a wholly armed service, but will have a permanently armed component, equipped with specialist police weapons and ammunition designed to neutralise only the selected target, and not military weapons and ammunition designed to kill as many people as possible as quickly as possible.

This was a contentious issue, not least because the SSD, known as 'Siaka Stevens' Dogs' in the 1980s, had been loathed and feared.[83] However, it had then gained much legitimacy amongst the local population for being one of the few arms of the state to fight back successfully against the RUF. Notably, therefore, this legitimacy did not come from policing, but from combat operations. This created tension between DfID, which was not necessarily supportive of retaining a domestic paramilitary unit – and particularly one that had been recently armed by the UK MoD with weaponry worth around $1.4 million – and the UK advisers within the

---

[81] *Ibid.*, p. 90. In turn, the SSD has its roots in two units: one British trained, the Internal Security Unit (ISU) 1, which focused on public-order policing and was set up before independence in 1961; and a second parallel body, the ISU 2, which was established in 1970. ISU 2 was given military training and was armed by Cuba, having been established to preserve the Siaka Stevens regime. ISU 1 and 2 were fused into one force, the SSD, in 1979 and were retrained by Cuba.

[82] Special Security Division, 'A Report on the Special Security Division of the Sierra Leone Police', Report No. 1, October 1999, unpublished.

[83] Albrecht and Jackson, *Security System Transformation in Sierra Leone*, p. 38.

CCSSP, who regarded security as the paramount requirement (the OSD had lost most of its weaponry, but it was only lightly re-armed). It was only by engaging the UK Chief of the Defence Staff directly in facilitating the establishment of the OSD that this was possible, since this would not be possible under the tenets of official development assistance, which prohibits the use of development funds for military purposes. There was also constant concern even amongst those advisers, like Ray England, who were most closely associated with the OSD that the unit would revert to old habits and become a well-armed security threat instead of acting as a force for good. The bottom line was, however, that already by 2002, the OSD was emerging as 'militarily prominent' in Freetown.[84]

After the war ended, it became possible to transfer SLP operations outside Freetown and move from developing a theoretical, strategic approach to implementing a more practical one. Deployment of the SLP across the country was made possible at this stage by the UK's extensive investment in necessary equipment.[85] Indeed, by 2004, as one assessment noted, 'the SLP has improved [its] responsiveness and its visibility. A major factor in achieving this situation has been the communications, vehicles and infrastructure support provided by the CCSSP'.[86] These investments were not sustainable in the long term, but their stabilising effect was undeniable; they were a crucial part of early state-building in Sierra Leone.

In 2003, Biddle handed over leadership of the SLP to Brima Acha Kamara, whom he had originally picked as one of the new leaders of the SLP. However, as per the 1991 constitution, Acha Kamara's appointment to IGP was made by the president on the advice of the Police Council, which had discussed the strengths and weaknesses of all of the candidates. In preparation, Acha Kamara – together with other potential candidates for the positions of IGP, deputy IGP and assistant inspector-general (the three highest ranks) – was frequently tasked by Biddle to present to the Police Council, brief the president and accompany him on official functions throughout the country.[87] As Biddle recalls:[88]

---

[84] Peter Albrecht interview with anonymous, Sierra Leone, July 2013. As the OSD emerged, its headquarters was put in a different location from those of the SLP and, as such, physical distance between the two seats of command was introduced. In addition, the new headquarters were given unprecedented authority over deployments and reassignments. Coupled with a separate self-image and a desire to stand apart from the rest of the SLP, this laid the foundation for a separate force (see Chapters III and IV for more on the OSD).

[85] Albrecht and Jackson, *Security System Transformation in Sierra Leone*, p. 87; Commonwealth Community Safety and Security Project (CCSSP), 'Visit Report', June 2004.

[86] CCSSP, 'Visit Report'.

[87] Albrecht and Jackson, *Security System Transformation in Sierra Leone*, p. 91.

[88] Biddle quoted in *ibid.*

> In the event the selection procedure was professionally conducted with some nine candidates being thoroughly scrutinized and analysed. Neither political consideration nor tribal preferences were brought into the selection equation. For my appointment, I had gone through the same process that culminated with an extremely thorough panel interview before the Parliamentary Select Committee, and I have to say that it was the most rigorous interview to which I was ever subjected. My successor's interview was equally thorough and more stressful, as it was televised and broadcasted on the radio – live! The selection process was as professional and as politically independent as those for selecting chief constables in the UK.

Although the CCSSP continued until early 2005, planning for its successor was underway as early as June 2002, reflecting new DfID thinking on security and justice programming, which had changed significantly since the two Commonwealth police programmes whose full implementation began in 1998 and 1999, respectively.

'Holistic' Justice-Sector Reform

The implementation of the Justice Sector Development Programme (JSDP), managed by the British Council and funded by DfID, began in 2005 and was initiated to support the Sierra Leone government's Poverty Reduction Strategy Paper by helping to improve access to affordable justice. Established much later than SILSEP or the CCSSP, the implementation of the JSDP thus began in a more benign environment than either of those programmes. The war had officially come to an end and Sierra Leone was transitioning from a peace-making to a peace-building context. Yet, although by 2005 the SLP in particular had already received considerable support through the CCSSP, the Law Development Programme had worked with the judiciary for less time and on a much smaller scale. This meant that support to the prison system and the broader justice sector, for example, had been limited or non-existent until the establishment of the JSDP.[89]

---

[89] Prison-service transformation, in particular, has been a central preoccupation of the Justice Sector Development Programme (JSDP), which is believed to have had a considerable impact on how the service is managed and directed. With no attention paid to prisons under the CCSSP, quick wins were more realistic because of the poor state of the prison infrastructure. For instance, the complete absence of juveniles in prisons in Freetown today is considered a significant achievement: with the building of a remand home, juveniles are now segregated from adult prisoners. Similarly, the building of an all-female prison in Kenema District was considered to have vastly improved the conditions for inmates and staff. See Piet Biesheuvel et al., 'Justice Sector Development Programme – Annual Review', March 2009, unpublished, p. 17. See also JSDP, 'Achievements and Lessons Learned', 2012, unpublished, p. 35.

The CCSSP's strong focus on the police was due to the programme's formulation, the personalities and professional backgrounds of the advisers (who were retired police officers), and not least Kabbah's keenness to establish and consolidate internal security, centred on the state. By the time the war ended, however – and with international policy-makers devising holistic approaches to SSR – it was thought that support to the police and the judiciary was not appropriately linked up.

The design of the DfID-funded JSDP had begun in June 2002. However, it was subject to considerable delay and was only approved in April 2004, with implementation beginning in March 2005. At the same time, the CCSSP officially came to an end in June 2005. This created significant start-up challenges for the JSDP, with some stakeholders impatient to see activities begin, while the police were concerned that the level of support that they had received through the CCSSP would end, or at least change significantly.

Under the JSDP, priority reform areas were expanded beyond single organisations and incorporated the indexing of customary law, prison overcrowding and delays in court, as well as efforts to address the lack of specialist justice provision for youths, and the lack of support mechanisms to meet, as one JSDP review noted in 2007, the 'needs of the poor, vulnerable and marginalised to access justice and the lack of connection between community needs and police operations'.[90] This took place as the previous focus on the SLP as an institution was eclipsed by both DfID's growing reluctance, especially after 9/11, to support programming considered too strongly oriented towards security and 'the state' rather than 'the people', and its ambitions to focus on the broader justice sector, and on the judiciary in particular. The JSDP also attempted to go beyond the formal court system to encompass the customary justice sector, which is estimated to provide justice for around 80 per cent of the population.[91]

---

[90] Geoff Bredemear, Kadi Fakondo and Laure-Helene Piron, 'Sierra Leone Justice Sector Development Programme: Output to Purpose Review Report', DfID, 2007, unpublished, pp. 9–10; Denney, *Justice and Security Reform*; Geoff Bredemear and S Lewis, 'Justice Sector Development Program – Annual Output to Purpose Review', DfID, 2008.

[91] Such estimates appear in most policy-related literature on informal or non-state justice. See, for example, OECD, 'Enhancing the Delivery of Justice and Security', 2007, p. 6; United Nations Development Programme (UNDP), 'Community Security and Social Cohesion: Towards a UNDP Approach', 2009, p. 9; Leila Chirayath, Caroline Sage and Michael Woolcock, 'Customary Law and Policy Reform: Engaging with the Plurality of Justice Systems', World Bank, July 2005; USAID, 'Field Study of Informal and Customary Justice in Afghanistan and Recommendations on Improving Access to Justice and Relations between Formal Courts and Informal Bodies', 2005. See also Peter Albrecht and Helene Maria Kyed, 'Local Actors in Security and Justice Programming', in Jackson (ed.), *Handbook of International Security and Development*.

The JSDP thus marked DfID's return to its perceived 'core business': that of bettering conditions for the poor. This shift was supported consistently by the JSDP in both Freetown and Moyamba District in the south, which became the 'pilot district' outside of the Western Area (the region around Freetown), where more concentrated reform efforts took place.

As noted, the UK had been involved in the justice sector since January 2001 and since the introduction of the Law Development Programme, which focused mainly on formal legal procedure. However, the bulk of UK support up to 2005 had been channelled into the SLP. Given the security situation of the late 1990s and early 2000s, coupled with the impact of increased drug trafficking in West Africa and an emerging drive from donors to address a post-9/11 agenda of counter-terrorism, it is clear that the police force was a critical element in the maintenance of internal security. However, at the same time, the perception of increased securitisation of development assistance and the militarisation of foreign assistance meant that it became more difficult for DfID to fulfil its role under international rules governing official development assistance. There had always been reluctance within DfID, a development agency, to venture too far into security programming; but with 9/11 and the militarisation of interventions that followed, this reluctance inevitably grew.[92]

As such, by 2005, DfID's priorities had shifted significantly and the concept of SSR was disappearing from its vocabulary, increasingly being replaced by another abbreviation: 'S&J' (security and justice) programming. SSR was now considered too strategic and too closely centred on the state level; the change in emphasis thus embodied a desire to move to a more people-centred approach to developing the justice sector, specifically in terms of levels of access on the part of the poor – something manifested clearly in the JSDP's focus on a fair and efficient court system, which had been one of the core gaps in previous approaches to security and justice. This, then, represented a rebalancing in the attention paid by DfID to security and justice elements, with growing prioritisation of the latter at the expense of the former.[93]

The Ebbs and Flows of National Ownership

One of the key reasons the SSR process stayed on track during the decade between 1997 and 2007 was that citizens as well as leaders bought into the overarching idea of UK engagement in the country. In short, as noted by

---

[92] For an analysis of this from a policing perspective, see Peter Albrecht et al., 'Community Policing in Sierra Leone – Local Policing Partnership Boards', *DIIS Report* 2014:16, Copenhagen, 2014, pp. 16–20. See also Albrecht and Stepputat, 'The Rise and Fall of Security Sector Reform in Development'.

[93] Chapter III of this Whitehall Paper details the full implementation of the JSDP from 2007.

Adrian Freer, commander of IMATT in 2003: 'there was no appetite to go back. It worked because the local population wanted us [the UK] to be there.'[94] Had this fundamental buy-in not existed – and had it not been there from the very start – it would not have been possible for so many reforms to be implemented, and so quickly. In the late 1990s and early 2000s, this benefited the focus on security as the top priority, which had been set by the president. At the state opening of Parliament on 22 May 1998, Kabbah stated: 'I take the security of this country as my number one priority and intend to pursue this objective with all necessary vigour'.[95] Similarly, at the state opening of Parliament on 11 June 1999, Kabbah adopted 'peace, security and development' as his main theme, pointing out that in 'developed countries of the world, peace and security have provided the foundation for their progress' and that, in Sierra Leone, 'human needs and human security must be the basis for our development.'[96]

However, there was also a clear understanding from the outset that some resistance – expressed on technical and political grounds – within the institutions that were being reformed (and built) should be expected, notably because of what such changes would mean for resource distribution. In the SLP, generally speaking, some senior officers would resist changes because they would have to put in more effort, and comply with new, demanding, and accountable systems and procedures. Many in the lower ranks would resist as they too would have to put in more work under better systems of supervision, which would also require them to be more proactive. Yet, within the SLP, the fact that an expatriate was leading the organisation made robust and at times drastic action in pursuit of reform a possibility.

With the handover from Biddle to Acha Kamara in June 2003 came fears that a Sierra Leonean leadership would slip into allowing methods of policing similar to those used before the conflict, and that UK support would disappear. Access to funding did indeed change significantly, but only in the sense that a Sierra Leonean inspector-general of police could not make the same demands as his expatriate counterpart on international donor resources.[97]

---

[94] Adrian Freer, roundtable, UK, 18 December, 2007.

[95] Ahmad Tejan Kabbah, 'Address on the Occasion of the State Opening of the Second Session of the First Parliament of the Second Republic of Sierra Leone', Freetown, 22 May 1998, <http://[www.sierra-leone.org/Speeches/kabbah-052298.html>, accessed 28 September 2014.

[96] Ahmad Tejan Kabbah, 'Address on the Occasion of the State Opening of the Third Session of the First Parliament of the Second Republic of Sierra Leone', Freetown, 11 June 1999, <http://[www.sierra-leone.org/GOSL/kabbah-061199.html>, accessed 28 September 2014.

[97] Albrecht and Jackson, *Security System Transformation in Sierra Leone*, p. 89.

Despite these fears, between 2003 and 2007 Acha Kamara gained considerable operational autonomy. In his words, once he had taken over as IGP:[98]

> [I]t became easier because we started to own the thing – everybody became involved in a very active way. The umbrella [of international leadership] was gone, and the message that had been very much conveyed to us was that in any situation there must be one leader, but that we could only make it as a team. There was that awareness among us that we should be seen to sustain what had been done. We started to review some of the policies, whether they suited us, and the Executive Management Board [the highest decision-making body in the SLP] became much livelier. Before, we said that whatever Keith [Biddle] decided was the right thing – without much discussion. Confidence started to come; we became bolder and dismantled a lot of the check points that existed across the country. Our own situation in the SLP had been unique. Keith was British, but the whole team was Sierra Leonean. In our various roles we were able to assist him; he worked through us. If you take Keith out, all the key players were still in place.

However, although the heads of Sierra Leone's security-sector institutions – including the SLP, ONS, CISU and RSLAF – were taking ownership of the SSR process, a number of other issues emerged. Notably, fractures were appearing within the political leadership. There was what can best be described as a 'perception–reality gap' with respect to what SSR actually meant. Principal stakeholders up to the presidential level might have supported SSR as a concept and as a process that would make state agencies more efficient in carrying out their functions. However, there were differing views with respect to what this would mean in practice.

Between the late 1990s and 2002, international support had been focused predominantly on winning the war, as well as stabilising the country and building the capacity of state institutions to continue this work going forwards. The different programmes that carried the SSR label were thus all engaged in the process of supporting the Government of Sierra Leone in achieving a sustainable victory. However, in the context of reform that followed the end of the war, effective intelligence-gathering could more easily be applied to expose the misuse of public funds within state institutions. Those officials with a vested interest in maintaining the status quo in this regard therefore began to resist SSR.[99]

Moreover, even though the newly established ONS was hailed as one of the key successes of externally supported SSR, there were clear indications that it had garnered more support from those external advisers

---

[98] *Ibid.*

[99] *Ibid.*, p. 4.

who had been instrumental in its establishment than from the president it was supposed to advise.

Indeed, while the ONS was being set up, Kabbah continued to use an informal group of trusted individuals to advise him on national security issues. Second, and following on from this point, because the country had generally been stabilised, Kabbah began to lose interest in the SSR process – and more broadly in the institutions and mechanisms established to support the provision of security. As then-National Security Coordinator Kellie Conteh observed:[100]

> By 2003 there was some attention [to the SSR process and national security matters in general], in 2004 less, in 2005 they were so comfortable [with the security situation] that they didn't listen at all. Defence Councils were postponed several times. The NSC [National Security Council] had not been convened for two years until we pushed for one major meeting, where we said that the government needed to be aware of the issues. By 2007 most ministries cared less about security.

While the various security agencies prepared for the 2007 general election, for instance, Kabbah displayed little interest in election security planning – and the fact that the election was ultimately relatively free of violence reflected the successful elements of the country's SSR process rather than the institutionalisation of a reform approach within State House.

Direction from London and In-Country Co-ordination

Another key issue in relation to the UK's involvement in Sierra Leonean stabilisation and peace-building was the continuing struggle to achieve joined-up government among UK departments. Although the High Commission is the principal political authority among UK institutions overseas, this was not reflected in the relationship between the High Commission, DfID and IMATT in Sierra Leone (indeed, until 2005 DfID did not have a permanent presence in the country). Each organisation reported back to London separately, and not necessarily in a co-ordinated way:[101] whilst IMATT was following Plan 2010 – the long-term strategy guiding its engagement with the RSLAF and eventual drawdown – from 2004, DfID pursued a country strategy that was considerably wider, incorporating the funding and implementation of SILSEP, the CCSSP and, later, the JSDP.

At the same time, while there might not have been a clearly outlined strategy for SSR in Sierra Leone that cut across the Foreign Office, MoD

[100] Conteh quoted in *ibid.*, p. 128.
[101] *Ibid.*, p. 171.

and DfID, there were regular meetings in the Cabinet Office about UK engagement in the country. With the backing of then-Prime Minister Tony Blair, the question of Sierra Leone and its recovery carried political weight in Whitehall. This circumstance was founded in strong historical ties between the UK and Sierra Leone, combined with a number of personal commitments by influential British politicians who had connections to the country. For instance, the fact that Blair's father had lectured in law at Freetown's Fourah Bay College during the 1960s is said to have influenced the prime minister's orientation towards Sierra Leone.[102]

Similarly, the personality of the then secretary of state for international development, Clare Short, was significant in putting Sierra Leone on the political map. She was 'almost an elemental force', one of her staff recalls. 'She was very, very committed personally – she met Kabbah and took this upon herself as a kind of personal crusade'.[103] In Short's own words: 'There were people like me, ringing Tony Blair, and saying: "We must not go [and leave Sierra Leone]". Blair, to his credit, decided, yes, they wouldn't just evacuate and leave, but stay there, which is what they did.'[104] The bottom line was that the decision to intervene and remain engaged in Sierra Leone was a notable one, with UK engagement in African affairs generally limited in the Labour government's first term.[105]

UK involvement increased during what became known as the 'Sandline affair', when a former British Army officer, Tim Spicer, representing the private military company Sandline, was accused of organising arms shipments to the country in violation of the UN arms embargo in place at the time (the arms shipment having been sanctioned in part by Peter Penfold, then-British high commissioner in Sierra Leone).[106] There was a clear understanding at the highest political level that such a situation could not occur again. Given that the Labour government had proposed an 'ethical foreign policy',[107] this scandal

[102] *Ibid.*, p. 170; Paul Jackson and Peter Albrecht, 'Introduction: The Roots of Security Sector Reform in Sierra Leone', in Albrecht and Jackson (eds), *Security Sector Reform in Sierra Leone 1997–2007*, pp. 3–15.

[103] Garth Glentworth, roundtable, UK, 2008.

[104] Peter Albrecht interview with Clare Short, UK, 2008. See also Clare Short, 'A Humanitarian Surge and its Demise, 1997–2003: A Personal Account', *Peacebuilding* (Vol. 1, No. 1, 2013), pp. 33–37.

[105] Albrecht and Jackson, *Security System Transformation in Sierra Leone*, p. 170; Albrecht interview with Clare Short.

[106] David J Francis, 'Mercenary Intervention in Sierra Leone: Providing National Security or International Exploitation?', *Third World Quarterly* (Vol. 20, No. 2, 1999), pp. 319–38.

[107] Chris Brown, *Ethics, Interests and Foreign Policy* (Cambridge: Cambridge University Press, 2009); David Chandler, 'Rhetoric Without Responsibility: the Attraction of "Ethical" Foreign Policy', *British Journal of Politics and International Relations* (Vol. 5, No. 3, August 2003), pp. 295–316.

prompted a significant amount of UK press attention and thus a response from the government.

High-level government ministers were clearly taking a keen interest in Sierra Leone. At the same time, joined-up work across Whitehall was also emerging as a relatively new phenomenon that centred on the African and Global Conflict Prevention Pools that were set up in 2001 and jointly owned by the Foreign Office, MoD and DfID. Within the development community, there remained resistance to the idea of involvement with the MoD and hard security issues, which were considered different to engaging in the establishment of a governance system that would lead to better managed and more democratically accountable security forces. Even in the late 1990s, when SSR was on the rise in DfID, it was still a relatively small group of people that pushed the agenda and there was an expectation that it would be challenged. As Clare Short recalls:[108]

> It might have been controversial for development people to talk about security sector reform … [However,] we decided to go for it, and we expected more flack than we got, actually, from the development world. I don't remember feeling very under attack – I think it was put to me that this was the right thing to do, that it might be controversial, that we had to be brave. I was just convinced of the case.

In Sierra Leone, DfID made the principled, if not necessarily practical, point of steering clear of operational matters and logistical support that would clash with official development assistance. The basic argument was that Sierra Leone's security system required the application of precisely the same principles and processes that apply to any other public-sector reform programme.[109] At the same time, whilst today resistance to engaging in security-related programming remains evident in DfID – and, indeed, is stronger than it was in the late 1990s – it is also the case that the department has made huge strides in working jointly with the MoD and Foreign Office since 2000.

Despite the political interest at the Cabinet Office level and the fledgling development of joined-up working across Whitehall in the early 2000s, however, there was little evidence by 2007 of coherent cross-departmental strategic direction regarding Sierra Leone. At the time, there were fears that this might have a negative impact on the changes to programming that would be necessary as Sierra Leone transitioned from a post-conflict to a fragile state, which would require long-term development planning. Indeed, without consensus on Sierra Leone's status across the three key departments in London, it would be difficult even to assess

108 Albrecht interview with Clare Short.
109 Albrecht and Jackson, *Security System Transformation in Sierra Leone*, p. 28.

whether the executive roles of international staff should be extended beyond the existing contracts.

Similarly, by 2007 it had yet to be decided what a realistic exit strategy for the UK would be or the point at which UK support to Sierra Leone should be reduced. This made it difficult to assess which programmes to scale down or which actions were needed to allow for a measured handover of responsibilities over time. Much of this would depend on political will and momentum – both in the UK and in Sierra Leone. This situation was exacerbated by the fact that no single department was in charge of – or willing to take responsibility or accountability for – SSR as a whole, and for the process in Sierra Leone in particular. The result was that personalities rather than processes or procedures often led decision-making. To a large extent, co-ordination became a function of individuals' ability to collaborate effectively on the ground.

Conclusion

Support from the UK and other external actors between 1997 and 2007 was provided to the Government of Sierra Leone to help win a war, to stabilise Sierra Leone and to begin the process of re-establishing the state institutions that had been destroyed or establishing those that had never existed in the first place. Subsequently, support was provided to re-establish an armed force under the slogan 'serving the nation', consisting of remnants of the collapsed army, rebel factions and traditional hunter militias. This support was consolidated as IMATT began to build up alongside, and partly as an extension of, Operation *Silkman* in November 2000.

In the early stages, the general state of emergency in Sierra Leone did not allow much time for the UK to develop a strategy. Prior to January 2002, when the war was declared over and the disarmament and demobilisation process was completed, support took the form of responses to consecutive crises. The lack of any domestic capacity to oversee the armed forces, which had carried out two coups in 1992 and 1997, was addressed by the DfID-led SILSEP. SILSEP also focused on the government's inability to co-ordinate responses to the security situation in the country and to collect coherent intelligence. The ONS and CISU were initially established to strengthen the Sierra Leone government's ability to perform these functions and were expected to evolve into peacetime conflict-prevention mechanisms.

Sierra Leone's new MoD was inaugurated as a 'joint civilian/military institution'[110] in January 2002. Although there were continued struggles

[110] Coker, 'Governance and Security Sector Reform', p. 114; Albrecht and Jackson, *Security System Transformation in Sierra Leone*, pp. 97–98.

between the MoD and its international advisers (IMATT officers in particular), a viable institution came into existence. A defence White Paper was produced which was thoroughly owned by the Sierra Leone government, MoD structures were reorganised to fit context and capacity, and IMATT produced Plan 2010 to guide its engagement with the RSLAF and its own eventual drawdown. Despite these gains, however, key challenges remained, including the recruitment and retention of qualified staff, and high levels of corruption, which had a detrimental effect on military and civilian staff and thus on affordability.

As previously noted, the establishment of police primacy had been an early priority of President Kabbah, prompting him to seek UK support to this end from as early as 1996. As programming got properly underway in 1998, the SLP was given a new ethos – that of Local Needs Policing – and vehicles, communication, equipment and uniforms were procured. In the late 1990s, however, predominantly as a result of the context in which efforts to re-establish the police began, but also partly because of the personalities of the advisers involved, integration of the range of security-related programmes being supported by the UK did not take place. It was a time when there was no coherent conceptualisation of the 'security sector' – or of the process of SSR – and thus no real sense of which security-related institutions should be included in the transformation process. This only emerged during the period from 2002 to 2005.

Relatively speaking, between 1997 and 2007, programming was dominated by security concerns, while the Sierra Leone government gave it progressively less attention in the latter part of the period. In turn, this meant that the broader justice system was given comparatively little support. It simply did not have the priority of the hard core of the security sector in the late 1990s and early 2000s. A Law Development Programme was initiated in 2001, but was comparatively small and relatively isolated from the CCSSP, SILSEP and IMATT. With the design of the Justice Sector Development Programme – a process that was initiated when the war came to an end – a much broader programme was set up, encompassing the justice sector as whole. The downside to the slow start-up of work in this sector was that while the police became more professional in its role, the ability to arrest criminals was of limited use if they could not then be given a fair trial. The JSDP grew out of this concern, as well as DfID's growing reluctance to engage in national security programming.

The period 1997–2007 was characterised above all by the end of open conflict and a transition from a state of emergency to a context of peace-building in the medium term. The first post-conflict elections were held in May 2002, with Kabbah and his Sierra Leone People's Party emerging as the clear winners. A Memorandum of Understanding was signed between the Government of Sierra Leone and the UK in 2002,[111] which bound both parties to an agreement until 2012, and committed the UK to spend £40 million per year for its duration.[112] As an expression of long-term commitment, the sense of assurance that the MoU gave to the transformation process was crucial, despite being vague on the deliverables.

Within the security sector, one of the key advances was producing a security strategy for Sierra Leone that was linked to the country's development objectives. In practical terms, this was set out in the partially interrelated Poverty Reduction Strategy Paper and security-sector review processes, with the latter reflected in Pillar One of the PRSP, on promoting good governance, peace and security.[113]

The importance of the security-sector review, conducted between 2003 and 2005, cannot be overestimated. First, it provided much-needed conceptual clarity on the institutions comprising the security system, and thus on who had a stake in defining what security meant for Sierra Leoneans. Second, it illustrated the functions and relevance of the ONS, as the co-ordinator of input from the wider security system and producer of a strategy document for the sphere. Third, the fact that the review was integrated into the PRSP meant that security and development were aligned to a degree that had not existed before.

These developments reflected significant strides forward across the security system, within which the political space for new organisations, such as the ONS and the revised MoD, was widening. In the SLP, the priority became to deploy across the country and move from a relatively theoretical, strategic position to a more practical approach. Leadership of the police was also handed over from an expatriate to a Sierra Leonean in June 2003 and with it, full national ownership of the organisation.

Meanwhile, the period leading up to 2007 was largely dominated by election preparations. Those held in 2002 took place in the immediate aftermath of conflict and in an environment that had not yet fully stabilised. They were also held with significant in-country security and logistical support from the UN. It was a testament to the SLP's rapidly built capacity that the force was able to oversee successful elections in 2007. The SLP published its election strategy in April 2006, with its main thrust to work within the national security architecture, thereby acknowledging the role of the ONS as the overarching co-ordinating body serving the overall strategic direction set by the National Security Council.

---

[111] For a general outline and the content of the Memorandum of Understanding between the governments of Sierra Leone and the UK, see *ibid.*, p. 85.
[112] *Ibid.*, p. 159.
[113] IMF, 'Sierra Leone', pp. 79–87.

At the level of the ONS, strategic discussions around election security started in mid-2006. The co-ordination forum provided by the ONS for the National Electoral Commission (NEC),[114] the SLP and other security institutions engendered a structured approach that covered all aspects of the elections. ONS leadership was vital in showing both domestically and internationally that the security system was coherent and spoke with one voice. That the elections were relatively free from violence was all the more significant when one considers that domestic political buy-in to security-sector reform had generally diminished by 2005 (and by 2007, NSC meetings had not been held for two years). When the votes had been counted, it became clear that the SLPP had lost elections to the APC under Ernest Bai Koroma. A new government had come to power.

[114] The National Electoral Commission (NEC) is the sole authority with a constitutional mandate under Section 33 of the 1991 constitution of Sierra Leone and Section 28 of the 2009 Chieftaincy Act to prepare and conduct all public elections and referenda. For more information, see <http://www.nec-sierraleone.org/History.html>, accessed 15 September 2014.

III. 2007–10: A NEW GOVERNMENT, A NEW BEGINNING

2007 was a watershed year because of the victory of the All People's Congress (APC) over the Sierra Leone People's Party (SLPP) in that year's general election. This was the first peaceful change of government in Sierra Leone since the war. Indeed, there was a general sense that 'people wanted peaceful elections', according to Garry Horlacher, UK adviser to the Office of National Security (ONS) during the election period.[1] Although this in turn meant that 'all we put in place wasn't really tested', it did also indicate a functioning security sector.[2]

The election may have been conducted in a professional manner, but the country also suffered severe financial difficulties throughout the course of the year. Salaries were paid to the armed forces and the police, but many other public-sector employees went unpaid for months. In the first quarter of 2007, the Sierra Leonean Ministry of Defence (MoD) received less than 5 per cent (412 million Leones, approximately $184,000) of its indicative quarterly allocation. One of the consequences was that the distribution of rice and fuel to the armed forces stopped until the suppliers had been paid the almost 3 billion Leones (approximately $1.25 million) owed to them. Furthermore, as then-Commander of the International Military Advisory and Training Team (IMATT) Brigadier Iain Cholerton noted, 'resources [within Sierra Leone's MoD] continue to be allocated to areas that are perhaps not critical to the most important activities of the RSLAF'.[3] For instance, despite having been allocated only 412 million Leones in total, 24 million Leones were spent on allowances for six RSLAF personnel attending a UK-funded military observer's course (this money could instead have been spent on moving almost 800 soldiers and their families into quarters donated by the Indian government that year).

---

1 Peter Albrecht interview with Garry Horlacher, over Skype, 2013.

2 *Ibid.*

3 IMATT, 'Commander IMATT (SL) – End of Tour Report', 2008, unpublished.

The transition of government also signalled the beginning of a more assertive leadership under President Ernest Bai Koroma and the APC. This was compounded by a general change in perception both domestically and internationally that Sierra Leone was moving from a situation of state failure to one of fragility and long-term development. This was matched by growing efforts to achieve consistency in terms of external support to government priorities. Looking back at the early stages of UK support while the war was ongoing, Emmanuel Coker (who headed up the Sierra Leone government's Governance Reform Secretariat)[4] recalls that 'the reform that was going on in [the] MoD was dictated by the British – the entire reform process was. The government at the time wanted SSR [security-sector reform], and the British were willing to do it'.[5] This was partly necessary, because during the life of the Sierra Leone Security Sector Reform Programme (SILSEP), 'the emphasis in terms of [the] public sector was to get the institutions up and running, restore peace and stability, reconstruction, rehabilitation – these were the priorities at the time'.[6] In some cases, as with the re-establishment of the Sierra Leone Police (SLP), British involvement was critical. As Coker observes:[7]

> There was no way that the police could be reformed if Keith Biddle [Sierra Leone's first post-war IGP – inspector-general of police], had not come in. When he came in, he was devoid of old school boy networks, connections and relations. He could take drastic steps to do certain things without being blamed. A Sierra Leonean IGP would have found it difficult, would have been pressured by his school, his tribe, his mosque. Keith Biddle was able to do what no one was able to do.

The UK had also promoted the MoD 'as the nucleus of wide-ranging reform':[8]

> The MoD was supposed to be the model. Not that they were imposing it directly. I wouldn't say that we were instructed to go that way, but the vibes that we were getting – in a very subtle way we were trying to adapt … We had a strategy for the entire public sector, but the MoD was being pursued separately from those broader reforms. Most of us did not like it, because primacy should have been given to the police, [and priority given to having] … the ONS up and running.

4 The Governance Reform Secretariat is the Government of Sierra Leone's internal co-ordination mechanism for public-service reform programmes to enhance the country's capacity to provide services.

5 Peter Albrecht interview with Emmanuel Coker, Sierra Leone, June 2012. Coker is now permanent secretary to the president.

6 *Ibid.*

7 *Ibid.*

8 *Ibid.*

The challenge in this regard was to align the specific reforms that were being proposed with the broader direction being pursued in rebuilding the civil service. This was also to an extent the case with the implementation of the DfID-led Justice Sector Development Programme (JSDP) – with its focus on the judiciary, prisons and other areas of the justice sector – from 2005. Initially, reforms were taken forward that were not actively co-ordinated with the government and the country's general direction of reform. 'We had to bulldoze our way in', Coker recalls, specifically regarding the UK's efforts to reform the MoD prior to 2007, and 'we did it by making management and functional reviews. While we conducted these reviews, we were able to make reforms that were to be implemented in ministries that were covered by other projects [such as SILSEP and the JSDP]'.[9] In sum, there was an acceptance of the fact that separate financing for discrete areas of reform might be necessary, but there was also a growing need for consistency in how external support was provided, especially following the accession of a new government in 2007.

From 2007, there was some cynicism within Sierra Leone both about what international support could achieve and about what the agenda of external partners actually was. As a Sierra Leonean official close to events during this period notes: 'let's face it, there is no free lunch. The donors come in, and in the process they create jobs for their own people'.[10] However, unlike the SLPP, which had only a 'truncated plan' for rebuilding Sierra Leone, the new APC government proved to be in a better position to clearly articulate its own priorities, first establishing 'An Agenda for Change' (2008–12) and, later, 'The Agenda for Prosperity' (2013–18),[11] the second and third Poverty Reduction Strategy Papers (PRSPs), respectively. Sierra Leone was moving beyond the immediate peace-building phase and the reactive management of crisis upon crisis. The approach of the new government reflected this.

This chapter explores the evolution of the security sector under a government which had not been directly involved in SSR efforts thus far. Moreover, given that the SLPP had initiated the SSR process in a context of war, it was inevitable that the APC would approach the security sector

---

[9] *Ibid*.

[10] Peter Albrecht interview with anonymous, UK, February 2013.

[11] Government of Sierra Leone, *An Agenda for Change: Second Poverty Reduction Strategy (PRSP II), 2008–2012* (Freetown: Government of Sierra Leone, 2008), <http://unipsil.unmissions.org/portals/unipsil/media/publications/agenda_for_change.pdf>, accessed 8 October 2014; Government of Sierra Leone, *The Agenda for Prosperity – Road to Middle Income Status: Sierra Leone's Third Generation Poverty Reduction Strategy Paper (2013–2018)* (Freetown: Government of Sierra Leone, 2013), <http://www.undp.org/content/dam/sierraleone/docs/projectdocuments/povreduction/undp_sle_The%20Agenda%20for%20Prosperity%20.pdf>, accessed 8 October 2014.

differently. The chapter goes on to analyse how institutions such as the ONS and the Central Intelligence and Security Unit (CISU) adjusted to the new political reality, before exploring the continued efforts to downsize the RSLAF and the emergence of a clear purpose in building the army's peacekeeping capacity. Finally, the chapter deals with the general implications of changing support to the justice sector and what holistic justice reform meant in practice, including in relation to the police.

Changing International Support to National Security

The biggest change in international support to the ONS and CISU was the termination of SILSEP on 31 March 2008 – a decision that had been made in mid-2007 following stable presidential elections, and due to the DfID country team receiving a smaller than expected allocation in the UK Comprehensive Spending Review.[12] Financial support from DfID to CISU through the ONS continued, but the role of the CISU adviser was picked up by the UK intelligence community for another year, before the position was cut in 2009. By 2007–08, DfID gave only limited programme-level direction for SILSEP, which throughout its life had 'clearly suffered from [the] lack of a coherent strategy and in particular lack of an exit strategy'.[13] This was partly because of reduced engagement as well as DfID's broadly limited expertise, understanding and appreciation of matters relating to national security and intelligence.

Generally speaking, it is also the case that the SSR community in DfID always has been small and, as argued earlier in this Whitehall Paper, was stifled by the changing approach to international interventions that followed 9/11 and the emergence of the UK's Stabilisation Unit, which is run by DfID, the MoD and the Foreign Office together.[14] Increasingly reluctant to engage robustly in security-sector matters, DfID instead sought to refocus on what were considered 'core areas such as growth and basic service delivery, which in the long term would be the only way to both prevent a return to conflict and allow progress towards achieving the MDGs [Millennium Development Goals]'.[15]

Peace-building and transformation of the security sector had defined DfID's approach since the late 1990s, and SILSEP was initiated

[12] UK Government, 'Project Completion Report (PCR): Sierra Leone Security Sector Reform Programme', May 2008, unpublished.
[13] *Ibid.*
[14] Peter Albrecht, Finn Stepputat and Louise Andersen, 'Security Sector Reform, the European Way', in Mark Sedra (ed.), *The Future of Security Sector Reform* (Ontario: Centre for Governance Innovation, 2010), pp. 74–87, 77.
[15] UK Government, 'Project Completion Report (PCR)'.

to address this need. However, following changes to the local context, by 2007 SILSEP had become:[16]

> [A] slush fund for SSR, there was no log frame. Originally, it was spot-on perfect, a way to put money into issues that had to be dealt with quickly; but Sierra Leone was moving from a conflict to a fragile context, and there had to be more accountability and transparency. SILSEP was brilliant, but time moves on.

Even so, no exit strategy was ever prepared for the SILSEP programme or for the wider UK engagement in SSR. Difficulties consequently arose in two areas. First, DfID played no part in defining a clear role and capacity for the RSLAF, which would have facilitated a stronger agreement with the Sierra Leone government about a sustainable size for the armed forces and an attendant reform programme. Second, although a joint DfID-IMATT work plan was developed in 2006 and was seen as the exit strategy for DfID, it was not taken up and implemented by the commander of IMATT in 2007 because it was an election year.[17]

This led to a situation in which DfID's 2008 decision to withdraw almost entirely from SSR in Sierra Leone was interpreted by the Foreign Office and the UK MoD as unilateral and unexpected. In reality, however, DfID continued to tackle development matters linked to the underlying causes of conflict through its poverty reduction-related work – an approach which ultimately fits well with the notion of upstream conflict prevention that is explored in detail in Chapter V. DfID also remained engaged specifically in SSR through its adviser to the ONS.

At this stage of the ongoing consolidation of the ONS, advisers were viewed as protectors of the political independence of both the ONS and CISU against external interference. Under the previous president, Ahmad Tejan Kabbah, tension had frequently built up between the executive and the ONS, resulting principally from the insistence of the first post-war national security co-ordinator, Kellie Conteh, on ONS political neutrality. Yet Conteh could rely, to some extent, on the protection of advisers from the UK, who not only strongly backed an independent ONS, but also benefited from good relations with President Kabbah. Perhaps unsurprisingly, therefore, after the 2007 elections there was also a sense within CISU and the ONS that more could have been done by external advisers to ease the transition from the SLPP to the APC, in explaining the two organisations' relevance as professional national security bodies, and underscoring

[16] Peter Albrecht interview with anonymous, UK, August 2013.
[17] Derek Poate et al., *Evaluation of DfID Country Programmes: Sierra Leone*, Evaluation Report EV690 (London: DfID, September 2008).

their political neutrality. In 2008, then-National Security Coordinator Kellie Conteh noted:[18]

> We need to maintain the level of advisers, whether they are visiting or permanent. They are still that protector. Perhaps after the next elections [we can do without advisers], because we are still transforming, we are still reforming, and we need those check and balances.

Indeed, there was an increasing realisation – including amongst international observers – that there was stronger support for the ONS among the British than there was in the Sierra Leonean executive. For CISU, meanwhile, the loss of a dedicated adviser following SILSEP's termination was extremely challenging and there was a sense that the organisation became less effective. This was partly seen as the consequence of the ONS's continuing control of CISU's budget. In a permanently resource-scarce environment, 'those were the most frustrating times', Ansumana Idriss, a director in CISU, noted about the period 2010–11.[19]

Finally, it is important to emphasise that DfID's adviser to the ONS was primarily tasked with co-ordinating ongoing DfID-funded support to the security sector (including within the MoD), rather than providing dedicated technical support to the national security co-ordinator.[20] This set-up partly reflected tension between members of the main UK players, with the Foreign Office preferring that IMATT take over DfID's civilian advisory role in the ONS and the Sierra Leonean MoD. On this matter, however, DfID – which was paying the bill – insisted on having a former police officer, rather than a serving military officer, fulfil the role of ONS adviser.

This evolving funding environment, and the shifting patterns of external support, formed the backdrop to the development of the Sierra Leonean security sector in 2007–10.

The Changing Overarching Security Architecture

National Security and Intelligence Collection

In 2007, the ONS and associated British support were generally viewed as a success story. By 2009, however, it was being argued that the ONS had become a victim of its own success, having evolved into a de facto Cabinet Office with a much wider remit than intelligence assessment and security co-ordination.[21] Indeed, it was suggested that the ONS was vying to

[18] Peter Albrecht interview with Kellie Conteh, UK, June 2009.

[19] Peter Albrecht interview with Ansumana Idriss, Sierra Leone, August 2013.

[20] Peter Albrecht interview with Piet Biesheuvel, UK, August 2013.

[21] Piet Biesheuvel, Tom Hamilton-Baillie and Peter Wilson, 'Sierra Leone Security Sector Reform Programme – Output to Purpose Review', April 2007, unpublished.

become accountable for the security sector as a whole. This was problematic because it raised the question of who would then be responsible for overseeing the ONS. External assessments by the UK were thus clear that the primary role of the ONS was to be one of co-ordination and information-gathering, analysis and dissemination. It would not be within the ONS's remit to manage or direct individual security-sector institutions, or to act as part of the state's security oversight architecture, even though it necessarily had a close relationship with CISU. Indeed, a May 2007 review concluded:[22]

> Underpinned by the wide definition of 'human security' adopted by the GoSL [Government of Sierra Leone], with HMG [the UK government's] encouragement, the ONS now aims to provide policy research and coordination to much of the Government...
>
> This expansion of the remit of the ONS carries benefits and risks. The ONS undoubtedly makes a positive contribution when it becomes involved in an issue. But there are dangers of 'mission creep' and an imbalance in Government, with an all-powerful ONS taking on ever more tasks at the expense of the less capable Ministries ... we risk creating a precedent of an over-powerful ONS which could be abused by future officials or politicians. This risk is exacerbated by the fact that the ONS is directly responsible to the President and does not have any effective Minister or Parliamentary oversight...
>
> What is now needed is senior, strategic advice to the ONS to help them define their precise role and relationship to other agencies and ensure that the ONS coordinates and supports rather than 'crowds out' the activities of the rest of Government.

While the ONS might have experienced mission creep, if only to a limited extent, its professionalism in carrying out its mandate during the 2007 elections was also undeniable. By this time, despite various Cabinet briefings on the proper use of the ONS as a conduit for all incoming intelligence and the National Security Council (NSC) as the proper forum for discussion of its implications, the traditional informal system began to re-emerge in parallel, as it appeared to have more utility for the task of electioneering.[23] Simply put, with the war over, security matters preoccupied the higher echelons of government to a lesser extent, which meant that the NSC met less frequently.

In direct response to this situation, the ONS – led by National Security Coordinator Kellie Conteh – established the National Security

---

[22] *Ibid.*

[23] Peter Albrecht and Paul Jackson, *Security System Transformation in Sierra Leone, 1997–2007* (Birmingham and London: Global Facilitation Network for Security Sector Reform and International Alert, 2009), pp. 116–17.

Council Coordinating Group (NSCCG) to serve as a co-ordinating and oversight mechanism, and as a form of executive committee to the NSC (advising on appropriate measures to safeguard the internal and external security of the state). By 2005 it had become a formal part of Sierra Leone's national security architecture.[24] This body brought together the heads of the implementing – rather than political – security institutions, incorporating the ONS, the heads of the military and the police, and their civilian counterparts. Its chief aim was to share and co-ordinate information and increase the professionalism of intelligence-tasking, collection, assessment and collation across all concerned services and government. Yet, its establishment and the way it operated reflected the limited political will at the top to engage in security-related matters. It was the national security co-ordinator who kept the NSCCG going.

Kellie Conteh's individual role during this election period was important, having been at the helm of the ONS since its inception in 2001–02.[25] Indeed, as a key actor within the SLP observes:[26]

> Kellie had a special passion in making the security sector succeed in whatever it did. That is how we [the police] looked at it – he would be after the police, we had special sessions, input was made, critiqued; there was that energy. He wanted everything to be better: 'Police, you are leading, but we all come around to support you' [he would say].

Naturally, the NSCCG became the forum in which all election-related activities, *inter alia*, were discussed, agreed and co-ordinated. In turn, it also provided an important support network helping the leaders of the key security-sector institutions and the National Electoral Commission (NEC) withstand the possible application of any pressure – political or otherwise – thereby enabling them to perform their functions with integrity. This was particularly important in an environment in which the executive was showing diminishing interest in security-sector matters.

An emphasis on strong links between central and local government institutions also played a critical role – both during and after the elections – within the country's intelligence structure, established after the civil war.

---

[24] Peter Albrecht and Mark Malan, 'Post-Conflict Peacebuilding and National Ownership: Meeting the Challenges of Sierra Leone', Center for International Peace Operations, Berlin, 2006, p. 117.

[25] In 2008, Robert Ashington-Pickett, adviser to the ONS between 2000 and 2003, noted that 'the timeline of establishing the ONS was not neat. The organization inherited a group of senior political figures who were part of the former personality-based arrangements of the Office of the National Security Advisor. This caused some initial confusion over the role of the ONS … By early 2002, [the] ONS and CISU had clearly separate roles.' Ashington-Pickett quoted in Albrecht and Jackson, *Security System Transformation in Sierra Leone*, p. 73.

[26] Peter Albrecht interview with anonymous, Sierra Leone, December 2013.

District and Provincial Security Committees (DISECs and PROSECs) were integral to the reach and functioning of the ONS beyond Freetown. Set up in the early stages of SILSEP, and formalised in the 2002 National Security and Central Intelligence Act, they became important vehicles for extending national security co-ordination beyond the central government in Freetown, and for involving the entire country in security governance. Bringing together key actors from the security sector as well as local leaders and civil-society groups, they supported increased local government and community co-operation with the security agencies, enabled more efficient co-operation between the security agencies, and improved the quality of information passed to the central government.[27]

From 2009, the concept was devolved further to chiefdom level with the establishment of Chiefdom Security Committees (CHISECs) in border regions of the country, funded by the UN Development Programme (UNDP).[28] Francis Keilie, director of research and planning in the ONS, noted that these institutions 'are actually conflict preventive bodies', further describing them as 'early warning mechanisms with more of an emphasis on human security. We noticed that most of the national security issues that came up around land ownership, lack of access to justice and so on were rife in the chiefdoms'.[29]

---

[27] Robert Ashington-Pickett, 'Intelligence and Security Service Reconstruction', in Peter Albrecht and Paul Jackson (eds), *Security Sector Reform in Sierra Leone 1997–2007: Views from the Front Line* (Zurich: Geneva Centre for the Democratic Control of Armed Forces and LIT Verlag, 2010), pp. 19–37, especially p. 35; Francis Wiafe-Amoako, *Human Security and Sierra Leone's Post-Conflict Development* (London: Lexington Books, 2014), pp. 86–87; Rosalind Hanson-Alp, 'Civil Society's Role in Sierra Leone's Security Sector Reform Process: Experiences from Conciliation Resources West Africa Programme', in Albrecht and Jackson (eds), *Security Sector Reform in Sierra Leone 1997–2007*, pp. 183–206.

[28] The emphasis on strong links between central and local government institutions developed out of the earlier decision to re-establish the chiefs under the DfID-funded Chiefdom Governance Reform Programme (CGRP), which was implemented between 1999 and 2001. During the conflict, chiefs and other authority figures had been targeted, and re-establishing chiefs, in particular, became a post-war priority for the Government of Sierra Leone. The CGRP was implemented in support of this, but as the programme got underway, considerable grievances were voiced about the chiefs, with one common complaint being that they rarely consulted locals but seemed ready to exploit them for personal gain. Nevertheless, paramount chiefs in Sierra Leone's 149 chiefdoms remain important authority figures today. See Richard Fanthorpe, 'On the Limits of Liberal Peace: Chiefs and Democratic Decentralization in Post-War Sierra Leone', *African Affairs* (Vol. 105, No. 418, January 2006), pp. 27–49; Richard Fanthorpe, 'Chiefdom Governance Reform Programme Public Workshops: An Analysis of the Facilitators' Reports', University of Sussex, September 2004, <http://r4d.dfid.gov.uk/PDF/Outputs/Mis_SPC/R8095a.pdf>, accessed 8 October 2014.

[29] Peter Albrecht interview with Francis Keilie, Sierra Leone, August 2013.

This more integrated and decentralised architecture was crucial in developing the potential for a more joined-up security sector. In 2008, however, the ONS raised concerns that although the police leadership was fully engaged in NSCCG meetings, lower-ranking officers, including in the regions, were not involved to the same extent – and this despite the fact that decentralised security committees had come to play an important role in co-ordination and conflict resolution at the local level.

The 2007 elections also proved to be an important turning point in other ways. Tensions between the Office of the President and the national security co-ordinator emerged immediately following the elections, with the latter pleading with the former not to bypass the formal security system by bringing the APC's election-period security team – comprised of ex-combatants who were not part of the formal security sector – to State House. Doing so would signal strongly that the new president did not fully trust the police.

Furthermore, the ONS and CISU – two young institutions of which the incoming party had no prior experience – now had to convince the new executive of their importance to, and relevance within, the security architecture. As one director of the ONS explained in retrospect:[30]

> Basically, of course, transitions are difficult to manage. When the new government came in, we had an open mind. I coordinate security affairs of this country, but they did not understand how we work[ed] … They thought we were spy agents, reporting to the President. We requested … meetings with the president and parliament, because the ministers should understand the responsibility of the ONS … We needed to explain the principles and policies we stand for.

Both the ONS and CISU also had to build trust with the new ruling party, addressing misperceptions regarding their status as politically neutral institutions. As Ansumana Idriss noted:[31]

> Politicians had the mindset that [the] ONS and CISU were created by the former regime, because of ignorant notions, because of what used to exist [before the conflict]. Their first challenge was whether to trust people in those institutions. People within government did not know … what CISU does and stands for.

This, Idriss continued, was partly the result of a 'cultural factor' and the belief that intelligence is a tool used to serve political interests. As such, CISU was erroneously considered a product of the SLPP government

[30] Peter Albrecht interview with anonymous, Sierra Leone, September 2013.
[31] Peter Albrecht interview with Ansumana Idriss, Sierra Leone, July 2013.

rather than a professional, legally defined body that would serve the government irrespective of the political incumbent of State House.

Similarly, although the Joint Intelligence Committee (JIC) worked well in terms of collating and assessing incoming intelligence,[32] the upper echelons of the APC government were not engaged, which, as one UK adviser noted, 'was a real problem from an ownership point of view'.[33] In other words, external support had helped to create organisations that were free from party-political association, but there was always a danger that those organisations could become alienated from the very government that they were established to advise and support.

For example, President Koroma came under pressure from both among his political advisers and within the APC to ignore the ONS and CISU and to use networks that existed outside the formal state system, which prior to and during the war had fed (inaccurate) information to State House, leading to inefficient responses to Revolutionary United Front (RUF) incursions. CISU was initially established to rectify this circumstance. As Sierra Leone emerged from conflict, CISU's main contribution to the provision of national security, including during the 2007 elections, had been to show claims of plots by parallel 'intelligence' networks to be nothing more than unfounded rumours. Quite simply, as one of CISU's key personnel stated about these informal, and unverified, information-gathering networks: 'The things they are doing are not things we can do. The things they do are political'.[34] In this regard, CISU continued to have a stabilising effect in its attempt to depoliticise the information that the executive was required to act upon.

One of the difficulties faced by CISU in establishing its own identity *vis-à-vis* the new executive – something that was prioritised in 2007–10 – was the relative strength of the ONS under Kellie Conteh. This was partly a reflection of how the two organisations were set up and of how funding was subsequently allocated by DfID. This dynamic provides important insight into the inevitability of institutional evolution.

Despite being operationally independent of one another, CISU was purposefully located under the ONS – an apolitical and entirely new institution – instead of under the control of the Ministry of Internal Affairs

[32] The JIC was established in 2001 and encompassed representatives of all security-sector institutions. It provides for a joint assessment of intelligence input and, through its multi-stranded composition, it provides a mechanism for checks and balances within the intelligence community in Sierra Leone.
[33] Peter Albrecht interview with anonymous, Sierra Leone, August 2013.
[34] Peter Albrecht interview with anonymous, Sierra Leone, August 2013.

(MIA) or the military. Thus, CISU was an element within the ONS structure, just as the Force Intelligence and Security Unit (FISU) was set up under the RSLAF and the Internal Intelligence Service (IIS – formerly the Special Branch) was a subsidiary of the SLP.[35] This meant that budgetary requests were made by the ONS on behalf of CISU and, by extension, the ONS decided what share of the funding CISU would receive. It seemed clear to CISU and its advisers that operational independence should be matched by administrative independence. Without it, the ONS could not be effective in co-ordinating the wider security sector because it was drawn into operational matters of co-ordinating and leading intelligence collection by its administrative role *vis-à-vis* CISU.[36] Discussions about separating the two agencies did not resurface forcefully until 2012, when Conteh retired from the position of national security co-ordinator.

Nevertheless, from 2007, the two institutions began to mature as distinct bodies, recruiting personnel independently of one another. CISU had only eleven staff members in 2005; however, with support from a UK adviser, this had increased within two years to twenty personnel and continued to grow. During the final years of the war, CISU's *raison d'être* had been to monitor paramilitary formations, including rebel groups such as the RUF and West Side Boys; with the end of the conflict, this switched to ex-combatants. By 2007, its focus had shifted again, adapting to the context in which it was operating, and it had been redefined around the government's emphasis on economic development – and specifically on tackling corruption, which was (and remains) a considerable challenge and politically extremely sensitive.

There was also an increasing concentration on countering organised crime. A good example of the role that CISU could play in post-war Sierra Leone was the seizure in July 2008 of a plane from Venezuela that had 703 kg of cocaine onboard.[37] From an intelligence perspective, this operation was considered a success, involving working closely with international partners, as well as developing and demonstrating the skill set required to monitor those involved. 'The cocaine case was like a movie script', one of the individuals close to events explained, 'already written, and people just acted it'.[38] It was also clear that the operation by CISU and the ONS took place in relative isolation from the broader security sector. While the two organisations acted professionally throughout the operation,

---

[35] Peter Albrecht interview with Joe Edkins, Sierra Leone, February 2014.

[36] Peter Albrecht interview with Andrew Cordery, UK, August 2013.

[37] *The National*, 'Law Agencies Close in on Vast Drug Ring', 21 July 2008; Chris Hawley, 'South American Gangs Flying Vast Quantities of Cocaine to Europe', *Guardian*, 15 November 2010.

[38] Peter Albrecht interview with anonymous, Sierra Leone, February 2014.

it was also largely carried out without police support because of a verified suspicion that individual officers were leaking information to smugglers based in Sierra Leone.[39]

The changing political context within Sierra Leone, combined with the turnover of key personnel and changes to international support over this period, thus undoubtedly transformed both the identity of and relationship between CISU and the ONS between 2007 and 2010.

The Evolving Focus of Defence Reform

Military Governance

One of the most significant post-election developments within the MoD was the appointment in 2007 of a full-time minister of defence, Alfred Paolo Conteh. Under the SLPP government, Kabbah had been double-hatted as president and minister of defence, with a deputy minister of defence overseeing day-to-day business in the MoD. However, the deputy did not have a seat in the Cabinet and therefore lacked the political clout to make decisions on behalf of the RSLAF.

The separation of the position of president from that of minister of defence thus ensured that the RSLAF now had consistent political representation in the Cabinet, as well as creating a healthy distance between the commander of IMATT and the president. It also meant that the army now came under diminished political pressure to recruit outside of the formal process, which had been the norm during the 1980s, when a so-called 'card system' gave the executive and other political figures the power to enlist loyal individuals into the army (and the police).[40]

An added benefit was that the president had less direct control of the army. This change did not automatically come with the appointment of a minister, but had as much to do with the personality of Paolo Conteh

[39] Following the seizure of the cocaine, suspicions arose that the minister of transportation, Ibrahim Kemoh Sesay, was involved in organising the flight and he was suspended. Kwesi Aning, 'Understanding the Intersection of Drugs, Politics & Crime In West Africa: An Interpretive Analysis', Policy Brief Series, No. 6, Global Consortium on Security Transformation, April 2010. When the case came to court, and when President Ernest Bai Koroma moved to prosecute and extradite three of the South American traffickers, the attorney-general and individuals from the Office of the President were accused of requesting a bribe from international partners for executing the president's order. However, the fact that prosecution and extradition took place in 2009 meant that overall the cocaine case is considered a considerable success, in particular for CISU. Ginger Thompson and Scott Shane, 'Cables Portray Expanded Reach of Drug Agency', *New York Times*, 25 December 2010.

[40] Albrecht and Jackson, *Security System Transformation in Sierra Leone*, p. 43.

and his intention to continue the institution-building process that had begun in 1999. By way of comparison, the existence of a separate minister of internal affairs has, for a number of reasons, not alleviated political pressure on the SLP – something that is most noticeable in the politically motivated recruitment of a considerable number of individuals to the SLP since 2007.

An illustration of the personality and goals of Paolo Conteh is provided by the latter's description of his experience of returning to Sierra Leone after twenty-one years in the UK, in order to take up his position as minister of defence:[41]

> I've been used to proper systems [in the UK] where everything is in place. Suddenly I am in a post-conflict country, grappling with SSR and all [the] other reforms ... The way people work here, I call it the Sierra Leonean way of doing things – they are laid back, they are not in a hurry. And I said: 'We should be in a hurry!' The war was only 11 years, but 25 years were lost ... Something I learned was that the President, he was in a hurry. He only had three years before the next elections would kick in. For him to get a second term, he needed tangible results. He was in a hurry and some of us were able to align.
>
> In the first three years, it wasn't easy; I changed three DGs [directors-general]. I don't think they were running with the same speed ... Initially, it was difficult for them, but then they always have the idea that he is a politician, he is here for a short while, he'll get tired. I recall the very first enlistment [under my tenure], I think it was in 2009. Normally this is where the politicians will say: 'Peter is my nephew, make sure he's enlisted'. They saw me, I wasn't getting involved in at all, even when XX sent me a note with his letterhead to help so and so.
>
> *Because of my strong ties in the party, they could not threaten me and dismiss me by saying that I work against the interest of the party. If I'd been one of the PMDC [People's Movement for Democratic Change] ministers it would have been different, but my uncle was the head of the party.*

Paolo Conteh's appointment also meant a reorientation of the approach taken by IMATT, which at that time was moving from an executive to an advisory approach, as set out in Plan 2010 (see Chapter II) and confirmed by the peaceful elections of 2007. While the commander of IMATT during

[41] Peter Albrecht interview with Alfred Paolo Conteh, Sierra Leone, December 2013 (emphasis added). The People's Movement for Democratic Change (PMDC) is the third main party in Sierra Leone. Following its backing of the APC in the 2007 elections, several of the party's senior figures became ministers in the APC government and have been a source of considerable political controversy during the tenure of President Koroma.

the election period, Brigadier Iain Cholerton, did not observe any changes in his interactions with the Sierra Leone government,[42] his successor, Brigadier Jonathan Powe (who arrived in early 2008), did:[43]

> The Minister had just been appointed, and the dynamic had changed a bit. Access to the President was less than for my predecessor. I went to see him [the President] with the Minister – once or twice on my own – our relationship was very different [than before], less intimate, less one-to-one. I did not feel I could tell any tales about RSLAF. It was up to the Minister to be up front and honest with the President.

As such, the focus of IMATT – and particularly of the civilian adviser to the Sierra Leonean MoD (a post that was moved from DfID to IMATT during this period) – increasingly gravitated towards the minister of defence. Paolo Conteh, for his part, wanted to see change but apart from a relatively short career as a soldier, he had limited knowledge of how an army is managed and, according to Adele McGookin, his first UK adviser, he had 'no idea of what being a minister was [about]'.[44] 'I was dealing with propriety, corruption, but a lot of my focus was on the Minister', McGookin further commented; but gradually, she observed, 'as he grew into the position he went from being bypassed to asking the right questions. The MoD was starting to function as a ministry'.[45]

Paolo Conteh also recognised the importance of the relationship that developed between him and his international advisers:[46]

> With the CIVAD [civilian adviser], the same as for the Commander IMATT, I cherished their views and opinions … when I was in a situation where I wanted an independent view, I'd always ask [the] Commander IMATT and [the] CIVAD. They have no attachments; they just say things. There are times they don't get it right, because of their background. They don't understand our society. I was coming from the UK, I was part of them, and they also … [thought] 'He is one of us'. I could see where they were coming from.

The appointment of a minister of defence after the 2007 elections thus constituted a further important step forward in democratising military governance, separating management of the RSLAF from the Office of the President. However, while it strengthened the MoD, it did not serve to underpin the civilian-military structure that external advisers had struggled to put in place since the late 1990s. One of the reasons for this was Paolo

---

[42] Peter Albrecht interview with Iain Cholerton, over Skype, August 2013.

[43] Peter Albrecht interview with Jonathan Powe, over Skype, August 2013.

[44] Peter Albrecht interview with Adele McGookin, over Skype, October 2013.

[45] *Ibid.*

[46] Peter Albrecht interview with Alfred Paolo Conteh.

Conteh's bias towards the army in which he had once served. There were also forces within the MoD and beyond that did not wish to put in place the checks and balances on the military that civilians' presence was designed to ensure.

The 2003 defence White Paper had sought to clarify relations between the MoD and the Joint Force Command (JFC), including between civilian and military personnel. By 2008, however, and coinciding with the termination of SILSEP and the shift in IMATT's mandate from an executive to an advisory role, the numbers of civilian personnel in the MoD had started to dwindle. While the director-general and his two secretaries remained, the assistant secretaries were removed – and not replaced. This, in effect, meant that due to reduced civilian capacity, rather than changes to the MoD's formal mandate, civilian control of the armed forces – one of the main goals when SSR was initiated in the late 1990s – was weakened considerably during this period.

Sierra Leonean military officers might have supported the weakening of the civilian element in the MoD. Like many armies across the world, the RSLAF was never comfortable with being legally dependent on civilians, whom they did not fully trust. As observed by one of the leading military figures in Sierra Leone in 2013:[47]

> Before this time, we used to have the RSLAF running its own affairs, wherein the chief of the army had the control; in the new structure, with civilian oversight of the armed forces, you now had the civilian Director-General. It is something that was not accepted with open arms, especially by the [army] hierarchy, who had their powers taken away. Civilians have their own procedures, especially in procurement, so naturally this breeds acrimony between civilians and the military. There is always that suspicion, apprehension. Up to now, it's there, it's not spoken about openly, but you see it, you feel it.

Nevertheless, it was a political, rather than a military, decision to stifle the civilian element in the MoD, which asked the 'wrong' questions – relating, for instance, to the selection of personnel for overseas training or corruption within the ministry. Civilian staff were thus simply removed and not replaced.[48]

Indeed, the civilian-military structure within the MoD was never fully operationalised because it was never fully accepted by the RSLAF or wholeheartedly embraced by the political leadership that came to power in the 2007 elections. Commenting on the relationship between the director-general and military staff, one IMATT adviser observed that 'each had their own agendas'. He further noted that: 'There needs to be

[47] Peter Albrecht interview with anonymous, Sierra Leone, December 2013.
[48] Peter Albrecht interview with anonymous, Sierra Leone, December 2013.

something in there that brings them together', given that 'one is a supporting element of the other, keeping propriety and oversight on behalf of the government'.[49] In short, and to state the obvious, systems, procedures and policies are important, but they still needed to be bought into and implemented by the individuals within those institutions receiving external support.

The Return of Patronage to the MoD

In 2007, a review noted that a 'self-confident, civilian-led team with a clear and well-coordinated line of argument' was in place in the MoD.[50] However, while it is true that procedures, expertise, and checks and balances had been introduced, there has been a tendency to underestimate the context in which this team worked – not least its political dimension, and particularly with respect to what is often referred to as 'corruption'. However, such terms do not facilitate understanding of how governance systems in Sierra Leone work, because they imply only that the rules of the 'game' – as introduced by the UK's advisers to Sierra Leone – have been broken. Rather, in order to comprehend how the 'system' works in Sierra Leone, it is essential to understand how neo-patrimonialism operates.[51] This section explores this general point through analysis of the specific case of Sierra Leone's MoD.

Before 2007–08, when the numbers of IMATT personnel performing executive functions within Sierra Leone's MoD were high, it is almost certain that levels of corruption within the ministry and the RSLAF were managed more carefully than in the civil service more broadly, because of the close involvement of UK advisers. This was underpinned by the general sentiment within the RSLAF immediately after the war that it was the people of Sierra Leone – not the army – that were in charge.[52]

As IMATT took on more of an advisory role, however, it became more difficult to control practices that were considered to be corrupt by external observers and advisers, and the good intentions of the minister of defence could not fundamentally alter the rules of dependence and reciprocity that govern social relations in Sierra Leone. Indeed, many of

[49] Peter Albrecht interview with anonymous, UK, October 2013.

[50] Piet Biesheuvel, Tom Hamilton-Baillie and Peter Wilson, 'Sierra Leone Security Sector Reform Programme – Output to Purpose Review', April 2007, unpublished.

[51] For an in-depth and historical review of neo-patrimonialism in Sierra Leone, see William Reno, *Corruption and State Politics in Sierra Leone* (Cambridge: Cambridge University Press, 1996).

[52] Peter Albrecht interview with Simeon Nashiru Sheriff, Sierra Leone, 2012. As Sheriff noted, 'The choice was not RSLAF's, but that of the people of this country – they were in charge, and we were really heavily defeated, so the decision about the military was really the people's.'

the formally employed civil servants had been recruited on the basis of patronage, thereby shaping their behaviour from their first day in the office.

A detailed discussion of patronage systems is beyond the scope of this Whitehall Paper.[53] However, in brief, in this system of patronage, civil servants owe an obligation to those who sponsored their employment. It is therefore commonly expected that they would become 'runners' for their sponsors, being the public face of corrupt arrangements and paying a proportion of their salaries to their patrons. They also look to their patrons, and the chain of patrons above them, to make things right if their actions are exposed. As they progress through the ranks, they are themselves obliged to become patrons to new recruits, who become runners in turn; and so the system goes on. This can be extended to political networks, with supporters expecting personal returns in exchange for votes or political support, which can lead to political regimes making appointments based on obligations owed, and not on merit.

These are extremely sensitive social and cultural matters that are not openly discussed.[54] In the case of Sierra Leone, this is compounded by the prevalence of secret societies that regulate social relations and lead to impenetrable (for foreigners) personal networks. Developing an ethos of propriety and transparency in such a situation is all but impossible, unless this process works with, rather than against, the neo-patrimonial network. The fact that this system has not been fundamentally altered means that one of the root causes of the conflict persists.[55] It also points to an

[53] See Michael Bratton and Nicholas Van de Walle, 'Neopatrimonial Regimes and Political Transitions in Africa', *World Politics* (Vol. 46, No. 4, July 1994), pp. 454–89; Jean-Francois Medard, 'The Underdeveloped State in Tropical Africa: Political Clientelism or Neo-Patrimonialism', in Christopher Clapham (ed.), *Private Patronage and Public Power: Political Clientelism in the Modern State* (London: Frances Printer, 1982), pp. 162–92.

[54] At the same time, as noted generally in a report discussing the transition between the Justice Sector Development Programme (JSDP) and the Access to Security and Justice Programme (ASJP): 'The effect of … corruption is ambiguous. While it is not in any way officially or politically sanctioned and is repeatedly condemned publically, corruption is pervasive and widespread. In practice it is simply not regarded by large sections of the elites as repugnant or unacceptable behaviour. For many, successful corruption is almost subject for congratulation for having the luck and opportunity'. Garth Glentworth et al., 'Sierra Leone: Transition Priorities in the Move from the "Justice and Security Development Programme" to the "Access to Security and Justice Programme"', UK Government, 2011, unpublished, p. 41.

[55] Peter Albrecht interviews with anonymous, June 2012 and October 2013; see Peter Albrecht, Osman Gbla and Paul Jackson, 'From Quick Wins to Long-Term Profits? Developing Better Approaches to Support Security and Justice Engagements in Fragile States: Sierra Leone Case Study', OECD, Paris, 2013, unpublished, p. 29.

inherent weakness in terms of development more broadly: addressing systems of patronage requires social transformation, but this is difficult to achieve through the technical solutions involved in building institutional checks and balances. Such mechanisms are only effective if they are bought into – and abided by – by everyone. Thus despite consistent and long-term efforts by SILSEP and IMATT, governance according to a neo-patrimonial logic could not be suppressed.

DfID's Pullback from MoD Support

In early 2007, DfID had decided to remove the deputy civilian adviser post and remove all discretionary project funding for training activities from the MoD. This meant that, thereafter, the civilian adviser to the Sierra Leonean MoD represented the only SILSEP contribution to broader defence reforms (excepting a few legacy projects that were in their final stages).[56] Thus, by November 2007, SILSEP – and DfID more broadly – was very much winding down its support to the RSLAF and MoD.[57]

Indeed, this move away from involvement in reform of the armed forces reflected a departmental change in approach to international interventions following 9/11. DfID was thus caught between not wanting to be associated with the military, which SILSEP – in effect – was at the time, and continuing to acknowledge that the RSLAF and MoD were central to ensuring Sierra Leone's stability. This was also a more general reflection of DfID's move away from strategic-level SSR towards a service-delivery approach – a focus on locally accessed, rather than centrally provided, services which came to dominate programming in Sierra Leone from 2010 (and which is explored in more detail in Chapter IV). This general development was encapsulated in DfID's 2009 White Paper, *Eliminating World Poverty: Building Our Common Future*, which stated that 'security and access to justice are essential for sustainable development in both fragile and more stable environments', and so these would be treated as a 'basic service'.[58] While this was implicit in how SILSEP and the Commonwealth Community Safety and Security Project (CCSSP) were implemented before the conflict's end, it became more explicit in the early 2000s and shaped future programmes, specifically the JSDP and especially the Access to Security and Justice Programme (ASJP), which were established in 2005 and 2012, respectively.

---

[56] One such example was Operation *Pebu*. See Aldo Gaeta, 'Operation Pebu', in Peter Albrecht and Paul Jackson (eds), *Security System Transformation Working Paper Series*, No. 6 (Birmingham and London: Global Facilitation Network for Security Sector Reform and International Alert, October 2008).

[57] Personal notes, Adele McGookin, 2012.

[58] DfID, *Eliminating World Poverty: Building Our Common Future*, Cm 7656 (London: DfID, July 2009).

Late 2007 thus saw discussions in London between DfID and the UK MoD with a view to moving responsibility for the position of civilian adviser to the Sierra Leonean MoD from the former to the latter. However, the MoD resisted the proposal because of the costs involved, and DfID rather grudgingly retained ownership of the post (with the intention that it would exist for only one more year, essentially to bring the position to a conclusion). As a consequence, the civilian adviser to the Sierra Leonean MoD was left on the periphery of SILSEP with little, if any, guidance from DfID.[59]

The main link between the civilian adviser and SILSEP thus became the adviser to the ONS.[60] Meanwhile, given the lack of an RSLAF- or MoD-oriented agenda within DfID, McGookin – who held the position in 2007 – aligned her workload with IMATT's Plan 2010 and gave political and policy input accordingly. This came with some benefits, as the adviser and IMATT now worked more coherently towards the same ends. Furthermore, given that President Koroma had appointed a full-time minister of defence in 2007, a new area of work had opened up. As McGookin explained, 'The Defence Minister was keen to realise the President's vision of governance and anti-corruption and I supported him in this, especially where he was being deliberately blocked by the less scrupulous members of the … [Sierra Leonean] MOD hierarchy'.[61]

In April 2009, the position of civilian adviser to the Sierra Leonean MoD was formally placed under the control of IMATT. This change of ownership from SILSEP to IMATT not only meant that the work of the civilian adviser was aligned even more closely with that of IMATT; it also meant that the role changed from project management (mainly in the area of institution-building) to providing higher-level strategic and policy advice to inform decision-making by the minister of defence, Chief of Defence Staff and the Defence Policy Committee. This was often reactive in nature, responding to changes in the environment.

Further Development of the RSLAF

From the start, the backbone of IMATT's support to the RSLAF was training, and the RSLAF's current capacity is largely a testament to that support. As was noted in September 2008 by Brigadier Alfred Nelson-Williams (who had become Chief of the Defence Staff a few months earlier in June): 'We can have all the equipment, but if there are not enough trained personnel for such equipment, the equipment becomes meaningless'.[62]

---

59 Personal notes, Adele McGookin.
60 *Ibid.*
61 *Ibid.*
62 Peter Albrecht interview with Alfred Nelson-Williams, Sierra Leone, 2008.

Immediately after the war in 2002, most RSLAF personnel went through the British short-term training courses and the Military Reintegration Programme overseen by Operation *Silkman* and IMATT. By 2007–08, training centres like the Armed Forces Training Centre had been established to train officers and other service personnel in basic military skills and to generate understanding of concepts such as neutrality and democratic accountability.[63] Following the RSLAF's positive performance during the 2007 elections, it was concluded that the latter had been achieved. Yet two other elements of the IMATT mission – achieving sustainability and affordability – were perceived to be lagging behind.

By early 2008, elections had dominated all activity for twelve months, which – from the perspective of IMATT – meant delayed progress in the transformation of the RSLAF. As Brigadier Cholerton, commander of IMATT in 2007, has noted, this was largely 'a plan to draw down' – that is, to downsize – the RSLAF to a more sustainable number of personnel. Nevertheless, elections were used to identify and consolidate a role for the RSLAF and, above all, to underscore the expectation that the army would stay out of the political sphere. In preparation for elections, through discussions and joint exercises across the security sector, emphasis was placed on police leadership in terms of internal security. Only under extreme circumstances was the RSLAF to be called in, and only in support of the SLP.

As such, it was within the Military Aid to the Civil Power (MACP) framework that the army provided support to the SLP during the election period, to counter any potential volatility or instability. In response to requests from the police – via the National Security Council Coordinating Group – the army positioned troops in agreed locations before, during and after the elections, despite apprehension on the part of some of the major stakeholders.[64] Even though it may have been appropriate to call in the army during the election period, there was also a danger that relying on its support via the MACP framework would become a gut reaction, a situation that then-National Security Coordinator Kellie Conteh cautioned against:[65]

> Overusing the MACP because people claim that the police are not able to do A, B and C is inappropriate. We hope that messages to the NSC [National Security Council] are heard: refrain from using the RSLAF too much. We want to keep in the police – if guns are needed, strengthen the OSD [Operational Support Division] rather than the RSLAF.

---

[63] Brigade Battle Schools were established in the field where personnel did level 3 training after completing levels 1 and 2 in their respective units.

[64] Albrecht and Jackson, *Security System Transformation in Sierra Leone*, pp. 151–53.

[65] Conteh quoted in *ibid.*, p. 139.

Despite such concerns, however, the deployment of troops during this period was transparent, with a press statement officially informing the public of its occurrence. Furthermore, the performance of the RSLAF during the election year was considered 'commendable', and indicated a high degree of success in terms of fulfilling criteria of democratic accountability – one of the primary reasons SSR was initiated in the first place. However, the other two elements of the IMATT mission, achieving sustainability and affordability, were 'as far from being achieved as ever'.[66]

This led to the intensification of training and a shift in support towards whole-of-career training for RSLAF personnel, particularly officers. This shift saw the consolidation of the Horton Academy staff college, which, in 2007–08, IMATT envisioned would become a regional centre of excellence that would generate income and be staffed mainly by Sierra Leoneans. Nevertheless, based on a judgement of RSLAF capability, in early 2008 these two objectives were considered difficult, if not impossible, to achieve in the short term (prior to 2012). This was further compounded by a perceived decrease in the ability of IMATT to influence the development of the RSLAF, as it gave up executive functions within the MoD and the Joint Force Command in favour of key advisory appointments only, as per IMATT's Plan 2010.[67]

Meanwhile, Sierra Leone's ongoing financial difficulties meant that the RSLAF was only kept fiscally afloat by the repeated intervention of the international community. The effect of this was that the 'Operational output of RSLAF [was] now probably at its lowest level since IMATT support first started. Units subsist and do little else.'[68]

With elections over, and with a continued emphasis on consolidating a role for the armed forces that went beyond distinguishing between internal and external security, it became critical to devise a strategy for making and saving money.

Apart from downsizing the army, it became increasingly clear that the air wing – which had been established in 1995 but was grounded in 2000, and which IMATT intended to develop as part of its Plan 2010 – was an untenable aspiration for the RSLAF.[69] Some personnel had been trained by the South African government over this period, and engineers, technicians, pilots and air-traffic controllers existed within the RSLAF. By 2007, however, much time had passed in which these personnel did not

[66] IMATT, 'Commander IMATT (SL) – End of Tour Report'.
[67] IMATT, 'Plan 2010', 17 July 2004, unpublished.
[68] IMATT, 'Commander IMATT (SL) – End of Tour Report'.
[69] The official strength of the air wing in 2004 was two MFI-15 Safari training aircraft, two Mi-8 transport helicopters and one Mi-24 heavy attack helicopter, but their status at the time was 'inoperable'. The RSLAF was essentially an infantry force.

have access to a functioning aircraft or refresher training, meaning that the knowledge gained had gradually faded. By 2008, redundant air-wing assets had been disposed of, and the failure to build the wing's capacity became one of IMATT's legacies.[70]

The maritime wing, however, represented a more positive story. IMATT had particularly high hopes for income generation as a result of the development of the maritime wing, which consists of around 500 personnel and a number of small patrol craft and barges. During 2007, the wing had some success in seizing trawlers fishing illegally off the coast and capturing armed pirates. In 2008, it was seen as an area in which a relatively small investment in terms of resources, legislation and interdepartmental procedures could reap significant financial rewards by establishing a licence-based process for fishing. Moreover, given concerns about piracy and the trafficking of illicit narcotics in West Africa, a maritime wing could contribute further to regional stability.

Also with respect to income generation, the RSLAF's leadership was keen to engage in international peace support operations (PSOs). This, in the words of the commander of IMATT in 2008, Brigadier Jonathan Powe, 'provided an external focus',[71] and in February 2007, Sierra Leone committed to the ECOWAS Standby Force (ESF) and signed a Memorandum of Understanding with the UN to participate in peacekeeping operations. Apart from providing the RSLAF with a positively defined role for the foreseeable future, this was also considered to reinforce the UK's success in transforming Sierra Leone's armed forces through IMATT.[72] The conflict had ended in 2002; yet by 2007–08 the country's army was emerging as a potential source of peacekeepers for deployment in hot spots across sub-Saharan Africa. To the RSLAF and IMATT alike, this development was considered an unqualified indication of success and the reflection of an army coming of age. The RSLAF began deployment of military observers and staff officers to UN peace operations in 2007 and by August 2009, twenty-three officers had served in various capacities on UN operations. Notably, in late 2009 an entire reconnaissance company was deployed to Darfur as part of the African Union/United Nations Hybrid Operation in Darfur (UNAMID), a more detailed discussion of which can be found in Chapter IV.

Therefore, while support to the maritime wing had been considered a priority for IMATT for some time, in 2007, contributions to PSOs were emerging as the predominant focus of the RSLAF. Both had the potential to define a positive role for the armed forces, rather than, as had often been the case since 2002, imposing limits on the army's mandate (which had

[70] Brima Sesay, presentation, Sierra Leone, February 2014.
[71] Albrecht interview with Jonathan Powe.
[72] This came out in numerous interviews with both Sierra Leonean and British officers conducted during 2013.

been restricted to deterring rebellion and maintaining internal security in support of the SLP, whilst staying out of politics). However, particularly with respect to PSOs, it was evident to IMATT in 2007 that the RSLAF lacked 'the ability to equip, deploy and sustain any element on operations without significant external support'.[73] This did not render the prospect of contributing to PSOs unrealistic, but it became clear that this would not happen without substantial international support.

Core Review: Rebalancing the Army

With the main emphasis in 2007–08 thus on saving money, priority was placed upon what the RSLAF officially referred to as 'rebalancing' – that is, 'downsizing' the force.

During the war, the armed forces had increased from 4,000 to 17,000 personnel with very little or no professional training provided to new recruits. In a September 2002 meeting of the Defence Council,[74] it was decided that downsizing the RSLAF should be a priority, but that this should be carefully controlled, ensuring that the age of retirement was adhered to, and that voluntary and compulsory retirements were carried out in a structured manner (with DfID support for redundancy packages). By 2007, the RSLAF – including the small maritime wing and non-operational air wing – was 10,300-strong (down from 14,075 in January 2003). The proposed optimum size of the RSLAF (8,500) had been laid out in 2004, in IMATT's Plan 2010, and it was proposed that the drawdown in total number of troops would be accompanied by a reduction in the number of battalions from eleven to nine, and in the number of brigades from four to three. 'A more realistic size [of the RSLAF] was 4–6,000', Brigadier Powe noted in retrospect, but 'we never pushed that, because it would have been politically unviable'.[75]

President Kabbah's general disinterest in the security sector during 2006–07 meant that the mid-year Defence Council was cancelled. At the next meeting, held by the new government following the elections, the intention to downsize the army, which had begun in December 2006 but not been carried forward, was reiterated. This process was built up around the Core Review that the RSLAF initiated in late 2005 and which was

[73] IMATT, 'Commander IMATT (SL) – End of Tour Report'.

[74] Albrecht and Jackson, *Security System Transformation in Sierra Leone*, p. 108. According to the 1991 constitution, the Defence Council is chaired by the president, and it is the president, acting on advice of the Defence Council, that appoints the Chief of the Defence Staff. The council advises the president on all major matters of defence policy and strategy, military budgeting, administration and the promotion of officers above the rank of lieutenant. 'The Constitution of Sierra Leone, 1991', Art. 167–69.

[75] Albrecht interview with Jonathan Powe.

undertaken over the following eighteen months 'under the advice of IMATT', as noted by current Joint Force Commander Brigadier Brima Sesay, to deal with 'excess numbers of personnel'.[76] It was becoming increasingly evident that while senior officers might agree with the principle of slimming down the army, given Sierra Leone's financial situation, its implementation was being resisted. Considerable effort was therefore expended by the UK country team (comprising IMATT, the British High Commission and DfID) and visiting UK government representatives to persuade their Sierra Leonean counterparts that an affordable RSLAF was better for the country as a whole. The Core Review, which carried the authority of the Chief of the Defence Staff, gave vital direction to the downsizing process, not only for the RSLAF, but also for IMATT.[77]

However, with an election looming in 2007, it was clear that any decision about the size of the RSLAF had to be made by the incoming government. The executive powers held by expatriates – civilian and military – had been greatly reduced during 2006–07, as Sierra Leoneans took over management of their own affairs, both within RSLAF structures and in the MoD. (UK decision-making on behalf of the RSLAF as well as within the MoD was always meant to be for a limited period of time.) The ability of IMATT to enforce difficult decisions on behalf of their Sierra Leonean counterparts was therefore decreasing. Thus, perhaps paradoxically, one enabling factor allowing the rebalancing exercise to move forward was the perception – as noted by Brigadier Powe – that 'security was lower down on the President's agenda than it might have been two–three years before. The country was more stable and secure, which in a way also allowed us to reduce the size of RSLAF. It gave us an opportunity to bring down numbers to an affordable size'.[78]

In February 2008, the findings of the Core Review of key functional areas within the MoD and JFC were agreed by the president-led Defence Council.[79] In emphasising the need for efficiency and economy, the review outlined a rebalancing process that would run from 2008 to 2010

---

[76] Albrecht interview with Brima Sesay; presentation by Jamie Martin, UK, September 2013; Albrecht and Jackson, *Security System Transformation in Sierra Leone*, p. 104.

[77] IMATT, 'IMATT Reorientation Phases 3 and 4 – Initial Thoughts', Freetown, 10 December 2008, unpublished.

[78] Albrecht interview with Jonathan Powe. Sierra Leonean military expenditure is equal to 0.7 per cent of the country's GDP, in comparison to Liberia at 0.8 per cent and Nigeria at 0.91 per cent. This can be compared to bigger spenders like South Africa (1.2 per cent), Angola (3.6 per cent) and South Sudan (9.4 per cent). See SIPRI and World Bank, 'Military Expenditure (% of GDP)', <http://data.worldbank.org/indicator/MS.MIL.XPND.GD.ZS>, accessed 9 October 2014.

[79] The findings of the Core Review promoted four areas of focus, including efficiency and economy, investment in personnel, management of equipment and infrastructure, and training for subsequent operations. With IMATT support and

and would be achieved through redundancies amongst the junior ranks only and through natural wastage. This planned reduction – which was considered 'quite modest' by then-Commander of IMATT Jonathan Powe[80] – would 'de-establish' one infantry brigade and two infantry battalions and associated infrastructure, although it was never made clear precisely what the operational implications of this would be.

However, during 2008, Sierra Leonean reluctance continued, centred on the immediate financial implications of making hundreds of personnel redundant, the logistical implications of doing so, and how this might affect morale overall.

It was clear that the role of the RSLAF could not be understood in purely military terms. In the words of Brigadier Cholerton, the RSLAF was functioning 'like a welfare state; each soldier probably keeps 10 others going. The military activity that took place was minimal, so [the] RSLAF was more like a welfare organization than a fighting force'.[81] Yet resistance to the RSLAF's downsizing was not openly articulated. The perception in IMATT, according to Wing Commander Richard Woodward – who joined IMATT in 2010 as an adviser on personnel matters within Sierra Leone's MoD – was that on the surface, 'there was no disgruntlement as such'; but there were 'a number of barriers to why things are not happening'.[82] Another adviser explained that during 2007–10:[83]

> We had a constant process of trying to help them draw up a plan for reduction, but there was resistance to our suggestions to reduce, constant delays. There would be an agreement, in principle, to reduce, and then discussions about how that could not happen in the next few months – always papers going through the office of the minister of defence, and the president. In the end, FCO had some tough discussions with the president, explaining why downsizing was pivotal. This was about ensuring that Sierra Leone was not falling off the wagon.

In support of achieving the Core Review's target of 8,500 personnel by February 2010, it was agreed that around 870 redundancies would be made in two tranches. Personnel made redundant would receive one year's salary (equivalent to £500) paid by the Government of Sierra Leone,

---

involvement, the activities conducted within the review realigned available funding with realistic and achievable goals.

[80] Albrecht interview with Jonathan Powe.

[81] Albrecht interview with Iain Cholerton.

[82] Peter Albrecht interview with Richard Woodward, UK, August 2013. Downsizing was further complicated by an unresolved issue around those Wounded in Action (WIA), who failed to come forward for the UK-funded programme in 2004. It was agreed that the UK's Africa Conflict Prevention Pool would financially support removal of that obstacle to implementing the Core Review.

[83] Peter Albrecht interview with anonymous, over Skype, August 2013.

and a gratuity, training and transport grants (worth £450) paid for by DfID.[84] By 2010, RSLAF numbers had dropped to 9,000 with significant support from the civilian adviser to the MoD, a post which since April 2009 had been funded by the UK MoD, rather than DfID.

Notably, the downsizing of the RSLAF was undertaken without a wider defence review; but as Wing Commander Woodward noted, by 2010 'they had downsized to such a level that they needed to do a defence review'.[85] Indeed, while defence papers set strategies from year to year, a longer-term, presidential-led view of how the RSLAF should evolve was lacking. In the early stages of the rebalancing process, the Sierra Leonean MoD expected that the savings 'achieved by this exercise will be ploughed back into the Defence Vote, which will alleviate some of the day to day problems we all encounter in dealing with resources'.[86] However, the creation of a smaller and leaner RSLAF was not matched by the build-up of force multipliers, as had been expected, because neither the Sierra Leone government nor the international community could provide the funding for the equipment.[87]

Thus from 2007, it was Sierra Leone's contributions to international PSOs that would shape the RSLAF's future priorities.

The Restructuring of IMATT

Peaceful national and local elections in 2007 and 2008, respectively, were considered a manifestation of Sierra Leone's transition away from conflict. In turn, this enabled the UK to re-evaluate IMATT's future size, shape, focus and eventual exit from Sierra Leone. The UK MoD's role in guiding IMATT's work was limited, and since Plan 2010 had been established in 2004, the general direction of the mission's work had been relatively clear. In 2007–08, however, there were also a number of other issues at stake, related to the UK's broader strategic focus. As recalled by Brigadier Powe:[88]

> The focus of funding had switched away from West Africa to East Africa, and the [UK MoD] had to a certain extent lost interest [in the former]. There were bigger fish to fry [in Afghanistan and Iraq]. So we were working it out on our own, based on the resources we had available. We had a standard set of tasks that we were given [set out in Plan 2010].

[84] In March 2008, the minister of finance approached DfID and IMATT for assistance in meeting the Government of Sierra Leone liability for Wounded in Action Tranche II (WIA II) – a sum of £350,000. He stated that the government could not afford this.

[85] Albrecht interview with Richard Woodward.

[86] *Ibid.*

[87] Capacity within the RSLAF to use and maintain such equipment in the long run may also have been in question.

[88] Albrecht interview with Jonathan Powe.

> I had a set of tasks, reasonably open, and after that it was up to me to decide, alongside the head of FCO and DFID [in-country], what the best way to use the resources was.

Although IMATT was allowed the flexibility to plan the process of reducing its presence before eventually withdrawing from Sierra Leone, it did not have the authority to decide on what timeline this would occur. As such, exit plans were dictated by the broader strategic direction set by London, and the attendant financial settlements; but they were planned in collaboration with the Sierra Leonean MoD and the RSLAF, with a view to continuing to 'concentrate on those areas where IMATT can make a real difference'.[89] What was referred to as the 'reorientation' was planned to take place between 2008 and 2012, thus going beyond Plan 2010. As confirmed by IMATT in October 2008:[90]

> It [the four-year period between 2008 and 2012] will see IMATT's effort evolve from a widespread team providing advice and support at all levels, to a much more focused team concentrating principally on training, education and peace supporting capability. It will see a reduction in the size of IMATT from a team of 90 in 2007 to a team of around 25 in 2011/2012.

Ultimately, these plans were largely implemented along the lines set out in 2007–08 (right up until the point in April 2013 when the International Security Advisory Team replaced IMATT, which will be discussed in detail in Chapter IV). During Phase 1 of this drawdown, IMATT's staff numbers were reduced from ninety to about seventy by the end of 2008. At this point, IMATT had begun disengaging at the tactical level, and instead concentrated its efforts at the strategic (MoD) and operational (Joint Force Command) levels, as well as on education and training. Funding for Brigade Advisory and Support Teams (BASTs) that had been dedicated to individual brigades was reduced considerably, and two teams responsible for supporting all brigades were established.[91]

During Phase 2 in 2009, IMATT staff numbers were further reduced to around fifty personnel, and it refocused its efforts on the delivery of training for PSOs and on education and staff training at the Horton Academy. The country-wide BAST was withdrawn at the end of 2009 and IMATT presence within the MoD, the Joint Force Command and the

---

89 IMATT, 'Commander IMATT (SL) – End of Tour Report'.

90 IMATT, 'Briefing Note – IMATT Reorientation', Freetown, 7 October 2008, unpublished.

91 These two five-man teams (BAST North and BAST South) were established to maintain links with the brigade headquarters, the Brigade Battle Schools and, to a lesser extent, the battalions. *Ibid.*

Combat Support and Combat Service Support units was minimised.[92] While IMATT was downsizing, and thus reducing its provision of dedicated, unit-specific advice, it placed greater emphasis on short-term training and advisory teams and facilitating participation by RSLAF officers in courses outside Sierra Leone.

Symbolically, if not substantially, the most significant change to IMATT was the change of its commander from a 1-star post (brigadier) to the appointment of a colonel – Hugh Blackman – in mid-January 2009. Combined with the transition from an executive to an advisory role that took place gradually between 2007 and 2009, a fundamentally different IMATT was emerging. 'Without being too dramatic,' Blackman noted, 'you had [Brigadier] Santa-Olalla [IMATT commander in 2005], who sacked 70 officers, [and then] ... somebody like me [in 2009], who was advising – from the perspective of leading IMATT that was quite a challenge'.[93]

This change inevitably had implications for IMATT–RSLAF relations, and there was a sense within IMATT that not enough thought had gone into the transition. In 2008, it was hoped and expected that a 'full colonel should be able to punch his weight', as then-Commander of IMATT Brigadier Powe noted in retrospect.[94] The High Commissioner had opposed the change but, ultimately, there was pressure from the MoD in London to make a 'deliberate signal of intent' and to say: 'We are now into a steady reduction of engagement'.[95] Yet this led to a 'rocky period':[96] in the Sierra Leonean MoD, power struggles arose around the minister of defence and the president as the leadership of IMATT and the RSLAF began working against one another. As Brigadier Brima Sesay of the RSLAF observed, the position of commander of IMATT was 'a very important function ... a powerful appointment', and the question of rank therefore 'created a lot of issues'.[97] In short, the change in rank of IMATT's leader from brigadier to colonel was not well-received by the RSLAF leadership. In Blackman's words:[98]

---

[92] Combat Support units relate specifically to the kinetic elements of the army (artillery, aviation, and so forth), while Combat Service Support units provide support *vis-à-vis* logistics, communications and mechanical engineering.

[93] Brigadier Santa-Olalla served as commander of IMATT in 2005. Whilst Commander IMATT had the status of 'adviser' in 2005, the level of influence in that role cannot be underestimated and to a large extent he was in operational command. Peter Albrecht interview with Hugh Blackman, over Skype, August 2013.

[94] Albrecht interview with Jonathan Powe.

[95] Albrecht interview with Hugh Blackman.

[96] *Ibid.*

[97] Albrecht interview with Brima Sesay.

[98] Albrecht interview with Hugh Blackman.

> Colonel is high, but not as high as a Brigadier – a grade down is a reduction; it was a signal of our intent to reduce in size, until we ceased to exist. Jonathan Powe [Blackman's predecessor] introduced me to the president – until that point it was reasonable to believe that they did not think it would happen. From that point there was disappointment in the irrefutable evidence that the UK was withdrawing. We were closer to the end than to the beginning.

The impact of IMATT's downsizing was also felt within the RSLAF, often positively. On the one hand, 'most of the support started to fade away', Sesay explained. On the other hand, 'there were things now, which [the] RSLAF had to decide on. It helped [the] RSLAF, it helped to prove what we've done, and [proved] that we can do things on our own, without IMATT involvement'.[99]

While IMATT was in 'draw-down mode', meanwhile, the implementation of DfID's new justice-sector programme was only just beginning. There had previously been clashes of personality and sometimes tension between those running the CCSSP, IMATT and SILSEP, but their overall strategic aim and approach had overlapped, centring on state-building. However, with the initiation of the CCSSP and the Law Development Programme's successor, the Justice Sector Development Programme, the difference between UK MoD (IMATT) and DfID priorities became more evident, reflecting both contextual changes in Sierra Leone and the broader shift in DfID's general thinking around its involvement in security-related programming.

Justice-Sector and Policing Reform

Holistic Justice-Sector Reform: Too Much, Too Fast?

The implementation of the JSDP under the British Council, which was wholly DfID-funded, officially began in 2007, but 'the two year inception phase [initiated in March 2005] was not enough' to get the programme up and running in earnest.[100] There were a number of reasons for this, which ultimately rested on unrealistic estimates of the time required to establish a new programme – something from which the transition in 2012 between the JSDP and its successor, the Access to Security and Justice Programme, also suffered.

The JSDP represented a fundamental shift in thinking and development within Sierra Leone's SSR process, which was now broadened to encompass the justice sector as a whole. It could be argued that together, SILSEP and IMATT had covered defence, security-system co-ordination

[99] Albrecht interview with Brima Sesay.

[100] Peter Albrecht interview with John Magbity, Sierra Leone, June 2012; Peter Albrecht interview with Peter Viner, UK, August 2013.

and intelligence-gathering comprehensively, and could therefore be considered a sector-wide programme. However, the JSDP was regarded by DfID from its inception in 2005 as 'the first Sierra Leone experience of a broad sector-wide programme'.[101] As such, the programme reflected two somewhat contradictory moves in international SSR policy-making circles. On the one hand, it reflected the systemic, 'holistic' approach to security that was gaining traction within DfID at the time, emphasising the provision of security and justice as public services (thereby excluding defence). However, it also reflected a reorientation within DfID with regard to working in the areas of security and justice, and the resulting wish to return to more 'conventional' development engagements. While CCSSP was initiated to enable the Government of Sierra Leone to reclaim its sovereign power to enforce order, the language and outlook of the JSDP was different. It explicitly targeted improving access to affordable justice, particularly for the poor, marginalised and vulnerable.

The Sierra Leonean context also shaped the JSDP, which was established in a time of peaceful fragility, unlike the CCSSP and SILSEP, which had been initiated while open conflict raged. As noted by Anthony Howlett-Bolton, a justice and security adviser within the JSDP, the programme represented 'a shift in focus from crisis and emergency management to one of sustainable economic growth and poverty reduction.'[102] The JSDP was more classically 'developmental' in its focus and approach – this being to 'establish the basis for long term sustainable reforms rather than what could turn out to be unsustainable quick wins'.[103] As such, the JSDP reflected a view within DfID that while the root causes of conflict might remain unaddressed, Sierra Leone had emerged from the immediate post-conflict phase.

In collaboration with national partners, the first two years of the JSDP were set aside to initiate priority reforms and assess the capacity of the sector to absorb and implement change. Prior to the 2007 elections, a draft Justice Sector Reform Strategy had been outlined, support had been given to individual organisations to formulate strategic plans, civil society was being involved to a greater extent than had previously been the case, and the prisons service (which had previously fallen between the

---

[101] DfID and Security Sector Development Advisory Team, 'Output to Purpose Review, Sierra Leone Security Sector Reform Programme III (SILSEP III)', London, September 2005, unpublished.
[102] Anthony Howlett-Bolton, 'Justice Sector Reform', in Peter Albrecht and Paul Jackson (eds), *Security Sector Reform in Sierra Leone 1997–2007*, pp. 93–106.
[103] Biesheuvel, Hamilton-Baillie and Wilson, 'Sierra Leone Security Sector Reform Programme – Output to Purpose Review'.

narrower focus of the CCSSP, SILSEP and the Law Development Programme) was being fully integrated into the JSDP.[104]

The protracted start-up phase saw the consolidation of the JSDP's new management arrangements. Unlike the CCSSP, IMATT and SILSEP, the JSDP was separate from, but designed to be led by, the Government of Sierra Leone – an option which had been less viable in the late 1990s and early 2000s. This had implications for the JSDP's ability to direct its spending without express approval of the dedicated Leadership Group, chaired by the Sierra Leonean vice president.[105]

The JSDP also attempted to establish formal national ownership within the justice sector by setting up a Justice Sector Coordination Office (JSCO) in 2007, with the aim of co-ordinating efforts and addressing the government's lack of capacity for sector-wide policy-making and planning.[106] Thus, while the JSDP was a multifaceted, sprawling programme, one of its primary objectives was to ensure better co-ordination across the justice system.

Located next to the attorney-general and solicitor-general's offices within the Ministry of Justice, the JSCO was from the outset branded as part of the government rather than part of the JSDP, even though it was funded by the latter. Reflecting its mandate, it came to play a crucial role in co-ordinating and producing the government's own sector strategy, the Justice Sector Reform Strategy and Investment Plan (JSRSIP) for 2008–10. Prior to the JSRSIP, there had been no strategic direction from the Sierra Leone government, and the donor community had consequently defined the sector's needs. This first JSRSIP essentially followed the established pattern of such strategy documents and, although it was put together by

[104] One of the most visible results of the JSDP's work in Moyamba District, the pilot district, was the refurbishment of the district prison. Prior to the JSDP, Sierra Leone's prison system had received no co-ordinated support. Under the JSDP, inmates in Moyamba prison were sleeping in beds rather than on the floor, received three meals a day and attended classes (having previously been unoccupied). More importantly, inmates knew why they were being detained, which is not necessarily the case in other prisons in Sierra Leone.

[105] The principal responsibility of the Leadership Group was to provide strategic direction and policy co-ordination, and to develop a sector-wide plan for the justice sector. The heads of the institutions represented in the Leadership Group – including the vice president as chair, and relevant ministers and the chief justice as members – each nominated two representatives to ensure regular attendance at meetings of the Technical Working Group, which was set up to guide the programme as it developed, to review progress and to identify any pressing issues that needed to be addressed. The Technical Working Group was also instrumental in ensuring that the programme's implementation was developed in line with a sector-wide approach to justice-sector budgeting and planning. Albrecht, Gbla and Jackson, 'From Quick Wins to Long-Term Profits?', p. 30.

[106] JSDP, 'Report for 2009 Annual Review for the period Feb 08 Jan 2009', 20 February 2009, unpublished.

external actors, it was done so with strong input from Sierra Leonean consultants, and in support of the JSCO.

As such, the JSDP was designed to establish a system whereby the government would take the lead in identifying and prioritising needs across the justice sector and in formulating and approving working plans. Within this push for national ownership, the JSCO became the main driver of change. As Peter Viner, who managed the JSDP from July 2008 until the programme was terminated in the second half of 2011, explained:[107]

> There has to be the capacity within the government to own the process. It's not a question of calling ministers together; you need a focal point that drives sector support. This means that in the longer term, you have to have that ownership within government and that's really the main reason for [the] JSCO ... You had a unit there that could continue post-JSDP, continue co-ordination [and] co-operation in the sector to ensure that the government itself was developing in an holistic manner rather than looking at the sector piecemeal.

This change in programming also signified a shift in external advice, which became much less personalised than under the CCSSP and when Keith Biddle had been the inspector-general of police. Biddle had benefited from direct access to President Kabbah as well as a close working relationship with Adrian Horn, who managed the CCSSP, providing him with access to a large policing programme. By contrast, relations with the government were institutionalised to a much greater extent under the JSDP.

This did not mean that the JSDP, a programme staffed by both expatriates and Sierra Leoneans, did not invest considerable time and effort in building relationships with their counterparts in the government. As the head of the JSCO Olayinka Creighton-Randall noted in 2012, the 'JSDP had very good interpersonal relationships with the agencies. They believed in building capacity and allowing institutions to grow rather than to micro-manage them'.[108] Development is inherently political work, not least when engaging with institutions that are involved in regulating power within society, as in the justice sector. Therefore, engaging the political leadership was considered crucial by Peter Viner:[109]

> The Attorney-General, you needed to be talking to him, the Minister of Local Government, if you did not speak to the minister you could not

[107] Albrecht interview with Peter Viner.

[108] Peter Albrecht interview with Olayinka Creighton-Randall, Sierra Leone, July 2012.

[109] Albrecht interview with Peter Viner.

> influence what was going to happen. It was about establishing those relationships quickly and saying: 'Look, we really need to push this or that'. It was almost like rewriting the programme with the individual leaders.
>
> We would work quietly behind the scene with the Vice President. It was about making sure that he would drive it, that he was there. Initially, I would do a lot of the work before meetings. When Olayinka was there, I made sure that she was given the space to do it. I would let Olayinka be the vice. That made things work a lot better.
>
> Building those relationships, including with the Vice President, meant that suddenly the head of prisons or police would be more accountable of their input. Ministers were put on the spot. Suddenly, they had to account for why things were, and were not, happening.

The relationships that the JSDP established were crucial to ensuring its planned activities were actually implemented – and as such, underscored the political nature of development programming at its very core.[110] Among these activities – as recorded by the JSDP Project Completion Report – was the construction of two new prisons, ninety-four accommodation units for prison staff, three new court buildings in Freetown, fifteen new Family Support Units and two juvenile facilities.[111] In addition, 85 per cent of all JSDP staff, including consultants, were Sierra Leonean, which was part of the programme's broader attempt to ensure a degree of national ownership. Unlike its predecessor, the programme also established close working relations with civil-society organisations such as Timap for Justice, which facilitated a community mediation project for settling disputes without recourse to any court, thus diverting them away from the state-governed justice system.[112] Such an option, which minimised the strain on both local and magistrates' courts, did not exist before the JSDP introduced community-based mediators through groups such as Timap for Justice.

---

[110] As is explored further in Chapter IV, the difficult relationship between advisers and the Sierra Leonean judiciary, in particular, was a considerable challenge to the JSDP's successor, the ASJP, which began implementation in 2012.

[111] In response to the mass violence that was experienced during the war, the Family Support Units were established in 2001 to deal with incidents of domestic violence. See Kadi Fakondo, 'Reforming and Building Capacity of the Sierra Leone Police, 1999–2007', in Albrecht and Jackson (eds), *Security Sector Reform in Sierra Leone 1997–2007*, pp. 161–69. See also Albrecht and Jackson, *Security System Transformation in Sierra Leone*, pp. 39–40, 142–43.

[112] Local courts constitute the lowest level of the formal justice system and are mandated to adjudicate on matters of customary law.

The Case of Moyamba District

The decision was made to choose a pilot district for the JSDP outside of Freetown and the Western Area, with the CCSSP and the Law Development Programme having worked mostly at the national level and primarily within the capital. The southern district of Moyamba – which encompasses fourteen chiefdoms and a population of 260,000 – was selected specifically because of the number of state-related justice institutions located there, including a prison, four police stations and five police posts, as well as being easily accessible from Freetown. The original programme concept suggested that further districts would be added, although this did not happen.[113] Instead, Moyamba came to act as a district 'test-bed' for new projects and ideas, from which those that worked might be rolled out, depending on levels of interest. In the final report outlining the achievements of the JSDP, the 'Moyamba pilot' was presented as an 'invaluable ... model that could be used to develop and test ways of improving people's access to justice elsewhere in the country'.[114]

Replicating management structures at the national level, a task force was formed from justice-sector institutions and civil-society organisations in the district. With support from the JSDP, the task force then prioritised areas for support and recommended a range of activities for approval by the national Leadership Group. Activities focused especially on itinerant courts, local courts, prisoner rehabilitation and infrastructure. As the JSDP came to a close in 2012, efforts towards the development of local courts and a circuit court were considered particularly successful.[115]

In line with DfID priorities since the mid-2000s, the general focus of the JSDP in Moyamba was thus on community access to justice. This was primarily done by focusing on the court system and informal mediation schemes, but also in line with a holistic approach to the justice sector by working with and consolidating the SLP's Family Support Unit and Moyamba's prison. The establishment of a circuit court meant that the physical – if not financial, linguistic or cultural – inaccessibility to most of the district was overcome. However, the population has remained dependent on the local courts, which are under the control of local authorities such as paramount and lesser chiefs. In interviews carried out in early 2011, it was noted that, generally, the Native Administration,

[113] Lisa Denney, *Justice and Security Reform: Development Agencies and Informal Institutions in Sierra Leone* (Oxford and New York, NY: Routledge, 2014), p. 105.

[114] JSDP, 'Achievements and Lessons Learned', British Council, Freetown, 2012, p. 12.

[115] The main focus of the JSDP in Moyamba was on community access to courts. A circuit (mobile) court, holding sessions across Moyamba, was established in an attempt to overcome the inaccessibility of many parts of the district. Albrecht, Gbla and Jackson, 'From Quick Wins to Long-Term Profits?', p. 16, note 5. See also JSDP, 'Achievements and Lessons Learned'.

which includes the Chiefdom Police,[116] had no resources. This and a lack of education, as well as reference to 'how things are commonly done', reveal limits to the reach of programmes such as the JSDP. Although illegal under the 2011 Local Courts Act, paramount and lesser chiefs commonly adjudicate on matters that fall within the jurisdiction of local courts and play a central role in the selection of chairmen of these courts.[117]

Nevertheless, the JSDP Project Completion Report recorded a 586 per cent increase in the number of cases heard at the magistrates' court in Moyamba in 2010, up from a baseline of eighty in 2007, with most cases also being resolved at the first hearing. Within these figures, it is notable that 391 women accessed the court in 2010, while only sixty-four had done so in 2007.[118] In isolation, these are impressive numbers that show how a programme such as the JSDP can have an impact. The question remains, however, whether its holistic approach led to a lasting, if not permanent, effect.

Balancing Prioritised Programming with a Holistic Approach

While there were evident advancements in ordinary people's access to justice under the JSDP, the JSDP Project Completion Report also acknowledged the difficulties experienced in pursuing a holistic approach. From the outset, its focus had been on making an effort 'to join up project components, not uplift sections in isolation creating the risk that cases fall between the cracks.'[119] Indeed, the 'justice system must be seen as one intertwined process with all aspects assessed and strengthened, as the

[116] A separate legal entity to the SLP, the Chiefdom Police appears in numerous pieces of legislation. Its primary role is to deliver summons for cases in local courts, enforce by-laws and assist with the collection of chiefdom revenue. The Chiefdom Police was previously the enforcement arm of the district councillors and paramount chiefs as 'court messengers'. Around 1956, as the British began to prepare Sierra Leone for independence, the SLP moved into the Protectorate (beyond the Western Area). The commissioner at the time was asked by the colonial secretary to take over the court messengers. He refused, almost for the same reasons as the leaders of police reform in the early 2000s: the financial and management burden of doing so. Peter Alexander Albrecht, 'Transforming Internal Security in Sierra Leone: Sierra Leone Police and Broader Justice Sector Reform', *DIIS Report* 2010:07, Copenhagen, 2010, p. 9; See Peter Albrecht et al., 'Community Policing in Sierra Leone – Local Policing Partnership Boards', *DIIS Report* 2014:16, Copenhagen, 2014, pp. 30–31.

[117] In the aftermath of the passage of the 2011 Local Courts Act, the chief justice set up a Local Courts Implementation Sub-Committee comprised of representatives from a number of agencies including the Ministry of Local Government and Rural Development, the Ministry of Finance and Economic Development, and the National Council of Paramount Chiefs.

[118] DfID, 'JSDP Project Completion Report', August 2011, unpublished.

[119] *Ibid*.

overall system is only as good as its weakest link.'[120] However, by the programme's end in 2011, prosecution procedures, for instance, remained a considerable concern. Criminal proceedings continued to be instigated with far too little evidence to secure a conviction – an unnecessary drain on resources, which in turn led to continued congestion of the justice system, and made overcrowding of the prisons worse.[121] A holistic approach may have been the foundation stone of the JSDP, but the programme also illuminated the considerable challenges in making a sustainable impact on the overall system. In short, being holistic does not mean that tasks and goals should not be prioritised.[122]

The sustainability of the JSDP's work was also brought into question by the absence of future donor funding. This was exacerbated by the Sierra Leone government's failure to prioritise justice as an area for intervention, and its allocation of low levels of funds to those sectors that it thought would be supported by donors instead. This is an example of the difficulties caused by the development of donor-dependent attitudes within a recipient government, which tends to focus on external sources of funding rather than on planning and budgeting for sustainable justice into the future.

The JSDP also faced difficulties in fulfilling its ambitions with regard to the Leadership and Technical Working Groups. It had initially anticipated that these would be replicated at the provincial and district level, to ensure effective sector co-ordination and collaboration. Although the JSDP did indeed carry out its activities across the entire country, the only district in which these co-ordinating structures were established was Moyamba. This reflected the wider challenge of branching out – across the full spectrum of its programme – into other districts, as was set out in the original JSDP programme document. This was likely due to the overwhelming ambition of encompassing the justice and security field in its entirety. Indeed, addressing the justice sector holistically in Freetown alone during the relatively short period of a programme cycle would be daunting enough. This indicates a general tendency of 'service providers' (the label used by DfID for companies or organisations that implement large-scale development programmes) to oversell what they are able to achieve, as well as the overblown expectations that donors have of them.

[120] *Ibid.*
[121] Glentworth et al., 'Sierra Leone', p. 5. In another example, 70 per cent of the prisons' budget was spent on food, but the prisoners received only rice. This, Glentworth et al. noted, 'suggests that there are related issues of corruption and low prison officer pay to be addressed'. *Ibid.*, p. 16.
[122] Mark Sedra, 'Introduction. The Future of Security Sector Reform', in Sedra (ed.), *The Future of Security Sector Reform*, p. 17.

In August 2011, the JDSP was replaced by the Access to Security and Justice Programme, which was run by Development Alternatives, Inc. (DAI). This change in service provider was in line with DfID's usual programming cycle (and the attendant legal requirement to tender large-scale programmes), but it also reflected pressure from London to respond to the guidance set out in DfID's 2009 White Paper, *Eliminating World Poverty: Building Our Common Future*.[123] This meant that firms other than the British Council could also make a bid to run the successor programme. In this instance, tension between individuals in the British Council and DfID at the time also played into the process, a point that again emphasises the importance of personal relationships. These processes are *never* just technical.[124]

Although implementation of the ASJP did not begin until 2012, planning was initiated in 2009 and it was tailored to address perceived weaknesses in the JSDP. In particular, these areas included: the failure to develop high-level governmental support and ensure the internalisation of justice as a core function of government; the need to extend justice provision beyond Moyamba District; and the requirement for 'joined-up' donor provision in the justice sector. Yet, for a variety of reasons – many of them beyond the control of those implementing the ASJP – the programme was initially problematic and the result was a year-long gap in UK support to the justice system as the transition from the JSDP to the ASJP took place (to be discussed in greater detail in Chapter IV).[125]

The JSDP and Reduced Funding for the SLP

The JSDP experienced notable challenges during its start-up, largely as a result of the programme's significantly broadened outlook, as well as the time required to identify the needs of the justice sector as a whole, and to establish management structures conducive to national ownership. These challenges also had implications for other programmes.

This was particularly evident with regard to the SLP. Under the Commonwealth Community Safety and Security Project between 2000 and 2005, £27 million (around $52 million) had been earmarked for the SLP alone, but under the JSDP, this sum was now to be shared across the sector, benefiting the police *as well as* the judiciary, prisons, Ministry of Internal Affairs and so forth. Although this might have been the right choice strategically, it came as something of a surprise to some within the SLP, with Sierra Leone's current inspector-general of police, Francis Alieu

123 DfID, *Eliminating World Poverty*.
124 Albrecht, Gbla and Jackson, 'From Quick Wins to Long-Term Profits?', pp. 36–37.
125 *Ibid*.

Munu, explaining that 'we did not know was that [the] JSDP was coming to *replace* the CCSSP.'[126]

At the same time, while the CCSSP had focused on supporting SLP equipment procurement, this was no longer the case under the JSDP, which took a different approach to working with the SLP. While buying vehicles, communication systems, uniforms and even weapons for the SLP may have been seen as necessary immediately after the war, DfID now argued – in line with discussions about sustainability within the justice sector – that the bill for equipment, buildings and welfare should be picked up by the Government of Sierra Leone rather than donors (DfID had never paid for weapons for the SLP, but it had overseen the CCSSP and paid Biddle's salary as IGP during the period in which the OSD was armed).

In the early stages of the JSDP (2005–06), this was compounded by the fact that individual UK advisers to the CCSSP resisted the broadening of reforms to the wider justice sector – perhaps reflecting a failure to differentiate between their professional role as external advisers and their personal conviction, perceiving that the new direction would have a negative impact on levels of support to the SLP. As recalled by Anthony Howlett-Bolton, justice and security adviser to the JSDP:[127]

> By the time I arrived, there was no balance and there were arguments [within the CCSSP]. Clearly there was an absence of a controlled hand and I didn't find any strategic direction. You could argue that they were at the end of [the] CCSSP, so there wouldn't be, but I then immediately asked the senior governance adviser [in DfID] about the closure report for the CCSSP. The answer I got was that 'we don't talk about closure'. The first decision I made in agreement with the IGP, he gave me a list of people who he felt were helping, were useful, and in the main kept them on. I also made it clear to the consultants that I'd ring them. The migration from CCSSP to JSDP was going to be a break.

This was a clash between two fundamentally different approaches to police reform: an actor-specific approach that relied on heavy investment – represented by the CCSSP (with the Law Development Programme) – versus a holistic, sector-oriented programme aiming to engender systemic change – represented by the JSDP. The latter's design also reflected the aforementioned changes in DfID's willingness to engage in matters of national security.

The reduction in funding available to the SLP had a significant effect in the following years. When the former head of the CCSSP was tasked by the defence attaché of the British High Commission – not DfID – to review

[126] Peter Albrecht interview with Francis Alieu Munu, Sierra Leone, July 2012. Emphasis added.
[127] Howlett-Bolton quoted in Albrecht and Jackson, *Security System Transformation in Sierra Leone*, pp. 93–94.

the SLP in early 2011, it was immediately evident to him that it was suffering as a result of scarce resources (as with all of the other security-sector institutions). While he observed that there were 'many good officers who are well trained, and the SLP has good policy-making capacity', he also noted that 'The SLP's current capability to provide policing functions in general … is assessed as poor',[128] identifying fundamental issues such as lack of basic resources and infrastructure, and poor leadership at the local level.

At the root of these issues was the lack of national resources, with the 2011 budget for officer salaries amounting to less than 30 per cent of that available in 2002 due to inflation, poor exchange rates and increases in staff numbers. A police constable's basic salary in 2010 was 148,520 Leones per month (roughly $62, equivalent to the cost of a sack of rice). As a consequence, police officers had great difficulty in meeting their families' housing, schooling and healthcare needs, and increasing numbers resorted to alternative means of providing for their families, such as petty corruption and maintaining small-scale businesses on the side. These practices were seen as corrupt or at best to constitute begging, with a consequent effect on public perceptions of, and trust in, the police.

In order to counter this dearth of funding, by the late 2000s the SLP had become increasingly reliant on income generated by hiring out armed Operational Support Division officers to banks and other institutions for the provision of security (at a rate of 500,000 Leones per officer – roughly $200 – with 20 per cent of this paid to the officer for food and transport). During 2010, around 3.8 billion Leones ($887,000[129]) was generated in this way – the equivalent of 776 officers being deployed full time on income-generation duties (excluding OSD officers deployed to provide protection to ministers and to guard key buildings and installations).[130] According to the deputy inspector-general of police, this income was used to run the force – a need compounded in 2011, for example, by the fact that there were delays in the first quarter's funding (indeed, money was allegedly borrowed from the welfare fund to keep the SLP functioning).[131]

It could be argued, then, that the build-up of the OSD reflected political pressure to recruit and strengthen the armed wing of the police, as well as the fundamental need to generate an income. In any case, the

---

128 Adrian Horn, Martin Gordon and Peter Albrecht, 'Sierra Leone Police – Review of Capabilities', London, 2011, unpublished, p. 6. As one of the authors of this Whitehall Paper (Peter Albrecht) was part of the team conducting this review, it is known who wrote the various parts of the final report.

129 *Ibid.* p. 20.

130 *Ibid.*

131 *Ibid.* pp. 19–20.

semi-privatisation of the SLP throws up a number of important questions about the extent to which the police force should serve private interests.

The Political Context of Policing

During the period 2007–10, the SLP was also under considerable political pressure – but it was a different *kind* of political pressure to that previously experienced. There is no denying the fundamental shift in the approach of the Kabbah government from that of the APC under Koroma, which to some Sierra Leonean observers reflected broader differences between the two political parties in terms of their willingness to meddle in the affairs of the security forces.[132] The APC's approach was further shaped by the context in which it came to power, with the country now stabilised but fragile.

By 2007, the SLPP had become identified with increasing corruption and greed (the metaphor of 'eating' is frequently used in Sierra Leonean politics and popular culture to describe this). Consequently, the APC was enjoying a revival as the only major opposition party, despite previously being identified with dictatorial rule and the one-party state between 1968 and 1992, and thus with the period leading up to the collapse of the state and subsequent conflict. The APC and Koroma won the elections in 2007 based on popular dissatisfaction with the pace of economic development, allegations of deep-seated corruption and because Charles Margai, the candidate of the PMDC, sided with Koroma in return for Cabinet posts.[133] As the historian David Harris points out, however, whilst Koroma is undoubtedly a reforming president, he also stands at the head of a relatively conservative party, with conservatism in Sierra Leone implying a continuation of patronage politics.[134]

This particular variety of Sierra Leonean conservatism has had profound implications for the SSR process, broadly speaking, and for police reform specifically. Under Koroma, recruitment into the SLP has become considerably politicised, for instance – a situation that resembles the pre-war context. The failure of the state before war broke out in 1991 was not caused by its inability to provide services *per se*. Rather, the leadership in Freetown failed to maintain the extensive neo-patrimonial network that had been established and consolidated during the post-

[132] The APC is traditionally associated with the north of the country, but ethnic – or tribal – tensions should not be overstated. It is clear that the APC victory was as much about the SLPP losing the election as the APC winning it. David Harris, *Sierra Leone: A Political History* (New York, NY: Oxford University Press, 2014).

[133] Jimmy D Kandeh, 'Rogue Incumbents, Donor Assistance and Sierra Leone's Second Post-Conflict Elections of 2007', *Journal of Modern African Studies* (Vol. 46, No. 4, December 2008), pp. 603–35.

[134] Harris, *Sierra Leone*.

colonial era.[135] Precisely because there is no history of a politically neutral bureaucratic system in Sierra Leone, the APC's trust in the institutions that had been built under the SLPP prior to 2007 was limited, as they were seen as the product of, and thus as serving, the SLPP and its interests.

Personality, politics and the level of stability within Sierra Leone thus played a part in the governments' differing approaches. President Kabbah was elected while the conflict was ongoing, in an unstable environment in which 'the whole system had capitulated', as noted by one of Freetown's long-serving journalists.[136] Kabbah's point of departure was therefore collapse and dependence on UK support. It was perhaps for this reason that his government:[137]

> [Did] not want to be overbearing and ensure that their own people were in the police. They allowed the process [that the UK had started] to go on and endorsed almost everything that was given to them. There were a few things that they challenged on the way, but the Sierra Leone police officers did not have the backing of Kabbah, who was always on the side of the British.

President Koroma, by contrast, came to power in a period of greater stability than Kabbah and was able to exercise greater control. He made an effort to build strong relations with the armed forces and the police prior to the 2007 elections, which, as one Freetown-based observer comments was 'typical of the APC', which 'never leave[s] things hanging like the SLPP'.[138] Differences in personality were also evident – the same observer commenting further that Koroma 'came in with his overbearing tendencies ... Kabbah would not call the chief of the police and direct him on what he had to do. [But] Koroma is a different person and he was dictating'.[139]

Furthermore, as the dust settled in the two years following the 2007 elections, the way in which the new president formalised the authority of his close-protection team revealed a growing politicisation of domestic security. It is worth pointing out that all of the parties running for government in 2007 made use of non-state actors, including ex-combatants, for their own security. While this delegitimised the formal security institutions, it also accentuated a lack of confidence in the SLP, which

[135] Reno, *Corruption and State Politics in Sierra Leone*; David Keen, *Conflict and Collusion in Sierra Leone* (Oxford: James Currey/Palgrave Macmillan, 2005); Krijn Peters, *War and the Crisis of Youth in Sierra Leone* (Cambridge: Cambridge University Press, 2011).

[136] Peter Albrecht interview with anonymous, Sierra Leone, September 2013.

[137] *Ibid.*

[138] *Ibid.*

[139] *Ibid.*

prevailed within the population at large. Koroma, most notoriously, had chosen fourteen ex-combatants as his security team in the run-up to the 2007 elections, including the well-known 'Leather Boot'. This group was retained as Koroma's bodyguards following his election, and was later implicated in attacks on SLPP party offices in Freetown in 2009.[140] The SLP was then used to legitimise their transition from informal security providers for Koroma during the election period to formal members of the Close Protection Unit of the OSD.[141] Not only were SLP recruitment rules bypassed in the process, but in the eyes of Sierra Leonean observers outside the security sector it also explicitly demonstrated the continued intertwining of formal and informal power.

Unsurprisingly, the use of state institutions to formalise the authority of ex-combatants was not viewed well within the police (or the Office of National Security); it was not discussed openly with the leadership of the police and reflected badly on the SLP as a whole. Reportedly, the ONS sent a letter to Koroma, stating that it was imperative that he use those officers within the OSD with formal training in providing close protection.[142] This suggestion was ignored however, and the fourteen members of Koroma's election security team continued to receive special treatment within the SLP, creating further tension. When they were drawn into the rank and file of the police, they were sent to Morocco in North Africa for training, instead of the national Police Training School in Hastings (Western Area). Furthermore, the most prominent of the group's members were subsequently promoted to the rank of superintendent. As stated above, it is common practice to set up party-political security groups, often referred to as task forces, but it was the first time that a task force was openly formalised as part of the state security apparatus, thereby further undermining the credibility of the SLP – and perceptions of its independence.

Similarly, when Francis Alieu Munu replaced Brima Acha Kamara as inspector-general of police on 20 August 2010, it was considered by some within the police to be a political appointment. It is worth remembering, however, that the APC did not make immediate changes to the SLP leadership upon its election to government, as had been anticipated. Moreover, the appointment (and replacement) of the IGP is by design a

---

[140] Erlend Grøner Krogstad, 'Security, Development and Force: Revisiting Police Reform in Sierra Leone', *African Affairs* (Vol. 111, No. 443, 2012), pp. 261–80, 279.

[141] See Maya M Christensen and Mats Utas, 'Mercenaries of Democracy: The "Politricks" of Remobilized Combatants in the 2007 General Elections, Sierra Leone', *African Affairs* (Vol. 107, No. 429, 2008), pp. 515–39.

[142] Peter Albrecht interview with anonymous, Sierra Leone, January 2011.

political act given that, under the 1991 constitution, the power to do so rests with the president acting on the advice of the Police Council, which is chaired by the vice president, and subject to the approval of Parliament. This proximity between the president and police – although in many instances sanctioned through an agreed division of powers within a democratic state – has nevertheless been of continuous concern.[143]

Conclusion

Following elections in 2007, the new political context that emerged had different implications for security-sector institutions. SSR had been initiated in a context of war by the SLPP government, which had little other choice – or wish – than to align its objectives with those of its closest international partner, and primary funder, the UK. When the APC came to power in peacetime in 2007, it inevitably took a different approach to the security sector, given its history of governing Sierra Leone as a one-party state before 1991, as well as the fact that it had not been part of the stabilisation process. Ultimately, many within the security sector experienced the change of government in 2007 as an escalation of political pressure.

Organisations like the ONS and CISU, which were established by the UK and received most of their funding from DfID, found themselves having to prove their relevance to an executive that did not fully understand or trust them. The pressure they came under was perceived – from within the two organisations – as political and partly tribal. Yet, as stated by a long-serving official within the ONS:[144]

> [Because] of the stance of the National Security Coordinator [Kellie Conteh], we were able to deal with these pressures … They [the APC] had their own idea of how to manage the institutions, so from day one, we saw pressure on us to play to the tunes of the political class.

Despite these difficulties in the transition from an SLPP to an APC government, and limited support from international partners during this period, the ONS and CISU not only proved their relevance, but demonstrated the professionalism that they had built up, with UK support. In particular, the way in which CISU (and the ONS) handled the seizure of a plane from Venezuela in July 2008 – along with its cargo of 703 kg of cocaine – provided clear evidence of their professionalism and

143 Horn, Gordon and Albrecht, 'Sierra Leone Police – Review of Capabilities', p. 58.

144 Anonymous, working-group meeting, Sierra Leone, February 2014.

international connectedness (although this incident also highlighted inherent weaknesses in the SLP and judiciary).

The RSLAF, meanwhile, now had a dedicated minister of defence, who took over responsibilities which had, until then, been constitutionally designated to the president (prior to 2007, a deputy ran day-to-day affairs in the MoD, while the president represented the RSLAF in Cabinet meetings). In the words of Brigadier Brima Sesay, the current joint force commander, having a permanent representative in the Cabinet meant 'an improvement in the way that the government reacts to our demands and issues'.[145] Furthermore, it appears that the new minister of defence was able to withstand political pressure targeted at the RSLAF, for example, by challenging attempts to force through politically motivated recruitments – something which afflicted the SLP to a much greater extent. However, this change at the political level did not fundamentally alter the RSLAF's difficult financial situation, and therefore did not notably change the conditions of service for ordinary soldiers.

Implementation of the Core Review between 2008 and 2010 led to the army being downsized from a force of 10,500 to one of 8,500. This significant reduction in size warranted a defence review, but this was never produced. Contributions to PSOs became the RSLAF's top priority – a step that was more about seizing an opportunity and maintaining force size and support than about following a planned strategic direction (this was the case within IMATT as well as the RSLAF). However, the stability and organisational pride that contributing to PSOs brought to the RSLAF was considerable, enhancing the troops' sense of purpose. It became a decisive factor in providing the RSLAF with stability but, tellingly, it was reliant on external support and the exigencies of international, rather than domestic, politics.

The day-to-day pressure on the police and court systems was perhaps the greatest among all security-sector agencies. Unlike the RSLAF, the ONS and CISU, the SLP's role in providing security as a basic service is continuous, and changes to its organisation are likely to have significant consequences for how that service is delivered, which makes the implementation of reform more difficult. In 2005, the SLP lost the dedicated support it had enjoyed under the Commonwealth Community Safety and Security Project, and while support continued under the Justice Sector Development Programme, this was provided in an entirely different way, and with much less emphasis on logistics and infrastructure. It was also becoming increasingly clear that stronger links were required

[145] Albrecht interview with Brima Sesay.

between the SLP and the Ministry of Internal Affairs, whose affiliation was historically weak. Indeed, as time passed, and as this chapter shows, by 2010 it had become evident that while the RSLAF's dedicated minister was able to withstand external pressure to recruit outside due process, the SLP, the ONS and CISU were less able to do so. 'Most of government', one Sierra Leonean official close to events noted, 'think they have to create jobs for "the boys", party boys ... We were not really able to withstand those kinds of pressures. You were side-lined; decisions were taken without your knowledge. Despondency crept in. It was against that background that we lost many of our colleagues'.[146] As the next chapter shows, the effect of irregular recruitment would be felt particularly strongly within the Operational Support Division.

Finally, this period saw greater focus on reform of the justice sector through the JSDP, the implementation of which was fully up to speed by 2007–08, following its establishment in 2005. However, within this sector, 'managing upwards' became problematic for external actors, particularly in terms of establishing meaningful national ownership. In general, DfID's retrospective evaluation of the JSDP made it clear that the Government of Sierra Leone assigns a low priority to justice and that there is a tendency to underfund areas likely to attract donor funding.[147]

In line with DfID priorities since the mid-2000s, the general focus of the JSDP in Moyamba, the programme's only pilot district, was on community access to justice. This was primarily pursued through a focus on the court system, but also through a holistic approach to the justice sector, working with and consolidating the SLP's Family Support Units and the local prison. The establishment of the circuit court meant that the physical – if not financial, linguistic or cultural – inaccessibility to most of the residents of the district was overcome.

However, the population has remained largely dependent on the local courts, which are under the control of local authorities, such as paramount and lesser chiefs. In interviews carried out in early 2011,[148] it was noted that the administrations of the paramount chiefs in Sierra Leone, of which there are 149, had only limited resources, if any. The lack of resources and education, but also widespread popular references to 'how things are commonly done', reveal limits to the reach of programmes such as the JSDP. Although this contravenes the legislation set out in the

[146] Anonymous, working-group meeting, Sierra Leone, February 2014.
[147] DfID, 'JSDP Project Completion Report'.
[148] Horn, Gordon and Albrecht, 'Sierra Leone Police – Review of Capabilities', p. 39.

2011 Local Court Act, it continues to be commonplace for paramount and lesser chiefs to adjudicate on matters that fall within the jurisdiction of local courts and to play a central role in the selection of the chairmen of these courts.[149]

The resilience of local systems to reform efforts is not surprising, nor is it unique to Sierra Leone. There may be several reasons that people prefer local courts, including cost, local culture and familiarity. However, the operation of justice at this level is primarily about the maintenance of social cohesion and, with it, political power structures. Local justice therefore deals with those regarded as deviant from the social norm in a specific way – for example, those who are female, poor or young. This is most obvious in the way in which rape and other sexual crimes are (not) dealt with, but also in terms of the specific criteria used to define someone as a 'youth', which have less to do with age and more to do with acceptability, economic independence and marital status.[150]

Abuse of the local justice system in Sierra Leone, often by chiefs, contributed to the outbreak of conflict, prompting thousands of 'youths' to become combatants.[151] It is not by chance that the first target of the RUF in each district during the conflict was the chief. Reconstituting justice is therefore not just a natural priority of SSR efforts; it is also critical in peace-building more generally. Although one could argue that the UK was right to concentrate on the security infrastructure whilst the conflict was ongoing and in the immediate aftermath of war, Moyamba's experience shows that justice reform is a long-term, messy and unpredictable process. In other words, whilst a military force can be reconstructed, armed and

---

[149] A similar argument around resource scarcity could be made with respect to Local Policing Partnership Boards (LPPBs), which is one of the SLP's practical expressions of community policing. While acknowledged as an important component of Local Needs Policing, for instance in cases of violence against women, they were not central to JSDP activities (see JSDP, 'Achievements and Lessons Learned', p. 45). In Moyamba District in early 2011, just one LPPB had been created for the Local Command Unit, which does not cover all of the district's fourteen chiefdoms (there is not complete overlap between the Local Command Unit and the district). Apart from scarce resources, the effectiveness of LPPBs is directly related to how important they are found to be by the local unit commander (LUC). In 2009–10, the only Local Command Units in which LPPBs were established in each chiefdom were Motema (western Kono) and Kailahun Districts. In both cases, the LUCs were strong proponents of Local Needs Policing and LPPBs.

[150] Nathaniel King, *Conflict as Integration: Youth Aspiration to Personhood in the Teleology of Sierra Leone's 'Senseless War'* (Uppsala: Nordic Africa Institute, 2007).

[151] Paul Richards, *Fighting for the Rain Forest: War, Youth and Resources in Sierra Leone* (Oxford: International African Institute/James Currey, 1996).

trained, reconstructing a justice system depends on multiple complex variables, including what the population thinks that 'justice' actually is and who it perceives to have legitimacy in providing it. This is not an argument *against* incorporating justice-sector reform into SSR, but it points to a need to think more carefully about the compatibility of local justice and international best practices.

IV. 2010–13: SUSTAINABLE CHANGE, OR REPOLITICISATION OF THE SECURITY SECTOR?

From 2010, the differences in the approach of the All People's Congress (APC) to managing the security sector were amplified. Chapter III describes the way in which political pressure on the security sector became more apparent when the APC came to power in 2007, and executive interference was stepped up. This pressure did not affect the whole sector evenly, but depended on the ability of key stakeholders to convincingly explain their respective institutions' role within the security architecture, as well as the exact nature of the concepts of 'political independence' and 'serving the government of the day'. Progressively, the rules of the neo-patrimonial governance system were again being enforced, with the result that state institutions, including those of the security sector, were governed by this logic rather than by principles of democratic governance. As such, it became a critical factor in the uneven distribution of scarce resources.

The defining event of the period 2010–13 was the general election of November 2012. The United Nations Development Programme (UNDP), the UN Integrated Peacebuilding Office in Sierra Leone (UNIPSIL),[1] DfID and the Access to Security and Justice Programme (ASJP – the successor to the Justice Sector Development Programme) all provided logistical and technical support, but security planning was shaped and driven by Sierra Leonean institutions, building on the experiences of the two national elections held since the end of the war in 2002. The Office of National Security (ONS) played a co-ordinating role

[1] UNIPSIL was established in 2008 to support Sierra Leone in identifying and resolving tensions and threats of potential conflict, and in consolidating governance reforms. It followed on from the United Nations Integrated Office in Sierra Leone (UNIOSIL), which was established by UN Security Council Resolution 1620 to begin operations in 2006, taking over from the United Nations Mission in Sierra Leone (UNAMSIL) that was terminated in December 2005.

and the Sierra Leone Police (SLP), with support from other agencies within the security architecture, was responsible for election security. In 2011, the SLP's capacity to police elections had been assessed as poor.[2] However, as the election approached it became evident that the SLP was prepared and 'the system was allowed to work', as observed by Lieutenant Colonel Joe Edkins, IMATT training adviser and director of Horton Academy from 2012.[3] The police certainly came under pressure in preparing for the elections, but there was no attempt to overrule or fundamentally undermine the national security architecture that had been established.

The SLP's plan involved all of the uniformed services within its framework of operation; the hierarchy within the Standard Response Guidelines was activated,[4] and the SLP chaired meetings to explain these plans and obtain support from the wider security sector. (For instance, the Provincial and District Security Committees (PROSECs and DISECs) provided fundamental support as early-warning and information-sharing mechanisms in this period.) With polling underway, police officers were sent out to rural areas in order to '[increase] their [the SLP's] footprint … there was always a police presence; always a police commander present'.[5]

As in 2007, the 2012 elections passed off peacefully. Although the Sierra Leone People's Party (SLPP) contested the legality of the results, the elections were – according to Colonel Jamie Martin, the last commander of IMATT – 'generally considered to be sufficiently free, fair and transparent to be acceptable to the people of Sierra Leone and to the wider international community'.[6]

Within IMATT, the 2012 elections were considered the litmus test of when and how the mission could and would exit Sierra Leone, having provided support for more than a decade. More broadly, it was a test of the assessment presented in the February 2010 paper setting out options for the JSDP's successor that Sierra Leone had 'transformed from a post-conflict and failed state into a fragile but developing nation'.[7] The question

---

[2] Adrian Horn, Martin Gordon and Peter Albrecht, 'Sierra Leone Police – Review of Capabilities', London, 2011, unpublished, p. 6.

[3] Peter Albrecht interview with Joe Edkins, Sierra Leone, February 2014.

[4] The Standard Response Guidelines delineate how Sierra Leone's national security architecture should respond to events under normal circumstances as well as in times of crisis. They present the instruments that are available to respond as well as command-and-control mechanisms, and establish operating procedures for decision-making by the National Security Council.

[5] Peter Albrecht interview with Joe Edkins, Sierra Leone, February 2014.

[6] Peter Albrecht interview with Jamie Martin, UK, September 2013.

[7] Libra Advisory Group, 'Interim Program Document for Improved Access to Security and Justice Programme – Sierra Leone', London, 2010, unpublished.

was whether Sierra Leone was now beyond the 'post-conflict recovery' phase and on a path of 'stable development'.[8]

Within the Sierra Leone government, there was no doubt that this threshold had been crossed. The country was experiencing an economic boom, as one of its highest-placed civil servants, Emmanuel Coker, noted in early 2014: 'if you travel out of Sierra Leone, on the way back, the planes are always full – they realize that the prospects for investment are good'.[9] By early 2013, Sierra Leone had fared well in macro-economic terms for half a decade. Annual GDP growth hit 21 per cent in 2012, largely due to iron-ore exports, and inflation was dropping. In December 2012, the International Monetary Fund graduated Sierra Leone from a 'fragile' to a 'low income' country.

Nevertheless, income distribution has remained extremely unequal, with a few rich citizens becoming visibly richer, whilst the many poor remain very poor. Ensuring that economic growth benefits the general population requires efforts to change how resources are distributed throughout the country. This needs to occur at both the national and the local level, where inadequate public services and corruption remain a reality. It was these very factors that led to tension and conflict in the early 1990s, and it is in the provision of basic services that corruption remains most rife.[10]

The 2012 elections coincided with fundamental changes to the way in which UK support was provided, driven by both the genuine advances engendered in the previous decade and by political dynamics in London. IMATT-related expenses were proving increasingly untenable and the organisation was being wound down, with plans being made for its replacement. Plans for the JSDP's successor, the ASJP, were also underway; with the design and tender processes completed in 2010 and 2011 respectively, programme activities began in earnest in 2012–13.

Specifically with respect to security-sector reform (SSR), the Sierra Leonean experience since 2010 provides important insights into how institutions fare after international funding and technical assistance are wholly or partly withdrawn, or transformed. By 2010, the Sierra Leone Security Sector Reform Programme (SILSEP) had been terminated; the SLP had for five years received considerably less funding than it had under the Commonwealth Community Safety and Security Project (CCSSP); and in 2010, DfID funding for the Central Intelligence and Security Unit (CISU) was cut. It is important to bring the experiences of these and similar

[8] Albrecht interview with Jamie Martin.

[9] Peter Albrecht interview with Emmanuel Coker, Sierra Leone, February 2014.

[10] Peter Albrecht, 'How Power Works in Sierra Leone', in Steen Andersen et al. (eds), *Developing Architecture: Learning From Sierra Leone* (Copenhagen: Arkitekter Uden Grænser and Forlaget PB43, 2013).

organisations to the forefront of the analysis: these provide insight not only into a SSR process that has been heavily influenced by external actors, but also more generally into the functioning of Sierra Leone's security and justice institutions in a resource-scarce and politically charged environment.

This chapter explores the impact of changes in the leadership and funding of some of the key institutions in Sierra Leone's security sector from 2010, and the consequences of a more direct politicisation of these institutions, underway since 2007 when the APC came to power. In 2010, these consequences were becoming obvious – notably in the ONS, CISU and SLP, where known supporters of the APC were installed as leaders and recruitment occurred outside due process. This was balanced by a heavy emphasis on community relations within the SLP, the continued professionalism and technical expertise of staff within the ONS and CISU, and the stronger strategic direction of the latter. However, there is no doubt – as this chapter shows – that the sector was under continued pressure. Within the RSLAF, a strong peace support operations (PSO) identity emerged, with deployments in Darfur having begun in 2009 – a development that had been inconceivable only a few years earlier.

Developments in Governance and Oversight

The ONS and CISU

In 2010, the ONS continued to play a crucial role in co-ordinating security-sector institutions, remaining of critical importance during pressurised periods such as the 2012 elections. By 2013, an external evaluation concluded that both the ONS and CISU continued to deliver professionally in their areas of responsibility, despite evident political pressure from the ruling party. Both were considered to be setting high standards of institutional integrity, management and competence, and provided a strategic vision to the executive that would otherwise have been absent.

In February 2011, the two organisations moved out of State House, where they had been based since 2002, and into a new building nearby on Tower Hill. Funding for the new headquarters had been allocated by DfID in 2007–08. Symbolically, the move emphasised their role in serving national rather than political interests, creating a physical separation between the executive and those bodies that collect, assess and analyse intelligence. In addition, the ONS and CISU were each given their own wing in the new building, representing a further separation between intelligence collection and analysis.

Yet this technical capability and professionalism has not automatically equated to buy-in from the executive. As under President Kabbah prior to 2007, the national security co-ordinator continued to struggle to stay relevant in the eyes of the executive while simultaneously maintaining political neutrality. Indeed, the relationship between Kellie Conteh and President Koroma grew increasingly 'frosty', as noted by one ONS staff member during this period,[11] resulting in a complete breakdown in communication between the ONS and State House in 2011.

Conteh, who had by then headed the ONS for over a decade, was known to be firm and principled to the point of being stubborn. This was both a curse and a blessing. Despite substantial pressure, the government had the *option* – although this was not always taken up – of basing decision-making on sound assessments and reliable intelligence, rather than on rumours or speculation, as had typically occurred during the conflict pre-SILSEP. Having a professional body meant, as one observer commented, that 'when something was happening, the ONS would be called upon, especially when … [the president] wanted to hear about something without political bias'.[12] On the other hand, when Conteh did not respond to pressure from the executive – for example, to call into use military aid to the civil power (MACP) and to bypass formal recruitment procedures[13] – the 'reaction was to isolate Kellie [Conteh] for a time. They did not try to manipulate the ONS, but moved it to the side', as noted by an observer close to events.[14]

The ONS therefore faced a delicate balancing act, given that fundamental trust between it and the executive was limited. Like his predecessor, President Koroma surrounded himself with a group of trusted individuals from both within and outside the formal security architecture. This inevitably stifled free communication between the higher echelons of government and the institutions established to serve Sierra Leone's national security interest. Yet while there was what has variously been referred to as 'internal intelligence', 'unofficial bodies' and 'informal networks' with direct access to State House – particularly during election periods – Koroma would also 'try to verify [what he was told] with Kellie [Conteh]'.[15] However, one adviser close to events noted that, as time passed, the 'periodic isolation became more and more'; Conteh 'would

[11] Peter Albrecht interview with anonymous, Sierra Leone, August 2013.

[12] Peter Albrecht interview with anonymous, over Skype, August 2013.

[13] Irregular recruitment began immediately after the new government came to power in 2007. The overuse of MACP was also a concern under Kabbah. Peter Albrecht interview with Kellie Conteh, over Skype, April 2014. See also Conteh quoted in Peter Albrecht and Paul Jackson, *Security System Transformation in Sierra Leone, 1997–2007* (Birmingham and London: Global Facilitation Network for Security Sector Reform and International Alert, 2009), p. 139.

[14] Peter Albrecht interview with anonymous, over Skype, August 2013.

[15] Peter Albrecht interview with anonymous, over Skype, August 2013.

knock on people's door once or twice, but then stop'.[16] The result was that Conteh became less persistent.

2012 was also a definitive turning point with respect to funding. Since 2010, pressure had been building upon (and within) DfID to reduce its support to the ONS. In particular, this pressure came from those who believed that it was not the role of a development agency to support an institution that fell squarely within the sphere of national security. In the stabilisation phase, the ONS may have been an appropriate focus for DfID – as stated by one observer who was involved in several reviews of Sierra Leone's SSR programming – but not as longer-term development got under way.[17] Furthermore, while the ONS had an important role in co-ordinating the security sector during elections or in times of crisis, it was not an accountability or oversight structure, although it appeared to be the ambition of ONS staff and its leaders that it should perform this function. The result was that DfID began its drawdown of direct budgetary support to the ONS in early 2012, coinciding with the commencement of the ASJP.

Kellie Conteh's near-simultaneous departure from the ONS in January 2012 left a significant gap within the security sector. Conteh was essentially the embodiment of the ONS under UK tutelage and he represented a significant part of the country's institutional memory of SSR as a whole. A press release from State House announced that the retired Brigadier Mustapha K Dumbuya would take over as national security co-ordinator.[18] With the formal transferral of CISU's leadership from Mustapha Abdullah to Christopher John, Conteh's former deputy, the heads of the two main national security agencies were thus replaced at the same time (although John had been acting director-general of CISU since 2010).

For CISU, this twin change in leadership meant that there was now more space to assert its role within the security architecture. To a large extent, the emphasis on these dynamics was personality-driven. Until John's takeover, CISU had remained hierarchically beneath the ONS and, as previously noted, entirely dependent on it for funding. This also meant that it remained somewhat isolated from potential users who were unaware of its existence. This was a matter that John sought to address, reflecting that, in 2013: 'nobody knew what we were doing; we … [had to] try to make ourselves relevant … though the operation is covert, I am not covert, and at the end of the day the information that we collected had to be operationalised'.[19]

---

[16] Anonymous, working-group meeting, UK, August 2013.

[17] Peter Albrecht interview with anonymous, UK, August 2013.

[18] State House, press release, 30 January 2012, <http://www.statehouse.gov.sl/index.php/component/content/article/34-news-articles/459-press-release->, accessed 13 October 2014.

[19] Peter Albrecht interview with Christopher John, Sierra Leone, September 2013.

For this reason, CISU experienced real difficulties between 2010, when DfID withdrew its funding, and 2012 – a period marked by limited interaction with international partners. This was compounded by the fact that some within the executive and other central figures of Sierra Leone's elite 'continued to say that we should not be trusted', according to a former director in CISU, speaking in 2013.[20] Indeed, there were fears that the country's first professional intelligence service would be disbanded altogether.

Despite its efforts to establish its political independence and relevance since it was founded in 2002, from 2010 to 2012 CISU continued to be seen as an institution belonging to, and therefore serving, the previous regime under the SLPP. In early 2012, it was still the case that 'Because of the doubt[s over political allegiance], the system was not functioning properly':[21] 'systems were created outside the system', as had previously occurred. It was a case of 'let's use our boys to collect intelligence and feed into the [Office of the] President'.[22] This was the political reality under which the ONS and CISU were established and operated. Parallel systems of information-gathering existed under both Kabbah and Koroma, particularly during election periods. However, 2012 constituted a turning point in this regard. Under John, meetings between CISU and the president became more regular, and the organisation was tasked with operations. This in turn helped to establish a degree of trust. As such, the difference of personality between Kellie Conteh and Mustapha Abdullah on the one hand, and Mustapha Dumbuya and Christopher John on the other, began to show immediately after the latter two had assumed their respective positions, underpinned by the fact that both were deemed faithful to the APC.

Following this, however, the particular set-up outlined in the 2002 National Security and Intelligence Act – which had established the nature of the link between the ONS and CISU – began to create tension. With a new director-general in place, CISU was positioning itself as an independent agency, rather than a unit subordinate to the ONS. 'They want to change their name from CISU [a unit] to CISA [an agency]', as one international observer commented, to denote the organisation's equal status.[23] This overturned the settlement agreed at the end of the war whereby military intelligence was subordinate to the RSLAF, the Special Branch was subordinate to the SLP, and CISU was subordinate to the ONS. Indeed, when the two institutions were created, it was thought they would benefit from having one pool of people to draw upon. Yet, ten years later,

[20] Peter Albrecht interview with anonymous, Sierra Leone, July 2013.
[21] *Ibid.*
[22] Peter Albrecht interview with anonymous, Sierra Leone, August 2013.
[23] Peter Albrecht interview with anonymous, Sierra Leone, September 2013.

the ONS and CISU had matured and created separate administrative structures. In 2012–13, CISU produced a 2013–16 strategic plan, and on that basis the president issued the directive that CISU should have financial autonomy. As one of the directors in CISU, Ansumana Idriss, observes, 2013 was thus the first year in which 'we [CISU] have singlehandedly prepared our own budget. We now give regular briefs to H. E. [the president]'.[24]

Security-Sector Review 2.0

Sierra Leone's first security-sector review was initiated a year after the end of the conflict, in 2003, and was published in 2005. It was based on an inclusive, nationwide consultative process and in the immediate post-conflict context identified threats to the consolidation of peace and stabilisation. Execution of the second review – a Sierra Leonean-led process which was initiated in 2011 at the formal request of the National Security Council (NSC) – exhibited the technical expertise that had been built up within the ONS during the previous decade and its wider institutional capability. It also exposed the limited attention paid by the government to security, as well as a feeling at the highest level that the ONS had received its fair share of scarce resources.[25] Initiated by then-National Security Coordinator Kellie Conteh, the process was completed in 2013 and the findings were launched by the president in 2014, on Dumbuya's watch.[26]

Three factors, in particular, challenged what Francis Keilie,[27] director of research and planning in the ONS, referred to as the aim of the first review's 'holistic implementation', and were taken into account as the second review process unfolded.[28]

---

[24] Peter Albrecht interview with Ansumana Idriss, Sierra Leone, July 2013.

[25] Peter Albrecht interview with anonymous, Sierra Leone, February 2014.

[26] State House, 'Key Note Address by his Excellency President Ernest Bai Koroma on the Occasion of the Launch of the Report of the Second Security Sector Review (SSR) for Sierra Leone 2012, Tuesday 22 April 2014, Miatta Conference Centre', <http://www.statehouse.gov.sl/index.php/component/content/article/34-news-articles/861-key-note-address-delivered-by-his-excellency-president-ernest-bai-koroma-on-the-occasion-of-the-launch-of-the-report-of-the-second-security-sector-review-ssr-for-sierra-leone-2012-tuesday-22-april-2014-miatta-conference-centre>, accessed 13 October 2014. There were considerable frustrations within the ONS over the delay in publishing the final report of the security-sector review, which was explained by unwillingness on the part of the national security co-ordinator to force through a publication date with the president who, perhaps understandably, was more focused on economic development.

[27] This section is indebted to a paper presented by Francis Keilie at a working-group meeting held in Freetown on 5 September 2013. Francis Keile, 'Sierra Leone's Security Sector Review Process', 2013, unpublished.

[28] *Ibid.*

First, by the time the review was finalised and formally agreed by the NSC, there was a perception within the ONS that donor fatigue had set in as Sierra Leone emerged from the immediate post-conflict phase. Combined with the government's inability to match international funding, as was initially pledged, the fund for the Security Sector Review Implementation Plan (SSR-IP), which had been established following the first review in 2005, was empty by 2007 (more information about the 2003–05 security-sector review can be found in Chapters I and II).[29] A second and related factor had to do with forward planning. The comprehensive nature of the SSR-IP was also a weakness, as it was based around a set of 'overambitious' and 'unrealistic SSR benchmarks', according to Francis Keilie.[30] A final factor that challenged the review's implementation lay in ownership of the process. In 2003, the ONS was still a new organisation. It was 'largely externally driven both in human and financial resources',[31] and whilst a 'flicker' of national ownership was reflected in the consultative process that formed the basis of the review, there were few Sierra Leoneans with sufficient experience at the strategic level and there was thus an overreliance on 'UK-loaned experts'.[32]

Learning from previous experience, it was thought that the second security-sector review would assist the government and the sector in developing a more 'realistic cost-effective resource requirement reflective of the current state of economic development'.[33] On this basis, the ONS developed a project proposal that was submitted to the NSC and endorsed in 2010, and the national security co-ordinator set up a Technical Working Group to oversee the preparation of the review, with representation from the SLP, RSLAF, immigration and prisons services, civil society and others. Through a participatory, countrywide consultative process, 'the ONS took the lead in conducting a strategic environmental analysis to determine the ordinary man's vision for Sierra Leone for the next decade and beyond, the threats associated with that vision and how these threats could be addressed'.[34]

---

[29] The Security Sector Review Implementation Plan (SSR-IP) was the mechanism through which DfID channelled funding (approximately $1.7 million) to the ONS. It was administered by the ONS, which reflected the trust that DfID had in Kellie Conteh. Decisions on allocations were made by the National Security Council Coordinating Group. For more information on the SSR-IP, see Mark White, 'The Security-Development Nexus in Sierra Leone', in Peter Albrecht and Paul Jackson (eds), *Security Sector Reform in Sierra Leone 1997–2007: Views from the Front Line* (Zurich: Geneva Centre for the Democratic Control of Armed Forces and LIT Verlag, 2010), pp. 71–91, 88–89.

[30] Keilie, 'Sierra Leone's Security Sector Review Process'.

[31] *Ibid.*

[32] *Ibid.*

[33] *Ibid.*

[34] *Ibid.*

The final report of this 2011–12 review represented an important shift in thinking from that of 2005. Notably, emphasis was no longer placed on a post-conflict agenda, but on long-term economic development in support of the government's 'Agenda for Prosperity' – its vision to become a middle-income country. The momentum towards such a shift had long been building, and this report highlighted that the transition from the provision of security as a national priority to security as an enabler of long-term national development was now complete – something that IMATT had concluded following the successful enforcement of security during the 2012 elections.

Defence: From Territorial Security to Income Generation

IMATT Draws Down

IMATT was reduced to around twenty-five personnel between 2010 and 2012. Its primary focus of providing training and education was reflected in the fact that from 2010 the IMATT Training Group was enhanced with additional staff from the Brigade Advisory and Support Teams (BASTs).[35] This resulted in the strengthening of the team at Horton Academy, for instance, and in the establishment of a small Collective Training and Outreach Team, which maintained links with the brigades and battle schools, albeit on a much reduced scale than had previously been the case.

Horton Academy had changed from what Hugh Blackman, commander of IMATT from August 2008 to February 2011, referred to as 'a bit of a British enclave' to an institution that was increasingly nationalised. At the same time, the academy's students were also being internationalised, as neighbouring countries started to send officers to attend courses there.

However, while progress was being made in terms of training, reports were emerging about growing disaffection amongst military personnel over issues ranging from transportation and accommodation to medical facilities and food rations. In 2010–11, concerns over the conditions of service in Sierra Leone's border areas were especially pertinent. However, the general culture within the Sierra Leonean MoD and the RSLAF made open expression of grievances particularly

[35] The Training Group was an integrated part of IMATT's structure, designed to deliver the high-quality training that was one of its core pillars. From 2008, the Training Group began transitioning from a structure predicated on the perceived need to deliver training support at the tactical level to one which sought to bridge the gaps in operational and strategic training support. Operational training support referred to collective training, deemed to be the responsibility of the Joint Force Command; strategic training support was deemed to be that which is required to identify, create and supervise training policy at MoD level.

contentious. Those who spoke out about ill-received decisions or corrupt practices often found themselves sidelined or defamed, meaning that individuals only shared concerns with IMATT on condition of anonymity. It was more usual for RSLAF and MoD personnel to remain silent about such matters.

Soldiers' concerns about the conditions of service reflected the generally difficult relationship that existed between the RSLAF and the MoD. While policies, procedures, rules and regulations were in place, they were not routinely adhered to by either civilian or military staff. A sense was emerging among civil servants that the military would get whatever it asked for, with very little challenge.

Meanwhile, although the task of bringing RSLAF troop numbers down to 8,500 dominated RSLAF–IMATT working relations after the 2007 elections, additional activities, such as building up the maritime wing, were also pursued over this period. By May 2013, however, this particular project had been stagnating for the better part of two years, 'primarily … [due to] a lack of maritime platforms on which to operate'.[36] It remained the aim to control illegal fishing and conduct search-and-rescue operations, and the maritime wing had certainly been able to stop some industrial crafts from entering the inner exclusion zone of 6 miles from the coastline; however, the wing's greatest success had been in acting as lifesavers off the coast. Despite external support, resources were insufficient. At the same time, attempts to save money through the implementation of the 2008 Core Review were prioritised and treated as the most realistic short-term goal. It had proven extremely difficult to generate income through the maritime wing as intended.

By 2010, it was the RSLAF's contributions to PSOs, initially in Darfur and then in Somalia, that had come to dominate.

Peacekeeping: The New Raison d'Être *of the RSLAF*

Aspirations to develop and deploy peacekeeping capacity had been building since 2007.[37] From late 2009, when a Sierra Leonean reconnaissance company was deployed as part of the joint UN–African Union mission in Darfur (UNAMID), contributions to peacekeeping missions became the predominant focus of the RSLAF – and they have remained so ever since.

It is difficult to overestimate the importance of the PSO focus as the downsizing of the RSLAF continued. As the current Joint Force Commander Brigadier Sesay explains: 'There was a belief that as the numbers

[36] Albrecht interview with Jamie Martin.

[37] Alfred Nelson-Williams, 'Restructuring the Republic of Sierra Leone Armed Forces', in Albrecht and Jackson (eds), *Security Sector Reform in Sierra Leone 1997–2007*.

went down [from 10,500 to 8,500], the soldiers would be replaced by force multipliers. This did not happen. What happened, really, [was that] the RSLAF aspiration of contributing to PSOs was actually a stabilising factor for the army. Had we not had that, the shock would have been difficult to accept'.[38]

Indeed, contribution to PSOs came to constitute an important *raison d'être* for the RSLAF in the context of severe financial constraints upon its role and activities. As such, PSOs were pivotal in giving the RSLAF a sense of purpose. After 2002 Sierra Leone did not face any immediate external threat, and it was in any case questionable whether the RSLAF would have been able to defend the country's territory on its own. In addition, the main internal threats were no longer considered to be military in nature, but rather to emanate from a lack of economic opportunity. Indeed, until the late 2000s, the armed forces' role had for the most part been defined negatively (that is, by downsizing); and the more positive development that did occur was both slow and confined to a single part of the RSLAF – the maritime wing.

Yet the emergence of a dominant focus on PSOs was not seen as positive in all quarters. Some observers within IMATT, for example, considered this shift in focus from territorial integrity to conflicts abroad – in Darfur (in 2009) and Somalia (from 2013) – to be problematic. An almost exclusive ambition to contribute to PSOs raised questions about the armed forces' ability to defend Sierra Leone's borders against an external attack. As one observer noted, 'the implications are that their skill base [for territorial defence] is being eroded';[39] only limited attention, if any, was given to preparing for the eventuality of an attack on Sierra Leonean soil.

Others, however, disputed the extent to which the growing focus on PSOs was distorting existing capacity. To the contrary, as Jamie Martin observed:[40]

> If it were not for PSOs, their [the RSLAF's] overall operational effectiveness would be degraded. Their contributions to PSOs allow them to keep some of their effectiveness. That 75 per cent [of RSLAF activity] in support of PSOs is in itself not a bad thing, because if they were not doing that, they would do no military work at all, so you could argue that the capability they now have is underpinned by the PSO activity. It's not a negative, it's a positive. The problem is that they don't have money to do anything else.

---

[38] Brima Sesay, working-group meeting, Sierra Leone, February 2014.

[39] Albrecht interview with Jamie Martin.

[40] *Ibid.*

IMATT, together with other international partners, came to play a crucial role in enabling RSLAF contributions to PSOs.[41] When it became clear that the Sierra Leonean MoD specifically, and the Government of Sierra Leone in general, could not meet the logistical and equipment requirements to contribute to UNAMID, an appeal was made to the UK, the US and Canada, which collectively agreed to donate most of what was required. The UK pledged $8–9.5 million, while the US gifted approximately the same amount through the delivery and maintenance of equipment. Canada pledged a significantly smaller amount, ring-fenced specifically for medical supplies.[42] The Government of Sierra Leone in turn agreed to buy the remainder of the equipment – mainly ammunition, which the US could not purchase on the country's behalf, and welfare kits.[43] The fact that Sierra Leone owned the equipment it used while contributing to UNAMID (known as 'wet lease') also meant that it was entitled to full reimbursement by the lead organisation (in this case the UN), thereby maximising the possible income from this activity. The RSLAF and the Government of Sierra Leone would earn less from the later contribution to PSOs in Somalia (under AMISOM – the African Union Mission in Somalia) for which it borrowed most of its equipment, primarily from the US, with the UK providing a much smaller proportion. With the equipment on 'dry lease', the money earned from the African Union (AU) in this case was only sufficient to pay for the army's training for the next deployment.

Beyond the donation of equipment, international support was also provided in terms of logistics and training, which was carried out by the US State Department's African Contingency Operations Training and Assistance (ACOTA) group,[44] with support from IMATT and short-term training teams from the UK. As recalled by then-Colonel Hugh Blackman, commander of IMATT from August 2008 to February 2011:[45]

> Over the years, we'd trained infantrymen in core combat skills (attack, defence, patrolling, etc.); also medics, intelligence, Military Police, logisticians, administration and mechanics. All of these were trained and prepared to a standard that we would have considered an

---

[41] Apart from supporting the RSLAF in pursuing its chosen direction, it was also in line with UK strategy to enhance African military peacekeeping capability. In some respects, IMATT's role was thus starting to resemble that of the two British Military Advisory and Training Teams in Eastern and Southern Africa, respectively.

[42] E-mail exchange, Hugh Blackman, 2014.

[43] E-mail exchange, Julian Bower, 2014.

[44] ACOTA's mission is to enhance the capacities and capabilities of its African partner countries, regional institutions, and the continent's peacekeeping resources as a whole so that they can plan for, train, deploy and sustain sufficient numbers of professionally competent peacekeepers to meet conflict-transformation requirements with minimal external assistance.

[45] E-mail exchange, Hugh Blackman.

> appropriate 'start-state' before launching on mission-specific training, i.e., for Darfur specifically. Thus, the UNAMID training was underpinned by IMATT's core training and education.
>
> ACOTA had the benefit of the in-Sudan tactical expertise; where IMATT were unable to travel (President Bashir and the ICC [International Criminal Court] ruling stymied any chance of Brits getting into Sudan and to the mission area) …
>
> Between IMATT, ACOTA and RSLAF (in the following order – expertise, money and manpower), we built a forward operating base [FOB] out at Benguema, with an ops room, briefing areas, accommodation, cookhouse, guard towers, etc. A company could then deploy to the FOB and operate out of it for a number of days/weeks in order to replicate normal UNAMID ops.
>
> It was an entirely complementary effort, with ACOTA delivering the money for training support and the tactical in-country experience from Darfur, but it would never have delivered to the necessary standard and within the required timeframe without either IMATT's historical investment to build the RSLAF over the 6–7 preceding years, or without IMATT's direct support to fund, equip, and train during the process.

On top of this, IMATT processed the significant amount of necessary paperwork and did most of the detailed staff work that enabled the deployment of a company to Sudan in 2009 and a battalion to Somalia in 2013, also supporting the drafting of formal diplomatic documents between the Government of Sierra Leone and the AU for the latter deployment.

Yet the RSLAF was also learning through these years of preparation for and deployment on PSOs. First, although IMATT made a significant contribution prior to the initial tours with UNAMID and AMISOM – both in difficult-to-access countries far from Sierra Leone – by the time the first company and battalion had been deployed, it was clear that 'IMATT needed to deal less with the subsequent deployments. It was a much simpler process to repeat'.[46] Instead, it continued to provide support, both in terms of training and equipment, throughout the six-month rotations that the RSLAF company served in Darfur, where it was engaged in such tasks as long-range reconnaissance and force protection.

In spite of this support, however, a number of issues arose. A significant concern throughout the Darfur mission related to the maintenance of equipment. 'If you keep it maintained', one IMATT officer noted, 'the UN will give you funding, but [the] RSLAF did not invest in that [maintenance], [or in repairing] flat tyres, gear boxes, and so forth'.[47] Thus,

[46] Albrecht interview with Jamie Martin. In the case of contributions to AMISOM, seven or eight IMATT officers worked full time in support of the RSLAF.
[47] Peter Albrecht interview with anonymous, UK, August 2013.

while the RSLAF undoubtedly made an important contribution to UNAMID, it failed to capitalise fully on the equipment it used in Darfur (and it did not maintain a full logistics record, meaning that it was impossible to keep track of equipment). This meant that it did not benefit as much as it could have from the UN-provided funding for the maintenance of equipment brought into theatre. This reflected a broader issue with managing overseas deployments, namely an awareness of the need to prepare soldiers for the task ahead in a comprehensive manner – incorporating financial, intellectual and organisational support.[48]

Other smaller, yet still significant, issues also had to be dealt with, for instance with regard to cooking facilities. In the grand scheme of things, such matters might seem relatively trivial, but this nonetheless became a real issue in theatre. When the cookers issued upon deployment broke, officers in theatre did not try to fix them but instead sought out charcoal, which is commonly used for cooking in Sierra Leone. However, it is not available in Darfur, so the officers attempted to have it sent from home. This case showed, on a small scale, the challenges that the RSLAF faced in terms of adjusting socially to mission life. Rather than using kitchen appliances available to them in Darfur, they turned to a more impractical solution.

Meanwhile, considerable tension arose at the ministerial level from questions relating to the distribution of funding gained from participation in PSOs for both the RSLAF as an organisation and for each soldier. This was the primary reason for participating in them, given that the UN, in the case of Darfur, paid $1,028 per soldier per month – of which the RSLAF retained around $200, which was then put into a 'PSO fund'.[49]

In administrative terms, the money was paid to compensate the Government of Sierra Leone for the investment made in that soldier to ensure he was fit to deploy. In effect, the government was '"renting" its soldiers to the UN and [was] being paid for that commodity'.[50] This, however, raised many key questions, such as how much of the $1,028 the soldier himself was to be paid for serving in Darfur. Technically, the individual soldier could lay claim to none of that money. All UNAMID receipts were paid by the UN to the central exchequer, which meant that the MoD would receive only what the Cabinet – and notably the Ministry of Finance – would agree to. It was a given, for instance, that the Government of Sierra Leone must first recover the money it had spent on equipment prior to the deployment (even though some within the RSLAF tried to resist to this). Yet care was also taken in ensuring that the MoD's related expenses – such as personnel, deployment, sustainment of the

[48] Peter Albrecht interview with Richard Woodward, UK, August 2013.
[49] Peter Albrecht interview with Joe Edkins, Somalia, October 2014.
[50] E-mail exchange, Adele McGookin, July 2009.

mission and equipment – were covered. Meanwhile, costs relating to the creation of appropriate mission structures had to be considered, particularly in the transition from the deployment of a company to UNAMID to that of an entire battalion with AMISOM.[51]

The payment of substantial bonuses to participating soldiers would have engendered other problems, such as the potential creation of a two-tier army in which small numbers of personnel made a lot of money at the expense of the 8,000-plus personnel who did not participate. In this scenario, and as McGookin comments, the 'morale of the many would ... be sacrificed to raise the morale of the few'.[52] Moreover, the bottom line was that the more that was given to the individual participants of UNAMID, the less that would be available to invest in the RSLAF. As such, it became a choice between the enrichment of the individual soldier and the betterment of the army as a whole, including its ability later to deploy a full battalion to AMISOM. It would also make it even more unlikely that the money from UNAMID, in particular, would be invested in housing, medical facilities and equipment enhancements, amongst other urgent requirements.[53]

Nevertheless, despite significant challenges in relation to the way in which the RSLAF planned and executed its PSO deployments, its participation in such operations was considered a significant success by both IMATT and RSLAF officers, not least because the army was operating in a resource-scarce and challenging political environment. As Minister of Defence Alfred Paolo Conteh stated in 2013:[54]

---

[51] E-mail exchange, Hugh Blackman. According to Julian Bower, adviser to the joint force commander during the period of the RSLAF's deployment to Darfur, the income paid to the Sierra Leone government for the month of April 2010 was: $135,000 for manpower; $71,000 for major equipment; $46,700 for self-sustainment (cook house, maintenance and so forth). In total per year this equalled approximately $3,032,400. Bower recalls: 'A portion of the money was required to sustain the force (e.g., vehicle spares) for training costs, for the next rotation and to buy replacement vehicles ... Some of the initial returns were used to pay back the commercial bank loan that GoSL [the Government of Sierra Leone] took out to cover the setting up costs'. Regarding the individual soldier, it was eventually decided that each should receive $15 while in theatre. E-mail exchange, Julian Bower. It is not clear how this compares to the total MoD/RSLAF budget at this time. 'It was an issue of real friction', one high-ranking adviser to the security sector prior to 2011 recalled, 'that we never (including the CIVAD [Civilian Adviser] IMATT), never had any real visibility over budgets, loans, deals with other nations, including the Chinese'. Peter Albrecht interview with anonymous, UK, August 2013.

[52] Peter Albrecht interview with Adele McGookin, over Skype, October 2013.

[53] Most RSLAF deaths are due to poor housing and sanitation.

[54] Peter Albrecht interview with Alfred Paolo Conteh, Sierra Leone, December 2013.

> When we ventured into Sudan in 2009, we had not been out with the UN for around fifty years. … [We had seen] Sierra Leone going from a war-torn country to a post-conflict country, and then a developing nation. We had 17,500 peacekeepers [in Sierra Leone during the conflict], and with our PSO contribution we are paying back humanity, the world, for what they did … for us. So when we went to Darfur, we did our rotations, there was a drawdown, and we came back. A few months later, we were invited by the AU to send a battalion – 850 personnel – to Somalia. For me that was pride; not only for me, but I think for the entire Sierra Leone.

From IMATT to ISAT: An Exit Strategy

As early as 2006, a working group was formed (along with DfID) to develop a workable model for future programming which, in the process, laid the foundation for IMATT's exit in 2013.[55] The idea was tabled to merge IMATT and SILSEP into one body that could work across the security architecture,[56] with members of the DfID and Foreign Office country teams and of IMATT being among the first proponents of an International Security Advisory and Training Team (ISATT), as it was called at the time. However, those who were part of the original working group left shortly after it was set up, and their in-country successors in DfID, the High Commission and IMATT failed to agree fully on what the scope of an ISATT should be. As a consequence, discussions about such a concept were not taken forward in 2006–07.[57] What did come out of these initial discussions, however, was an awareness of the opportunity for closer co-ordination between IMATT, SILSEP, the JSDP and the High Commission.

---

55 Albrecht and Jackson, *Security System Transformation in Sierra Leone*, pp. 186–87.

56 With the de facto separation of the civilian MoD adviser from DfID's SILSEP in 2007, and the transference of the role to IMATT in April 2009, this is in effect what happened.

57 This speaks to a general issue about co-ordination among British departments in country, about turf wars and the ability of a department to pull rank, and the power to make decisions on behalf of the other departments. The High Commission is formally in the lead in Sierra Leone; however, unlike IMATT, DfID tended not to accept this hierarchy. First of all, DfID gained considerable leverage both from its role as the manager of UK development activities and from the ten-year Memorandum of Understanding that pledged at least £40 million per year (around $61 million). By extension, DfID also sought – entirely legitimately – to avoid unnecessary politicisation and securitisation of development funding by allowing the Foreign Office or IMATT to take the lead. However, the absence of a formal, institutionalised relationship between the three departments made it difficult for the High Commission to lead assertively and define what DfID could and could not do (see Chapter II for further discussion of the difficulties in creating a joined-up approach within Whitehall, 1997–2007). This meant that, to a large extent, co-ordination and the alignment of agendas became a function of individual relationships and the ability to collaborate effectively on the ground.

The role of the DfID-funded adviser to the Sierra Leonean national security co-ordinator was created, initially within the ONS under SILSEP, to pursue such co-ordination.

Five years later, in mid-to-late 2011, IMATT had entered the final stages of developing an exit strategy, having been reduced considerably in size and having largely completed the transition from an executive to an advisory mandate in the interim. DfID played only a limited role in this process. By this stage, SILSEP no longer existed, and the DfID-funded position of the national security adviser within the ONS had been cut. The result was that the link between IMATT and DfID – which had never been strong, and was often tense, despite the strong overlaps between the two organisations and the presence of formal advisers from each in the ONS and the MoD – was further weakened.

This tension and limited interaction between IMATT and DfID at the time of the conceptualisation of the International Security Advisory Team (ISAT – as it came to be called) was noticeable to the team that developed the scoping paper for the IMATT-to-ISAT transition,[58] which was informed by fieldwork carried out in early 2012. Also clear was the desire on the part of DfID to focus on community justice and poverty, rather than strategic security, which was to be the core focus of the proposed ISAT.

Indeed, ISAT was conceived partly to fill the gap, at the strategic level, left by the end of SILSEP and the reorientation of DfID's priorities within Sierra Leone; throughout the transition, this gap continued to inform the way in which the shift from IMATT to ISAT was rationalised. As part of this process, assessments were made as to the levels of support that were needed across the security sector as a whole. Following ten years of close support, it was thought that the military was ready for IMATT's withdrawal. By contrast, the IMATT-to-ISAT options paper concluded that the 'Sierra Leone Police and justice sector institutions have not benefited from the same close and sustained engagement and support over time enjoyed by the RSLAF'.[59]

Unsurprisingly, this statement was not well received by DfID, given its investments in the justice sector as a whole through the JSDP and the ASJP. It also did not take into consideration the fundamentally different peacetime

---

[58] Jeremy Astill-Brown, Patrick Davidson-Houston and David Morgan, 'Stability and Prosperity in Sierra Leone: International Military Advisory and Training Team (IMATT) to International Security Advisory Team (ISAT)', London, March 2012, unpublished. Upon request from IMATT on 15 December 2011, a team consisting of Jeremy Astill-Brown (former diplomat), Patrick Davidson-Houston (former Brigadier and the first commander of IMATT) and David Morgan (former police officer) was tasked by the Stabilisation Unit with carrying out the review. Unlike in 2006, the team did not include anyone from DfID, or with a development background, indicating the distance between DfID and IMATT, both practically and politically.

[59] *Ibid.*, p. 8.

tasks that are expected of an army and a police force: away from public view, the army had the time and space in which to develop; by contrast, the police force has to sustain daily interaction with – and the support of – the public. This situation was further intensified by the fact that 'increasingly the need has shifted away from the transformation of military institutions towards a focus on the more complex needs of citizens'.[60] Thus the issue of how to manage such a shift in emphasis became a critical one in the evolution of UK involvement in Sierra Leone.

By December 2011, funding from the UK's Conflict Pool – created in 2009 under the joint control of the Foreign Office, DfID and the MoD in order to provide a ready source of funds for use in the prevention of conflict – was agreed in principle in order to reformat IMATT and pursue this shift in focus (although this was not reflected in the UK government's approach as a whole, despite the argument that the transition could and should have had government-wide implications).[61] Of course, the unknown factor when transition options were being considered was whether Sierra Leone's 2012 elections would be successful and whether the reasonable level of stability the country had experienced would endure throughout and thereafter. If these goals were achieved, 'IMATT ... would have completed its primary task of mentoring and advising the ... RSLAF and ... would be in a position to change its shape, size, focus and emphasis'.[62] If this was the case, 'current thinking', it was noted in March 2012 ahead of the elections, 'is that it [IMATT] will be replaced by a small International Security Advisory Training Team (ISATT) of between six to eight permanent UK staff, military and civilian ... The aim would be for ISATT to promote security internally – through carefully targeted civilian policing and military activity – and externally – in the form of maritime security, regional co-operation and the provision of support to peacekeeping operations'.[63] (Indeed, when ISAT officially began its operations in April 2013, this was largely the shape it took.)

As IMATT's exit strategy gathered pace in 2012, there were inevitably concerns within Sierra Leone about the impact of the impending withdrawal, even though IMATT had been reduced in size year-on-year since the publication of Plan 2010 in 2004. To allay these concerns, it was deemed imperative that the Government of Sierra Leone, the RSLAF and the Sierra Leonean MoD in particular were consulted on the process. As

---

[60] *Ibid.*, p. 17.

[61] Funding of IMATT as it transitioned into ISAT during fiscal year 2012/13 was £4.6 million (approximately $7.4 million), while ISAT, during its first two years (fiscal years 2013/14 and 2014/15), was allocated £3.2 million per year (approximately $5.2 million). IMATT, 'International Military Advisory and Training Team (Sierra Leone) Transition Study – Terms of Reference', Freetown, 15 December 2011, unpublished.

[62] *Ibid.*

[63] *Ibid.*

noted by Jamie Martin, the last commander of IMATT (2011–13): 'we did a lot of work to prepare the ground, particularly with the Sierra Leoneans to ensure that they were comfortable with the change. [The] RSLAF shouldn't feel that we were just walking away'.[64]

Meanwhile, although the peaceful conduct of the elections in November 2012 provided a certain level of confidence in the ongoing stability of Sierra Leone, this was just one of a number of factors that fed into the UK's decision to bring IMATT's presence to an end. As noted in Chapter III, the UK's investment in African security was becoming increasingly focused on East Africa, and in this context IMATT was seen as an expensive asset to maintain. There was also continuing pressure in the UK to reduce public spending as a result of austerity measures and, crucially, the 2010 Strategic Defence and Security Review (SDSR) and the 2011 Building Stability Overseas Strategy had prompted changes to the UK's investment in overseas security initiatives.

With the UK increasingly beset by what were perceived as more pressing priorities, knowledge within Whitehall of the ongoing efforts in Sierra Leone was partially dissipated, at least beyond those who retained a personal interest in the country. This problem of institutional memory, common to governance systems confronted by regular staff turnover, poses something of a dilemma to organisations with long-term aims, since direct support within the machinery of government tends to decrease over time. There is thus a tendency to 'reinvent the wheel'; in the case of IMATT, this required the explanation and re-explanation of the programme's importance over time. In light of this, and as priorities in London shifted, it was concluded that IMATT's termination was timely – having made a considerable contribution to stability in Sierra Leone – and that a leaner, more strategically and internationally oriented body was required.

This new body would also reflect the changed international context in which it was conceived. Lieutenant Colonel Joe Edkins – who continued to serve as training adviser to the RSLAF under ISAT – has highlighted the importance of experience gained in Afghanistan and Iraq in shaping the top-down, strategic approach that was built into ISAT's structure:[65]

> IMATT, when it was set up, did not have the benefit of what we learned from Iraq and Afghanistan; it was post-Balkan [Wars], and we did not want to see that happen again. Now, we are looking back with a different set of eyes. With IMATT, there was initially an unwritten assumption that the end-state would be a normal training mission, a BMATT [British Military Advisory and Training Team]. Success was not

[64] Albrecht interview with Jamie Martin.

[65] Peter Albrecht interview with Joe Edkins, Sierra Leone, February 2014.

> having IMATT, but a standard BMATT, which would have meant that we maintained a bottom-up approach [of training soldiers].
>
> The idea of focusing top-down was a bit of a no-brainer after Afghanistan and Iraq. There was recognition that with fewer resources, you had a choice of sustaining a training base or [trying to achieve] … influence at the strategic level – you could not do both…
>
> If I have to make a choice between top-down or bottom-up, I would choose top-down, because without political buy-in, and the resources that go with it, you are not addressing long-term problems. Unless you do that, the minute you take away support it will all fall over; if the politicians do not see it as important, then it doesn't matter how good the soldiers are.

The result was that, after more than twelve years in existence, in April 2013 IMATT was replaced by the much leaner ISAT which, crucially, is headed up by a UK civil servant rather than a military officer. Whereas IMATT's focus was entirely on the development of the RSLAF and MoD, ISAT has a much broader remit, looking strategically across the security sector as a whole.[66] In addition to continuing to advise and support the RSLAF and MoD (it is recognised that the MoD still needs significant support), it is more closely aligned with the ASJP and will work with the other security-sector agencies – from the SLP to the ONS, the National Fire Service, the Prisons Department and the Immigration Office. It also aims to play a greater role in the Mano River Union – a regional association established in 1973 to foster economic co-operation between Sierra Leone and Liberia, later joined by Guinea – and the wider sub-region, predominantly through training offered at Horton Academy. In the medium-to-long term, ISAT will also seek to secure greater participation and investment by other international partners to fund both its operational and training requirements across the security sector. In this way, ISAT represents a fundamental shift away from traditional 'downstream' activities, such as training, towards more 'upstream' activities, including policy influence and co-ordination.

However, because support to the SLP was a new area for ISAT, which grew out of a military establishment, getting it up and running 'took a while';[67] indeed, as Joe Edkins explains: 'it was much quicker to reduce what the military advisers were doing to a new baseline than to build up advisory capacity that is trusted and seen as a safe pair of hands'.[68]

---

[66] Ashlee Godwin and Cathy Haenlein, 'Security-Sector Reform in Sierra Leone', *RUSI Journal* (Vol. 158, No. 6, December 2013), pp. 30–39.

[67] Peter Albrecht interview with Joe Edkins, Somalia, October 2014.

[68] *Ibid.*

Nevertheless, ISAT experienced a 'breakthrough moment' at the strategic level in its support to the ONS in developing its own national security policy and strategy (which at the time of writing has not been published). At this point, it became clear that ISAT was crossing the line between being a military and security advisory team. 'We were quite literately establishing a holistic construct', Edkins commented, with ISAT providing technical support to an ONS-led process.[69] Furthermore, a year after ISAT was established, the police component was starting to ramp up its activities, pursuing a focus on human-resource management and a review of the Operational Support Division (OSD) as a first step in discussions about how reform of the SLP's armed wing might be pursued. On the military side, support continued to be provided to the Sierra Leonean MoD, to the RSLAF with regard to PSOs and to Horton Academy, still considered the key driver for change within the RSLAF. Likewise, support to the maritime wing continued, despite setbacks and limited progress, in anticipation that the oil exploration currently underway off the Sierra Leonean coast will be successful – which, as a key element of the country's economy, would therefore require protection.[70]

Defining IMATT's Success

In stark contrast to historical popular perception, by March 2012 the RSLAF had become one of the better-respected organisations in Sierra Leone – a success largely attributed to UK support.[71] In the wake of its drawdown, it is essential to identify the defining features of IMATT's success, in order both to recognise the genuine achievements attained and to learn from its experiences. In this regard, it is important to be realistic and to accept that incremental change is the best that can be hoped for, because wholesale transformation in the short term is rarely feasible – nor is it often desirable because, as development experience in Sierra Leone and elsewhere has shown, abrupt change would not be sensitive to the political interests at stake in fragile situations.

Wing Commander Richard Woodward, who served with IMATT between February 2010 and January 2013, provides one perspective on how IMATT's success might be presented. It deserves full quotation, not for its objective truth value, but as an observation by someone who was part of IMATT in its final three years. This Whitehall Paper has so far explored the overall process of re-establishing an army in Sierra Leone and the clarification and delineation of its role – internally *vis-à-vis* the

[69] *Ibid.*
[70] *Ibid.*
[71] Astill-Brown, Davidson-Houston and Morgan, 'Stability and Prosperity in Sierra Leone', p. 1.

police, and internationally as the RSLAF embarked on PSOs in Darfur and Somalia. Woodward articulates a nuanced and perhaps realistic conception of what can be defined as 'success', given the political and economic reality that Sierra Leone continues to face. He also highlights a fact that is sometimes forgotten: in the end, it will be up to Sierra Leoneans, and *not* external actors, to decide the direction of travel for the RSLAF and for the country more broadly.

Speaking in August 2013, eight months after he had returned to the UK from Sierra Leone, Woodward explained:[72]

> [IMATT] was one of the success stories of the British military that is not very well publicised. Following David Richards' intervention we put a military organisation on top of it, and threw resources, human and financial, into it, reintegrating the armed forces into society. From that, in 2000, to when I left in 2013, we had downsized IMATT to six people. The difficulty now is to ensure that there is sufficient support to the RSLAF and MoD, giving Sierra Leoneans enough rope to carry on their own way of doing business – and to take their armed forces in the direction that they want them to go.
>
> Success is shown in the fact that the RSLAF was able to deploy, with international success, over 500 people to Somalia ... It does not only show that Sierra Leone is doing well in the big wide world. It also shows to Sierra Leoneans that the strife is over ... Success was demonstrated by the elections in 2012, where the RSLAF and the SLP worked together in MACP [Military Aid to the Civil Power]. That you could put soldiers on the street, and that their show of presence [was] considered helpful was a measure of success. The understanding by the Chief of [the] Defence Staff, from the Minister of Defence and down of the role of the armed forces within the country; and the fact that the police has a primary and the army has a secondary role. All this is a demonstration of success.
>
> *Within its capability, it's a huge success – that is, within the constraints that are put on them, the RSLAF and MoD, financially and in terms of policy. If they had a multi-million pound organisation, things might look different, but so far they don't.*
>
> There are some very capable junior officers, who work very hard to try to achieve what the hierarchy wants. Key to maintaining their skills will be to invest in their training. They know that it is important that they invest in their people.

As Woodward highlights, success must be measured on the basis of the context in which processes of systemic transformation take place. IMATT support was consistent for over a decade, with the RSLAF evolving from a

[72] Albrecht interview with Richard Woodward. Emphasis added.

point of collapse to being able to contribute to PSOs. This is a considerable feat. It is also evident, however, that considerable challenges remain.

The SLP: Local Needs or Paramilitary Policing?

By 2010, the combination of limited international support and general resource scarcity in Sierra Leone had taken its toll on the SLP. This did not mean that development of the police was at a standstill; Francis Munu, who took over from Brima Acha Kamara as inspector-general of police (IGP) in August 2010, not only oversaw a considerable expansion of the force from around 10,000 to 12,000 officers (the consequences of which are discussed below), but he also initiated a number of important reforms of the police organisation. As Munu observed in 2014:[73]

> We needed to review the structure of the organisation so that it could carry out its mandate. We needed to include modern concepts of organisational management, and to do so we were able to cluster certain departments into directorates. The Crime Services Directorate was established from all the departments that deal with crime-related issues such as legal and justice support, transnational organised crime, Interpol and the CID [Criminal Investigation Department]. We also made … [a] Support Services Directorate that came to include the department of transport, the procurement department and the finance department. I also increased the number of regional commands, from four to six.

The SLP did receive some support from the JSDP (2005–11), but only as a small component of the overall programme (encompassing strategic elements of policing, police–community relations and the integration of policing into the justice system). In 2012, a member of the UK team sent to Sierra Leone to assess potential options for an IMATT successor observed that 'The police did not speak about [the] JSDP';[74] this was not interpreted as a denial of the important work done by the JSDP with the police, but merely as recognition of the fact that the programme's centre of gravity was elsewhere.

The SLP's financial situation had continued to deteriorate over this period, meaning that by 2012–13, only limited funding – if any – was

[73] Peter Albrecht interview with Francis Alieu Munu, Sierra Leone, February 2014. Other notable institutional innovations included the establishment of a Transnational Organised Crime Unit (TOCU) that was based on the former Joint Drug Interdiction Task Force (JDITF). It was set up to support the implementation of the ECOWAS Regional Action Plan to Address the Growing Problem of Illicit Drug Trafficking, Organized Crime and Drug Abuse in West Africa. An inter-agency unit, TOCU is supported by the UN Office on Drugs and Crime (UNODC) and other international donors.

[74] Peter Albrecht interview with anonymous, over Skype, October 2013.

available for operations, while no funding other than salary payments was sent to Local Command Units up-country. This situation was confirmed in an unpublished external review in March 2012.[75] A presidential announcement prior to the 2012 elections – in an attempt to bolster support – that all SLP officers, like armed-forces personnel, would receive a rice ration was not underpinned by any additional budgetary allocation. Thus, in 2014, the SLP has spent 26 billion Leones on rice (approximately $582,000), amounting to 38 per cent of its non-salary budget. This has apparently caused significant problems for the SLP, necessitating cuts and increasing the overall percentage spent on salary and benefits. It has additionally created a further opportunity for tactical-level corruption, with rice being drawn in the name of absent staff; and the transparency of the procurement, handled centrally by the government, has also been questioned. (Furthermore, the impact of this promise on the government's finances is broadening; unsurprisingly, the prison and fire services are currently demanding similar allocations.)

Since 2012, however, a significant number of police officers have been deployed with PSOs in Darfur and Somalia. As with the RSLAF, this is a testament to the high levels of professionalism among some police officers but, unlike the RSLAF, such deployments have not been – and cannot be – the SLP's primary focus. While SSR activities with respect to the RSLAF were primarily initiated to reorient it away from involvement in politics, there was an expectation that the SLP's capacity should be built up so that it could maintain internal security. From this perspective, police contributions to PSOs were potentially a considerable drain on human resources within the SLP. In 2011, for instance, twelve out of sixty-one trainers at the Police Training School in Hastings were deployed to Darfur. Similarly, by 2011, the Corporate Services Department (CSD), the policy-development and information-gathering hub within the SLP, had lost four of its staff (which usually stands at between ten and fifteen members) to UNAMID. As noted by Horn, who led the Commonwealth Community Safety and Security Project (CCSSP) between 1999 and 2003, 'it was doubtful [that] those staff would be replaced' and even 'if they were, the replacement would likely have no technical skills that would be useful in CSD'.[76] However, in terms of the income generated, police PSO contributions were important, and particularly so for the individual officer. Unlike soldiers, police officers were deployed as individuals, and therefore personally received mission subsistence allowance to reimburse 'accommodation, food and incidentals'. Given that the UN allowance in Darfur

---

[75] Astill-Brown, Davidson-Houston and Morgan, 'Stability and Prosperity in Sierra Leone', p. 9.

[76] Horn, Gordon and Albrecht, 'Sierra Leone Police – Review of Capabilities', p. 50.

was about $100 per officer per day, this represented a vast increase on the individual officer's salary, which for a constable was 148,520 Leones a month (approximately $62).[77]

In 2010, while Acha Kamara was still IGP, the Police Council agreed to increase the strength of the SLP to 12,500 personnel (up from 8,500 in 2005). As Francis Alieu Munu, who succeeded Acha Kamara in August 2010, explained in retrospect: 'Police consolidation [since the war came to an end in 2002] led to an increased demand for police services. We strengthened the numbers, went on a recruitment drive. We also needed to prepare for elections in 2012, and I barely had 1.5 years to do that. All of this provided justification for increasing police numbers'.[78]

However, it was also perceived by donors and civil-society activists that this expansion was politically driven, with the police perceived to be less resistant to such pressure than the RSLAF, which benefited from both the involvement of IMATT and the resilience of the minister of defence. Further evidence that the SLP was indeed susceptible to political pressure came with the appointment of Musa Tarawali as minister of internal affairs in December 2010. Earlier that year, Tarawali – when he still held the position of resident minister, South – reportedly bypassed the local unit commander (LUC) by bringing in the OSD to oversee by-elections for vacant parliamentary and local council seats in Pujehun District.[79] Although other candidates – including from the SLPP – also allegedly brought in ex-combatants in support of their campaigns,[80] Tarawali stood accused of politicising the OSD to the advantage of the APC.[81] His

---

[77] *Ibid.*, p. 6. The SLP takes a share of the individual officer's allowance. Before 2013 it was said to be $200, but the amount greatly increased in 2012–13 (rumoured to be several thousand dollars, though the authors were unable to verify this). Those who refused to pay the police organisation its share were subsequently sent to less attractive posts in Sierra Leone.

[78] Albrecht interview with Francis Alieu Munu.

[79] Both Pujehun and Kono Districts have experienced significant political tension; indeed, 'a combustible fault line is magnifying between APC youth and chiefs or elites supporting the SLPP'. Amnesty International, 'Continuing Human Rights Violations in the Post Conflict Period: Amnesty International Submission to the UN Universal Periodic Review, May 2011', 11th Session of the UPR Working Group, 2011, p. 6.

[80] *Ibid.*; UN Security Council, 'Fifth Report of the Secretary-General on the United Nations Integrated Peacebuilding Office in Sierra Leone', S/2010/471, New York, 17 September 2010, p. 4. Similarly, following a closely contested general election in 2007, the SLPP headquarters in Freetown were attacked, with subsequent clashes between supporters of the two main parties occurring in Pujehun, among other places. Andrew Lavali, Charlie J Hughes and Mohamed Suma, 'Sierra Leone: Elections and Diversity Management', UN Economic Commission for Africa, 2011, p. 3.

[81] The possibility of doing so was eased by the fact that the OSD is controlled and managed centrally, albeit with a presence across Sierra Leone's regions and police

appointment as minister of internal affairs just months later was seen as a reward for serving the party, underpinned by a belief that he would be in a good position to prepare the SLP for the 2012 presidential elections. Such accusations of politicisation of the police, both at the ministerial level and within the OSD, clearly point to perceived differences between the progress made by the RSLAF and SLP respectively (however, as noted earlier, direct comparisons between the two institutions are unhelpful, given their fundamentally different roles).

Meanwhile, from 2010, a fundamental contradiction emerged in the SLP's execution of its internal security tasks. The SLP leadership continued to define its style of policing as Local Needs Policing (LNP), involving 'working closely with the community, sharing information, working together on crime prevention and developing an overall policing approach that suits the community's needs'[82] – a model which was initiated in 1998 by the Commonwealth Police Development Task Force (CPDTF) and was supported thereafter by the CCSSP, and which the JSDP was then specifically tasked with developing further.[83] This was done primarily through an 'extensive training programme' that addressed the 'development needs of most senior and middle managers and the training of criminal investigations and intelligence staff'.[84]

When the CCSSP was terminated in 2005, however, the JSDP refused to take on the hard edge of policing that the OSD represented. Echoing DfID's broad sentiments about its involvement in SSR from 2007 onwards, the JSDP had taken the view 'that because of the different orientations of justice and security sectors, it would not be appropriate, either theoretically or practically, to combine them into one sector'.[85] Thus, although SILSEP picked up elements of the CCSSP's work with the OSD,[86]

---

divisions (Local Command Units). There is a regional co-ordinator at each regional headquarters. This co-ordinator acts as an adviser to the regional assistant inspector-general. Horn, Gordon and Albrecht, 'Sierra Leone Police – Review of Capabilities', p. 20.

[82] JSDP, 'Achievements and Lessons Learned', British Council, Freetown, 2012, p. 42.

[83] *Ibid.*

[84] *Ibid.*, p. 46.

[85] Anthony Howlett-Bolton, 'Justice Sector Reform', in Albrecht and Jackson (eds), *Security Sector Reform in Sierra Leone 1997–2007*, p. 97.

[86] Among the 'security' elements of policing that SILSEP took over were public-order management, police intelligence and the provision of kit, whilst the development of Local Needs Policing fell under the JSDP. This divorced hard from softer policing and was reinforced by the appointment of an adviser with both policing and special-forces experience to train the OSD to be the 'paramilitary wing' of the SLP (this adviser had also served under the CCSSP). See Garth Glentworth et al., 'Sierra Leone: Transition Priorities in the Move from the "Justice and Security Development Programme" to the "Access to Security and Justice Programme"', UK Government, 2011, unpublished, p. 11, note 13.

the result was that proactive programming *vis-à-vis* the armed wing of the police was dwindling. This split between the two DfID-funded programmes, with the JSDP and SILSEP looking after justice and security elements respectively, was intended as an interim solution before OSD support was phased out in 2006–07.

Through its direct access to the vice president, via the Justice Sector Leadership Group,[87] the JSDP could potentially shape his and the Police Council's approach to the OSD. However, this relationship did not yield the benefits one might have expected, in that changes were either not made or not consolidated. This may have simply reflected the fact that good relations do not necessarily lead to fundamental change in practice. Indeed, there is no direct correlation between limitations to international assistance and the decay or politicisation of state institutions, individually or collectively; this would give too much credit to the transformative effects of international support and take away responsibility from those institutions' governance structures.

With little external support for the previous three years, by 2010–11 considerable incongruence had emerged between the OSD's line of development and the SLP's promotion of Local Needs Policing as its overall ethos, and its emphasis on the need to engage communities in service provision through community policing. The rapid expansion of the OSD – which was poorly managed – meant that the armed wing of the police had grown from around 3,000 to more than 4,000 officers,[88] a third of the SLP's total numbers. From 2011, increasing numbers of shooting incidents involving OSD officers exposed their insufficient training and consequent tendency to panic when under pressure. Such incidents are likely, ultimately, to severely undermine the SLP and its broader community-based approach.

According to Guy Collings, one of ISAT's first police advisers, this growing incongruence was due to the way in which the Local Command Units were managed:[89]

---

[87] The Justice Sector Leadership Group was set up by the JSDP and chaired by the Sierra Leonean vice president, with ministers and the chief justice among its membership (for more discussion of the Leadership Group in the context of the JSDP, see Chapter III). Its overall responsibility was to provide strategic direction and policy co-ordination, and to develop a sector-wide strategic plan for the justice sector.

[88] In 2004, it had been decided that OSD numbers should grow from 2,400 to 2,900, a figure based on contemporary threat assessments and the likely demands of an expanding portfolio to man some 600 protection posts. In September 2004, for example, the OSD took over responsibilities for security from the UN in the east of the country. Albrecht and Jackson, *Security System Transformation in Sierra Leone*, p. 90.

[89] Peter Albrecht interview with Guy Collings, Sierra Leone, September 2013.

> Every LUC [local unit commander] has an OSD component attached. Whilst the OSD operate [alongside] the LUCs, they are controlled directly by … [and] answerable to the head of the OSD. They can be tasked by the LUC and theoretically they are [also] answerable to the LUC, but if they don't like what they are told, they can run to the HQ.

Collings further observed that the OSD 'say that they are supportive [of Local Needs Policing], but they are not. When you ask them how, they look blankly at you'.[90] It was evident that a gap existed between the rhetoric of Local Needs Policing and community policing on the one hand and the strengthening of the SLP's operational arm, the OSD, on the other.

What to Do with the OSD?

An external review carried out in 2007 in support of SILSEP concluded that because the OSD could not be deployed for normal policing, in 'the longer-term, the SLP will need to consider how the OSD can be absorbed into the main police structure in order to ensure best use of available resources'.[91] After the 2007 elections, UK advisers recommended that the SLP conduct a further review of the entire establishment to clarify the appropriate size, structure and focus of the service and the prospects for the absorption of the OSD (UK advice was offered in support of this activity). This review was not carried out until early 2011, however, and it was only done so upon the specific request of the defence attaché in the British High Commission. The result was that DfID did not see it as useful guidance on future planning, and it dismissed the review's recommendations for the provision of logistical support in particular. The High Commission, meanwhile, did not have the financial means to enforce the review's implementation. Thus the review epitomised a broader struggle between the Foreign Office and DfID in their approaches to police reform – with DfID rightly interpreting the review as a criticism of its efforts; it also encapsulated the aforementioned tension between the DfID and Foreign Office in-country teams, with the latter formally in charge but the former holding the coveted purse strings.

Nevertheless, the review, conducted in early 2011 by Adrian Horn,[92] raised particular concerns over the status of the OSD. The OSD was considered by former IGP Keith Biddle to have been on 'the front line of policing' in the immediate aftermath of the war.[93] By the early 2010s, however, it was seen as a destabilising force, operating in isolation from

[90] *Ibid.*

[91] Piet Biesheuvel, Tom Hamilton-Baillie and Peter Wilson, 'Sierra Leone Security Sector Reform Programme – Output to Purpose Review', April 2007, unpublished.

[92] Horn, Gordon and Albrecht, 'Sierra Leone Police – Review of Capabilities'.

[93] Albrecht and Jackson, *Security System Transformation in Sierra Leone*, p. 96.

the rest of the SLP and becoming increasingly opaque. Indeed, as then-Defence Attaché Sam Seward noted in early 2011, reflecting the sentiment of most external actors: 'I don't think anybody really understands [the] OSD; [or] how it's now used'.[94]

The 2011 police review also assessed that while there was 'no supporting evidence that there are plans to militarise the OSD ... some of the activities, particularly the change of uniform [from general duty to military-style blue camouflage], are creating that perception, and perception can become reality'.[95] The paramilitary appearance and training of the OSD awakened memories of the Special Security Division founded by then-President Siaka Stevens in the 1980s, which served the regime rather than population. The procurement of arms worth $4.5 million for the OSD in late 2011 – including 2,500 assault rifles, fifty heavy machine guns and 100 grenade launchers – from a Chinese company further reinforced this view. The police argued that this delivery was simply to replenish wastage – something that many in political opposition to the APC, and notably within the SLPP, rejected, arguing that it was an attempt, pre-election, to provide the OSD with weapons that had not been made available to it via the CCSSP. In the end, the equipment was transferred to the RSLAF following severe criticism from international partners and civil-society groups.

The potential politicisation of the OSD was one of two major issues that continued to be of concern to the UK – with poor training being the other. As part of the expansion of the police force initiated by Acha Kamara in 2010, around 735 OSD personnel were recruited;[96] but much of this recruitment occurred outside due process. Then, without appropriate formal training or scrutiny, some of these recruits were immediately transferred to Kono, in eastern Sierra Leone, to police the by-elections taking place in late 2010. Likewise, before the 2012 elections, a similarly unco-ordinated OSD recruitment process took place. Training was rushed and scrutiny of the individuals recruited was deemed insufficient by UK advisers.[97] It was even alleged that the majority of new OSD officers were APC supporters, even though many of them did not come from the north

[94] Peter Albrecht interview with Sam Seward, Sierra Leone, January 2011.

[95] Horn, Gordon and Albrecht, 'Sierra Leone Police – Review of Capabilities', p. 7.

[96] Albrecht interview with Francis Alieu Munu.

[97] Before the war, new recruits were commonly selected on the basis of a 'card system', whereby assistant inspector-generals, the inspector-general, ministers and other powerful individuals could order the recruitment of loyal individuals outside due process. Potential or serving army and police officers of all tribal backgrounds would approach a politician, for instance, to influence the inspector-general of police and were, for a fee, given the politician's 'calling card'. On the reverse side of these cards there was an instruction that the officer was to be appointed to a particular position or that he or she was to be recruited into the security force.

of the country, the traditional stronghold of the APC.[98] Clearly, in a system in which the OSD enjoys significant power and privileges, any such politicised recruitment is dangerous – and it suggests a shift back to former practices. Indeed, even the perception that this is happening can be destabilising.

The lack of proper documentation of recruitment also facilitates the politicisation of the process, because it makes full verification impossible. In early 2011, one senior officer noted that the recruitment process for the OSD had been carried out separately because it was decided at a political level that their numbers should be boosted and because of a general reluctance among new general-duty recruits to join the OSD.[99] The government's plan, articulated by the Police Council, was to recruit 500 in total, with the north, south and west each to recruit 100 individuals, and the Western Area, containing Freetown, to recruit 200. However, the executive put pressure on the SLP to take on a further 200 OSD personnel, with the minister of finance pledging to allocate additional funds in order to quell the protests of the SLP, which argued that it could not afford to pay for their uniforms, boots or training. By the following year, it was not possible to say for sure who amongst the new recruits had been trained and in what skill set. Whilst most attended the OSD Training Centre at Samu in Kambia District and were given what can best be described as military-style training, it is unclear how many, if any, went to the Police Training School in Hastings for general-duty training.

Despite UK concern over such practices, in early 2011 then-National Security Coordinator Kellie Conteh told Horn and the rest of the team reviewing the SLP that 'If the UK underlines this point too strongly, it will undermine the SLP'[100] – a recommendation that was taken into account in the team's final report. Conteh also emphasised the need for patience. Over time, it was observed, one way of addressing the issue would be to develop focused training for these recruits, to set standards, and then discard those officers who were not qualified (this in fact happened at the beginning of 2014). Indeed, Conteh noted that fifty recruits had already been dismissed through internal police procedures.[101]

Nevertheless, events in the following years revealed the consequences of insufficient training. For example, in 2012–13, a number of controversial shooting incidents involving the OSD across the country resulted in civilians being wounded and killed. During one such incident

Merit mattered but not as much as personal loyalty and conformity. Albrecht and Jackson, *Security System Transformation in Sierra Leone*, p. 45.

[98] This was noted by a number of high-level security officials during conversations and interviews between 2010 and 2014.

[99] Peter Albrecht interview with anonymous, Freetown, January 2011.

[100] Kellie Conteh, meeting, Freetown, January 2011.

[101] *Ibid.*

in Koidu, civilians wrested a gun from an OSD officer. Following these and other events, including the shooting of a teenager in the east of Freetown in late 2013, 700 OSD officers were sent to the Police Training School in Hastings to undergo general-duty training. These incidents had a marked impact on public perceptions of the OSD, which in turn heavily influenced perceptions of the wider SLP. Unsurprisingly, when ISAT began operations in April 2013, exploring ways of supporting the OSD was one of its first priorities. 'We can invest in training', one of the newly arrived advisers noted:[102]

> [But] its political orientation [towards the APC] is so strong, facing in the entirely wrong direction. [When there are problems] the government response is to send in the OSD, which aggravates the problem … Being honest with them [the government] at this stage will give them here and the CPP [Conflict Prevention Pool] a sense of whether there is an appetite for ISAT. If you ask us, you'll get an honest answer.

This remained a problem in 2014, when one international observer concluded that the relationship between the OSD and the rest of the SLP was 'that of between two separate organisations. The OSD is essentially a force within the force'.[103] Later that year, ISAT, in collaboration with the SLP, conducted a full review of the OSD.

'All Change' in the Justice Sector

The Legacy of the JSDP

As one DfID official noted in 2013, the 'justice sector was [actually] beginning to look like a sector at the end of [the] JSDP'.[104] The programme began winding down over the course of 2011, and when it was terminated in September of that year it left two main legacies: first, a justice system that was accessible to greater numbers of people, and in particular to segments of the population that had previously had limited or no access; and second, the development of new legislation and practices aimed at improving the justice system's efficiency, investing in local justice processes, and increasing the number of cases that could be dealt with either in local courts or through mediation.[105]

---

[102] Peter Albrecht interview with anonymous, Sierra Leone, September 2013.

[103] Peter Albrecht interview with anonymous, Sierra Leone, February 2014.

[104] Peter Albrecht interview with anonymous, Sierra Leone, December 2013.

[105] The phrase 'common law court' is used to describe the courts in Sierra Leone that apply the common law, as opposed to the local courts that apply customary law. The terms 'formal' and 'informal' courts are inapplicable in Sierra Leone, as the local courts (sometimes erroneously referred to as 'informal') derive their jurisdiction from an Act of Parliament which also regulates their activity (Local

As such, the JSDP had begun a process of transforming access to justice in Sierra Leone, but it would have been unrealistic to assume that all of the programme's activities could have become self-sustaining by its end. As was observed in the report outlining the UK's priorities in the transition from the JSDP to the ASJP: 'Development in what is called collectively primary justice (activity at chiefdom level – e.g. local courts, community mediation) … [is] much more likely to become sustainable than those programmes which have to depend on significant amounts of GoSL funding'.[106]

Whilst the JSDP's work with legal aid, for example, was regarded as effective, it was also clearly unsustainable in the absence of continued donor funding, given the pace of change that could be expected within a five-to-six-year timeframe. The passing of the Legal Aid Act in early 2012 was a legislative victory for the JSDP, given the Act's elaboration of a mixed model of criminal and civil legal aid, and the provision of legal information and mediation services through to representation in court.[107] The provision of legal aid also alleviated some of the pressure on common law courts, which have long been characterised by lengthy delays and backlogs. As part of this process, the JSDP made visits to police stations and referred cases back to the community, thus succeeding in settling cases out of court.[108] However, without external funding, the state lacks the capacity and incentive to continue providing legal aid.

Another remaining issue relates to the judiciary. In 2013, two years after the end of the JSDP, there remained a refusal to accept that change within the judiciary was needed, even though it is still small and highly politicised. By 2008, for example, there were still fewer than 200 members of the Sierra Leone Bar Association, all of whom were located in Freetown.[109] Similarly, in February 2010 there were only eleven legally qualified staff in the Ministry of Justice's Department of Public Prosecutions, two of whom were consultants, 'indicating that the Ministry is

---

Courts Act, 1965, which was replaced by the Local Courts Act, 2011). This touches on a broader discussion around problematic and empirically inaccurate discussions of state versus non-state security and justice actors. See Peter Albrecht and Helene Maria Kyed, 'Introduction: Non-State and Customary Actors in Development Programs', in Peter Albrecht et al. (eds), *Perspectives on Involving Non-State and Customary Actors in Justice and Security Reform* (Rome and Copenhagen: International Development Law Organization and Danish Institute for International Studies, 2011).

[106] Glentworth et al., 'Sierra Leone', p. 43.

[107] See Sonkita Conteh and Lotta Teale, 'Sierra Leone Parliament Passes Landmark Legal Aid Law', NAMATI, 11 May 2012, <http://www.namati.org/newsposts/sierra-leone-passes-legal-aid-law/>, accessed 13 October 2014.

[108] Peter Albrecht interview with John Magbity, Sierra Leone, December 2013.

[109] Albrecht and Jackson, *Security System Transformation in Sierra Leone*, p. 42.

understaffed and under-resourced'.[110] Thus, as one observer from the donor community stated in 2013:[111]

> The judiciary is politicised from the top; even small cases that the political elite should not be concerned about, they are concerned about. With our support, we don't think we can do a lot about the politicisation. However, you can speed up cases and make citizens' experience of justice much better, but we are not even getting traction on that [in late 2013]. It's partly a leadership question – if the chief justice and consultant master and registrar ... are not capable of taking these issues on, we are not [going to] get ... very far.

Despite some progress, meanwhile, the formal court system remains difficult to access for most Sierra Leoneans, especially for the poor, women and other marginalised groups in rural areas. Many courts still fail to resolve disputes promptly, fairly, effectively, and often even conclusively. The processing of cases is slow and costly (resulting in a growing backlog), while the capacity of the justice system to address serious crimes appears to remain very low. For example, close to 1,000 cases of sexual abuse and over 1,500 cases of domestic violence were reported to the police in 2010; however, none of these cases has yet resulted in a conviction[112] – and data collected by the ASJP in 2013 show that improvement in this area remains very limited.[113]

Alongside issues around management and leadership, financial instability has also been of concern. Between 2007 and 2011, Sierra Leone government funding for the justice and security sector fell from a high of 90 per cent of the budget requested in 2008 to a low of 68 per cent in 2011 (exclusive of salaries handled by the Human Resource Management

[110] This information is drawn from the document outlining the design of the ASJP. It is also pointed out that many low-level prosecutions are undertaken by more than 300 police prosecutors who have virtually no legal education, training or compilations of law with which to fulfil their obligations. A consequence of the absence of compilations and digests of law is that magistrates and judges hand down 'illegal' sentences because they are rendering judgments that do not reflect the law. The fact that much of Sierra Leone's legal framework is obsolete – with laws relevant to the justice and security sector dating back to the early 1960s and with little new legislation pending – is yet another indication of what may be a general lack of commitment to justice development. Libra Advisory Group, 'Improved Access to Security and Justice Programme – Options Paper', 2010, unpublished.

[111] Peter Albrecht interview with anonymous, Sierra Leone, December 2013.

[112] Sierra Leonean Ministry of Finance and Economic Development, 'Fragility Assessment', 2013.

[113] The ASJP's own data, collected from magistrates' and high courts in target districts, indicated a 5 per cent conviction rate during the three-month sample window in 2013.

Office).[114] This reflects a shortage of resources, but also the Government of Sierra Leone's tendency to reduce funding in donor-supported areas. The government demonstrated its commitment in principle to reform of the sector through the drafting of two Justice Sector Reform Strategies (for 2008–10 and 2011–13) and its willingness to cover an increase in running costs for the sector (from $6.8 million in 2007 to $9.3 million in 2011) – although this was not sustained across the sector, with it being limited to the police and the ombudsman in 2011, for example. Indeed, government funding (excluding salaries) across justice and security has been erratic over the past five years; most ministries, departments and agencies apart from the SLP suffered a significant decrease in budget in 2011, with funding falling to 2007 levels or below.[115]

One of the notable strengths of the JSDP, however, was its ability to build robust partnerships with key actors in the justice sector and the executive, with good relations between programme staff and government partners considered a cornerstone in programme implementation. There is, however, limited evidence that these relationships have had any long-term effects on how the justice sector has performed subsequently (as observed above).

The role of the Justice Sector Coordination Office (JSCO), which had become the embodiment of the JSDP's institutional memory since its creation in 2007, was crucial as the JSDP drew to a close. Indeed, the programme's legacy has depended on it. There has been some tension between the JSCO and the Ministry of Justice over turf. This was inevitable as the former was established as part of, yet also outside of, existing institutions, partly as an extension of the JSDP, gradually taking over policy development and co-ordination within the sector. Indeed, it was built into the JSDP's strategy that the JSCO would assume this role as quickly as possible, certainly before the termination of the JSDP, and that it would take an important, strategic lead in co-ordinating two Justice Sector Reform Strategy and Investment Plans (JSRSIPs). However, this capacity and knowledge developed in the JSCO was not simultaneously nurtured elsewhere in the sector, giving rise to friction.[116]

The JSCO also made moves to bring itself closer to the ONS, and thus to bring the justice and security sectors closer together. In 2010, discussions were held between the heads of the two organisations with regard to strengthening co-ordination, while the head of the JSCO was also invited to present the organisation's work to the National Security

---

[114] Between 2007 and 2011, for every £1 the Sierra Leone government put into the justice sector, the JSDP (on behalf of DfID) contributed 62 pence.

[115] Glentworth et al., 'Sierra Leone', p. 46.

[116] This is not dissimilar to the role played by the ONS in the security sector and its role in developing two security-sector reviews.

Council and was given a permanent seat on the National Security Council Coordinating Group.

At the time of writing, however, and despite its crucial role in bringing together a better co-ordinated justice sector, the JSCO has not yet been established as a legal entity and is therefore – in technical terms – not yet a formal government body (the bill has yet to be put before Parliament). This has resulted in an ongoing lack of clarity around its precise role and mandate, and confusion over whether it is a donor or a government project. In turn, this has meant that it has sometimes been sidelined because, in the words of the current head of the JSCO, Olayinka Creighton-Randall, it has seemed to others to be 'neither here nor there'.[117] Another consequence is that the justice sector has sometimes been viewed as secondary to the security sector, because the ONS, by contrast, was established by a legal statute in 2002.

The process for establishing the JSCO as a legal entity started as far back as 2009, following a DfID review. The Justice Sector Leadership Group, which was originally set up by the JSDP, approved the legal establishment of the JSCO in 2010. This was also one of the key recommendations made during the retrospective Cabinet-level review of the 2008–10 JSRSIP and during the development of the second JSRSIP, for 2011–13. However, the idea was rejected, and it was only in mid-2013 that the government agreed to move forward on making the JSCO a formal government institution.

In the meantime, pressure on the JSCO was heightened and the continuation of JSDP gains was complicated with the transition to the ASJP. While there were more similarities between the JSDP and ASJP than there had been between the approach of the CCSSP and Law Development Programme and the JSDP, it is still worth emphasising the significant, negative impact that the transition had on support to the justice sector – a general point that applies to the termination and transition of other programmes in the sector (such as SILSEP).

Indeed, such transitions are bound to have repercussions for collaboration between donors and partners, and particularly where many of the gains made are directly linked to the establishment of successful relationships, as in the case of the JSDP. These relationships were put under pressure with the transition to the ASJP, which brought a variety of difficulties – both because the new programme was starting from scratch and because there was no formal handover between the British Council and the new contractor, global development company DAI.

[117] Peter Albrecht interview with Olayinka Creighton-Randall, Sierra Leone, September 2013.

The Difficult Transition from the JSDP to the ASJP

Thinking around the JSDP's successor began in mid-2009, with the new programme then referred to as the Improved Access to Security and Justice Programme (IASJP – the 'I' was later dropped). Based on DfID's White Paper, *Building Our Common Future*, fundamental to the ASJP was a conception of security and access to justice as 'basic services' that should be delivered to 'ordinary people' to improve their lives. Within DfID, it was also considered the appropriate time to 'complement HMG's [Her Majesty's Government] largely "top-down" approach to the security and justice sectors in Sierra Leone with a "bottom-up" focus on basic security and justice service provision for the poor'.[118] While the JSDP had moved beyond Freetown and had a broader focus than the Commonwealth Community Safety and Security Project, it was still, in 2009–10, considered a state-orientated and largely supply-driven programme.

The design phase of the ASJP was initiated in early 2010 by a team from the consultancy firm Libra Advisory Group, which was to follow an elaborate process of consultation with DfID's Sierra Leonean counterparts as the new programme was developed. It quickly became evident that the approach of the design team was out of sync with Government of Sierra Leone expectations of DfID support. The earlier termination, in 2008, of the Sierra Leone Security Sector Reform Programme had meant that within national security institutions – notably the ONS – it was expected that the JSDP's successor would involve support to the security sector, as well as to the justice sector, at the strategic level. Indeed, the ONS appeared to expect that it would manage elements of the ASJP when it began implementation, when in fact the programme was to be justice-led.[119] As such, it was the JSCO that was to take the lead within the Sierra Leone government.

There was thus a sense within the design team that the ministries and departments within the wider Sierra Leone government had not been properly prepared for what the team was in the country to do; that is, to design a demand-driven programme. Being demand-driven meant that the programme would be centred on 'a local approach to problem solving' and exhibit a strong focus on 'non-state actors' through support to paralegal and

[118] DfID, 'TOR for Improved Access to Security and Justice Programme in Sierra Leone (IASJP)', London, 2009, unpublished.

[119] This became clear to the team that designed the ASJP in early 2010. Indeed, it appeared that the ONS saw itself as an accountability mechanism of the security sector as a whole, a role that was resisted by the UK because it was seen to undermine an already weak Ministry of Internal Affairs. Quite simply, as noted further in 2013 by Sophy Thomas, who was safety and security adviser with the ASJP from January 2012 until June 2014, 'there is no one to implement the plan in MIA [Ministry of Internal Affairs]'. Peter Albrecht interview with Sophy Thomas, Sierra Leone, August 2013.

mediator organisations, as well as to the SLP's Local Policing Partnership Boards.[120] In other words, the ASJP would target those institutions used by ordinary people in their daily lives, rather than focusing solely on state institutions that struggled to deliver basic goods and services. This reflected a change in policy within DfID itself, but it also hints at a false understanding of the JSDP, which had never taken a purely top-down approach, both in Moyamba and also in its support of paralegals. As such, the 'new' approach should really have been seen as a change in balance between elements within the programme, with some of the bottom-up elements first piloted in Moyamba now coming to the fore, in place of a greater emphasis on formal state justice and ministerial control.

It was inevitable that tensions would emerge as a result of this focus on 'demand' for justice, rather than its 'supply'. Evidently, the outcome of prioritising the former was that control of the programme's management and funding would be diffused away from the central governance institutions in Freetown. As such, whether the programme should be supply- or demand-driven was not simply a technical matter, but a deeply political one because it touched on how resources would be distributed, and was therefore a bone of contention.

This was reinforced by the crucial role of external financial support in Sierra Leone's national economy. Indeed, the Government of Sierra Leone explicitly warned of the dangers inherent to prioritising local, or 'non-state', actors over centrally governed institutions in its 2010 report responding to Libra's suggested programme options, calling it 'a recipe for friction'.[121] Instead, the government suggested that building the capacity of key state institutions should continue, and that emphasis should be placed on working *in concert with* non-state actors to implement demand-driven services. This would lead to a more balanced security system and would limit the 'dangers associated with building the capacity of non-state actors to demand and expect more service, whilst declining to build state actors' capacity to deliver'.[122]

---

[120] Libra Advisory Group, 'Interim Program Document for Improved Access to Security and Justice Programme. In addition, complications arose from the fact that the senior governance adviser who was overseeing the design phase left in the middle of the process. Local Policing Partnership Boards (LPPBs) are the institutional expression of the SLP's community policing model. They function as a de facto interface between the SLP and local communities, enabling the resolution of minor offences, as well as ensuring that criminal offences such as cases of murder and rape are reported to the police. See Peter Albrecht et al., 'Community Policing in Sierra Leone – Local Policing Partnership Boards', *DIIS Report* 2014:16, Copenhagen, 2014; SLP, 'Local Policing Partnership Board Constitution', 2011; SLP, *Handbook: Local Policing Partnership Boards* (Freetown: Sierra Leone Police, 2014).

[121] Government of Sierra Leone, 'Response to ASJP Suggestions', 2010, unpublished.

[122] *Ibid.*

The tension between DfID and the Government of Sierra Leone in this regard was predictable; so too was the fact that the ASJP would not be able to deliver on all of the varying priorities of the different elements within the UK government. There was a sense within IMATT and the Foreign Office that while the RSLAF had enjoyed consistent support from the UK and was a more professional organisation for it, the SLP had been largely ignored since the termination of the Commonwealth Community Safety and Security Project – and this was reflected in the standard of basic policing services. The Foreign Office in particular was equally concerned about the potential withdrawal of DfID's support from the ONS – an issue similarly highlighted by the Sierra Leone government in its observation that '90% of the [ASJP] Options Paper dwells exclusively on the justice sector'.[123] However, neither the Foreign Office nor IMATT had the funding to initiate comprehensive security-related programming at the strategic level (a circumstance partially responded to by the establishment of ISAT).

The approach set forth in Libra's final programme document, presented in mid-June 2010, remained decidedly justice-orientated and in this regard reflected the priorities of DfID in both Freetown and London. However, the level on which it sought to make an impact was modified and the ASJP now struck a balance between strengthening individual ministries, departments and agencies, addressing local justice and security concerns, and improving trust and confidence in the key providers. Reaction and flexibility were replaced by an emphasis on building accountability and trust, given that Sierra Leone had 'completed the transition from a post-conflict to a fragile state'.[124] This was in part a reflection of perceptions of SILSEP, which had reputedly been strong on flexibility and quick to react to events as they unfolded on the ground, but weak on accountability, transparency and clarity of direction. Of course, it also reflected a desire for a 'normalisation' of programming. Indeed, while DfID remained concerned about Sierra Leone's stability, its purview was development and therefore it now focused more broadly on justice and security programming (rather than SSR), and it did so to support Sierra Leone in becoming a 'democratic and stable state' that was 'making significant progress in reducing poverty'.[125]

Unfortunately, however, the transition between the two programmes was afflicted by several issues that had hampered previous justice-sector programming. The first of these was timing: the JSDP ended in August 2011, but the new contractor for the ASJP was not announced

---

[123] *Ibid.*

[124] Libra Advisory Group, 'Interim Program Document for Improved Access to Security and Justice Programme', p. 5.

[125] DfID quoted in *ibid.*, p. 13.

until November and the programme was intended to launch in January 2012 – by which point JSDP staff had already left. The net effect of this was to leave the Sierra Leonean justice sector in suspension, without even domestic support which, as noted earlier, had been reduced as the Government of Sierra Leone began to focus on other priorities. Furthermore, DfID pushed back its programming further to allow the ASJP to align itself with the Sierra Leone government's 2011–13 Justice Sector Reform Strategy and Investment Plan II, delaying the beginning of implementation by a further six months. In the end, instead of the one-month overlapping transition that was supposed to occur, the messy transition – which was completely out of the hands of the Government of Sierra Leone – meant that the hiatus lasted almost a full year (the fact that 2012 was an election year also meant that moving reform efforts forward was difficult, given the executive's preoccupation with campaigning).

This was compounded by the fact that the initiation of the ASJP had been presented as a 'new start'. In fact, the opposite was true, but the result was that in 2012 many activities, including those underway outside of Freetown, ground to a halt. In conversations with the paramount chief of Kayamba in 2012, for example, he appeared confused, noting that while the JSDP, in its pilot programme, had ensured closer co-operation among Moyamba District's paramount chiefs, the establishment of a circuit court and the provision of training, these activities had not continued after the JSDP had left.[126]

In practical terms, this exposed a number of critical considerations with regard to the nature of programming in general and, in particular, how donors relate to – and are perceived by – local actors.[127] Whilst this episode was damaging to the contractors, it was also somewhat damaging to DfID's reputation in Sierra Leone, with local actors expressing dismay at the transition, the lack of information available, and the fact that activities previously held up as important simply ceased for a full year. This is not to suggest that the relevant contractors did not make efforts to pass on information to the incoming contractor (although DAI did not enjoy access to all of the written information generated by the previous programme under the British Council); but it does illuminate potential difficulties when working in partnerships, and how transitions involve more than a simple switch between contractors, given the emphasis on developing relationships with national and local actors.

[126] Peter Albrecht interview with Foday Momoh, Sierra Leone, June 2012.

[127] This problematic transition is dealt with in more detail in Peter Albrecht, Osman Gbla and Paul Jackson, 'From Quick Wins to Long-Term Profits? Developing Better Approaches to Support Security and Justice Engagements in Fragile States: Sierra Leone Case Study', OECD, Paris, 2013, unpublished.

ASJP: Falling into the Holistic Trap?

The fact that the ASJP was initiated in an election year fundamentally shaped what could be achieved in the short term, with, for example, the programme's staff barred from working directly with then-Minister for Internal Affairs Musa Tarawali until after the elections, due to perceptions of politicisation. At the same time, the election period also proved to be an opportunity for the new programme, providing an event on which the early stages of implementation could focus. As such, the ASJP began implementation with targeted support to the SLP, ONS and civil society in preparation for the elections; for instance, support was given to the Local Policing Partnership Boards and to finalising an election manual. These activities may not have been at the very centre of Sierra Leone's election-planning process, but they were significant in kick-starting ASJP–partner relationships.

Most of 2012 was thus spent in building momentum within the ASJP, and in handling the general elections in November and their aftermath. In 2013, with the ASJP under increasing pressure to deliver, efforts were directed towards establishing a broad-based presence outside Freetown and beginning implementation in earnest (initially in the districts of Western Area Rural, Kenema, Koinadugu and Moyamba, before expanding to four additional districts in 2014).[128] A broad range of activities was launched through which the ASJP sought to split its attention considerably more equally between the central government and the local level (reflecting the acknowledgement that the effects of government-level reform did not always trickle down, as well as the prevalent emphasis within international development policy-making circles on 'non-state' justice- and security-sector activities).[129]

This split in support also meant that while the ASJP's overarching focus was on delivery, the spirit of the holistic approach continued to be manifest. For instance, the ASJP pursued its goal of making local policing services more responsive by supporting the training of the SLP's middle management *vis-à-vis* Local Needs Policing, and of Local Policing Partnership Boards members with regards to their roles and responsibilities. At the same time, technical advice was provided to the permanent secretary in the Ministry of Internal Affairs on policy and planning for the ministry as well as security agencies. Other key areas of intervention included increasing the efficiency of local courts and the availability of

---

[128] Albrecht et al., 'Community Policing in Sierra Leone', p. 15.

[129] Peter Alexander Albrecht, 'Transforming Internal Security in Sierra Leone: Sierra Leone Police and Broader Justice Sector Reform', *DIIS Report* 2010:07, Copenhagen, 2010, p. 9.

skilled informal justice services, while ensuring that the justice sector was effectively co-ordinated and managed by relevant agencies to facilitate the delivery of JSRSIP II.

From these brief deliberations on the ASJP, which is still being implemented, it is evident that the balance of support has shifted explicitly to the local level, even as work is also carried out centrally. There is a danger, however, that the ASJP – in its emphasis on a holistic approach – could ultimately make the same mistake as the JSDP by trying to do too many things in too short a timeframe. Good programming requires difficult prioritisations – a lesson from the JSDP that must be acted on as well as understood.[130]

Fundamental to this is accepting that although wholesale transformation may not be possible, gradual changes and to improvements of the scope and quality of service provision are – something which DfID and the ASJP appear to have accepted in their efforts to improve the formal and informal justice systems, even though the country's political dynamics are much more difficult to shape. Often, expectations of what can be achieved by a particular policy within a short period of time are formulated far away from the area of implementation, and from a macro-level perspective. This leads to frustration with what are considered limited results on the ground, when in fact limited and context-specific change is all that can be hoped for in the short-to-medium term.[131]

Conclusion

The end of March 2013 marked the termination of IMATT, the longest and most consistent programme of support to a security-sector institution in Sierra Leone. By then, the RSLAF's role as a security force was well understood and accepted within the rank and file. There had been obstacles along the way, including the downsizing of the army. The failure of 'Pebu' and 'Pumas' – the programmes of building barracks for the RSLAF and of re-establishing the air wing – was still fresh in the minds of the RSLAF leadership and IMATT was, rightly or wrongly, held accountable for this failure.

Yet the bottom line was that IMATT had been considered an integral part of Sierra Leone's defence sector following the civil war; and it left behind a stable armed force that stayed out of politics and was oriented around contributing troops to peace support operations overseas. By

[130] ASJP, 'ASJP 2014 Work Plan', Freetown, 2014, unpublished.
[131] Peter Albrecht, 'Local Actors and Service Delivery in Fragile Situations', *DIIS Report* 2013:24, Copenhagen, 2013, p. 47.

2013, this focus took up an estimated 75 per cent of the RSLAF's resources. While some IMATT advisers may have considered the dominance of the PSO agenda to be too one-dimensional, it gave the RSLAF a purpose, which it had lacked in the early 2000s. As Brigadier Sesay explained: 'If you take the transition period from 2002 to today, we had [played host to] UN peacekeepers, and now we are a major player in peacekeeping ourselves. It's a serious positive'.[132]

The ONS, meanwhile, has experienced considerable challenges since 2010, including the appointment of a new national security co-ordinator in early 2012 and limited receptiveness to its work on the part of the executive, which remained in the hands of the APC. Indeed, the role of the ONS had changed since it was first established during the civil war and in the years immediately after: as early as 2005, when the SLPP was still in power, the possibility of renewed conflict was seen as unrealistic, and the executive's attention was shifting to economic development. The 2013–18 'Agenda for Prosperity', which was formulated by the re-elected APC government, cemented this shift in focus and inevitably had consequences for the attention devoted by the executive to the ONS specifically, and to the security sector as a whole. In line with this, the security-sector review produced by the ONS in 2011–12 emphasised the role of the security sector in support of the country's long-term development. Sierra Leonean-led, it was also the manifestation of an organisation which had come into its own, having adapted to new roles and functions.

The greatest changes during this period occurred within CISU. The combined shocks of a new government in 2007, the termination of external funding in 2010, and the relative isolation of CISU from international support were a hard blow. Rather than leading to institutional collapse, however, CISU was able to articulate a clearer organisational identity within the remit of the 2002 National Security and Intelligence Act. This entailed CISU's de facto separation from the ONS and enhanced attempts by CISU to show its 'clients' – that is, government departments – how the organisation could support their work. CISU was able to illustrate that while its operations might be covert, the organisation itself was not, and that as an apolitical body it could play a useful role in preparing intelligence reports upon which relevant government bodies could act. Before the 2012 elections, it had some success in showcasing its capabilities, even if continued doubt and a lack of trust on the part of some elements of the executive meant that parallel systems of politically motivated information-gathering continued to exist. Nevertheless, in 2013

[132] Brima Sesay, working-group meeting, Sierra Leone, February 2014.

the president pledged to make CISU's budget independent from that of the ONS.

Institutional development, adjustment and preservation in an ever-changing context was always going to be a challenge as Sierra Leone moved along the continuum from stabilisation to peace-building to long-term development. As external funding of CISU was terminated, and greatly reduced in the case of the ONS, and as executive interest in the two organisations remained low, questions of funding became critical, as did concern with whether the human resource base could be sustained. For example, the matter of who will prepare and train the next generation within CISU and the ONS remains an open question.

Within the police, a split in focus was emerging over this period: on the one hand, there was a continued rhetorical emphasis on Local Needs Policing; on the other, the poorly managed and rapid expansion of the Operational Support Division meant that the armed wing of the police had grown to more than 4,000 officers.[133] From 2011 onwards, increasing numbers of controversial shooting incidents involving OSD officers exposed their insufficient training and consequent tendency to panic under pressure. Both Local Needs Policing and armed policing remain strong characteristics of policing in Sierra Leone, and it is evident that the inherent contradiction between the two has yet to be dealt with. While there continue to be numerous sources of tension between the police and the public, including petty corruption, curbing the OSD's irregular use of force would help to alleviate some of the most serious of these.

Within a long-term timeframe, one of the most dramatic changes in programming has occurred in the justice sector. There has been a rebalancing from an approach dominated by law and the formal system towards one that incorporates many more local, non-government providers. This partly reflects the justice provision available in most parts of Sierra Leone, but also the negative public perceptions of formal justice in

[133] As noted by Albrecht and Malan in 2006: 'The police are largely unarmed (with the exception of the operational support division amounting to around 30%) and rely on building relations with local communities for intelligence gathering. The decision in 1999 to have a largely unarmed police service deserves special mentioning as something unusual for Africa – and the rest of the world. The underlying rationale of this decision has been that police officers carrying firearms is a barrier to interaction between them and the public.' Peter Albrecht and Mark Malan, 'Post-Conflict Peacebuilding and National Ownership: Meeting the Challenges of Sierra Leone', Center for International Peace Operations, Berlin, 2006, p. 131.

the country.[134] In one way, this may be presented as a shift from a top-down to a bottom-up approach, but it should be noted that the ASJP still incorporates significant support to formal justice provision and ministerial-level oversight.

[134] An Afrobarometer poll undertaken in 2012 shows that 50 per cent of those surveyed think that all or most judges and magistrates are 'involved in corruption'; see Afrobarometer, 'Survey Results: Afrobarometer Round 5 Survey in Sierra Leone, 2012', <www.afrobarometer.org/files/documents/summary_results/srl_r5_sor.pdf>, accessed 14 October 2014; Mohamed Suma, *Sierra Leone: Justice Sector and the Rule of Law*, a review by AfriMAP and the Open Society Initiative for West Africa (Dakar: Open Society Initiative for West Africa, January 2014).

V. UPSTREAM CONFLICT PREVENTION

In 2008, former UK development secretary Clare Short noted in an interview that, in the post-Cold War era, the legitimacy of combining development, foreign policy and military power as an integrated intervention instrument in conflicts overseas was lost. It had been possible in Sierra Leone in the late 1990s, she argued, but with 9/11 and the subsequent wars in Afghanistan and Iraq, the legitimacy of this model had vanished. She would later refer to these events as the 'humanitarian surge and its demise'.[1] The UK government's response to the fundamentally altered context of intervention that emerged in the early-to-mid 2000s was *stabilisation*,[2] a term and set of practices that describe the prevention or reduction of violence, accompanied by socioeconomic programming to develop state legitimacy. Stabilisation was a continuation of the efforts to merge security and development, but with an emphasis on the former over the latter in the context of the wars of the early twenty-first century.

The end of the first decade of the new century, however, saw what may constitute an important, formal shift in the UK's approach following a decade in which international interventions have relied predominantly on military strength. This was manifested in the 2010 Strategic Defence and

---

[1] Peter Albrecht interview with Clare Short, UK, 2008; see also Clare Short, 'A Humanitarian Surge and its Demise, 1997 to 2003: A Personal Account', *Peacebuilding* (Vol. 1, No. 1, 2013), pp. 33–37.

[2] For a broader discussion of UK government stabilisation efforts, see Richard Teuten and Daniel Korski, *Preparing for Peace: Britain's Contribution to Stabilisation*, RUSI Whitehall Paper 74 (London: Taylor and Francis, 2010), pp. iv–177; Foreign Office, MoD, DfID and Stabilisation Unit, 'The UK Government's Approach to Stabilisation', London, 2014, <http://www.stabilisationunit.gov.uk/attachments/article/520/TheUKApproachtoStabilisationMay2014.pdf>, accessed 17 October 2014. Institutionally, the emergence of stabilisation as the primary concept underpinning UK efforts in this area prompted the creation, in 2004, of the Post-Conflict Reconstruction Unit (PCRU) to provide a standing UK civilian capacity for deployment to post-conflict situations. In 2007, the PCRU was renamed the Stabilisation Unit.

Security Review (SDSR) and the 2011 Building Stability Overseas Strategy (BSOS). At the very least, the two White Papers opened debates on what an alternative or more multifaceted approach might look like.

First, the SDSR established the need to 'focus on those fragile and conflict-affected countries where the risks [of instability or insecurity] are high' and noted that to 'help bring enduring stability to such countries, we will increase significantly our support to *conflict prevention* and poverty reduction'.[3] The concept of 'upstreaming' was then fully articulated a year later in the BSOS as a joint initiative between the UK Ministry of Defence (MoD), the Department for International Development (DfID) and the Foreign Office. 'Investing in upstream prevention', the BSOS states, means 'helping to build strong, legitimate institutions and robust societies in fragile countries that are capable of managing tensions and shocks so there is a lower likelihood of instability and conflict'.[4]

'Upstream conflict prevention', significant for its emphasis on prevention, may be defined as 'a long-term approach that seeks to understand and respond to the *underlying causes* of conflict and instability *before* they result in violence'.[5] Strictly speaking, therefore, security-sector reform (SSR) and development efforts in Sierra Leone since the 1990s cannot be characterised as upstreaming, since the process began downstream, during open conflict and as a peace-making effort. However, as Saferworld – an influential peace-building non-governmental organisation (NGO) in the UK – has pointed out, a 'defining feature of an "upstream" approach is not when in the conflict cycle it takes place, but that it seeks to address the underlying drivers of conflict'.[6] In this light, the experience in Sierra Leone offers important lessons for the practical application of upstream conflict prevention. Indeed, when analysed more closely, it is clear that the fundamental principles of upstreaming match those which have variously shaped elements of SSR programming in Sierra Leone over the years, such as the necessity of being context sensitive, holistic and people-centred.[7] This shows that, far from constituting an entirely new concept, the building blocks of upstreaming have been part of long-term and evolving policy developments in the UK and elsewhere *vis-à-vis* intervention in fragile situations since the end of the Cold War.

---

[3] HM Government, *Securing Britain in an Age of Austerity: The Strategic Defence and Security Review*, Cm 7948 (London: The Stationery Office, October 2010), p. 44. Emphasis added.

[4] *Ibid.*, p. 18.

[5] Saferworld, 'Upstream Conflict Prevention', <http://www.saferworld.org.uk/what/upstream-conflict-prevention-1>, accessed 17 October 2014. Emphasis added.

[6] Saferworld, 'Upstream Conflict Prevention: Addressing the Root Causes of Conflict', Saferworld Briefing, September 2012.

[7] *Ibid.*

This chapter outlines in detail how components of upstream conflict prevention are reflected in the past fifteen years of SSR in Sierra Leone, which began before both stabilisation and upstreaming entered mainstream policy discourse. It first emphasises the historicity of the concept of upstreaming and then discusses a number of its characteristics, including context sensitivity, being holistic, and taking a people-centred approach to programming and intervention.

Rebranding Old Principles of the Security-Development Nexus

Upstreaming constitutes a shift in policy thinking from the past 10–12 years of intervention, but the concept is not fundamentally new. It articulates a key lesson learnt by UK policy-makers since the end of the Cold War – namely, that international interventions, including in the security sphere, are more likely to succeed if they go beyond military engagement and involve diplomatic efforts and development expertise (the combination of which, as noted above – and as discussed in greater detail in Chapters I and II – was the underlying rationale for the UK's involvement in Sierra Leone in the late 1990s).

The notion of upstreaming further nuances this conception of what constitutes an effective intervention in its emphasis on preventive measures, and specifically the underlying drivers of conflict. As such, upstream conflict prevention reflects a growing reluctance in the global North to intervene militarily in complex conflict environments. Of course, and as the current US-led military campaign against the extreme Sunni insurgent group ISIS shows,[8] military force remains an essential instrument in response to insecurity.[9] However, the intention is that upstream conflict prevention will be a stronger fixture of international interventions, in recognition of the fact that violence and conflict rarely arise spontaneously; rather, they often have deep roots in the way that political power and wealth are distributed.

Indeed, this recent shift in policy suggests that development practices may once again be coming to the fore in setting the agenda for security-related programming, as was the case in the late 1990s and early 2000s. However, for this to happen development agencies will require the necessary space – in both political and policy terms – in which to define an approach to national security matters on their own terms. As long as development is subordinated to a militarised security agenda this will not be possible.

---

[8] The Islamic State of Iraq and Syria, also known as the Islamic State. See Adam Withnall, 'Iraq Crisis: Isis Declares its Territories a New Islamic State with "Restoration of Caliphate" in Middle East', *Independent*, 30 June 2014.

[9] Patrick Cockburn, 'War against Isis: US Air Strategy in Tatters as Militants March On', *Independent*, 12 October 2014.

SSR in Sierra Leone: Merging the Security and Development Agendas
Before the full impact of 9/11 was felt on international policy-making, and before military force came to dominate intervention in fragile contexts, it was DfID that – to a large extent – drove the SSR agenda,[10] both in the UK and in multilateral forums such as the Organisation for Economic Co-operation and Development (OECD), the UN and the EU. Thus the emphasis was on a process that is governance-oriented, holistic and multi-layered (see Chapter I for discussion on this point).[11]

At the time, critics saw the merging of security and development, which SSR came to represent, as the progressive 'securitisation of development'.[12] Indeed, it was increasingly accepted in policy circles that there was a causal connection between poverty and insecurity, with the former having previously been seen as 'merely' an issue of inequality and injustice.[13]

However, precisely because the SSR concept emerged from within a government department focused on international development, it could also be said that SSR – as it was practised in the late 1990s to mid-2000s – was an attempt to 'developmentalise security'.[14] Development agencies, and DfID in particular, were redefining the ways in which security actors should be engaged in fragile situations. Key to this 'developmentalisation' of security, as with the more recent policy of upstream conflict prevention,

---

[10] While space does not allow a detailed discussion of the period in international politics between the end of the Cold War and the beginning of the War on Terror, it is clear that the decade between 1991 and 2001 was unique. Clare Short explains: 'With no great conflict dividing the world, there was an increasing possibility that reducing poverty and creating a more equitable world order might become the focus of international policy'. Clare Short, 'Foreword', in Mark Sedra (ed.), *The Future of Security Sector Reform* (Ontario: Centre for Governance Innovation, 2010), pp. 10–14. It was in this context that security support was emerging as a mechanism to advance development and peace-building.

[11] Jennifer Sugden, 'Security Sector Reform: The Role of Epistemic Communities in the UK', *Journal of Security Sector Management* (Vol. 4, No. 4, November 2006), pp. 1–19.

[12] Mark Duffield, *Global Governance and the New Wars: The Merging of Development and Security* (London and New York, NY: Zed Books, 2001); Frances Stewart, 'Development and Security', *Conflict, Security and Development* (Vol. 4, No. 3, 2004), pp. 261–88; Lars Buur, Steffen Jensen and Finn Stepputat (eds), *The Security-Development Nexus: Expressions of Sovereignty and Securitization in Southern Africa* (Uppsala and Cape Town: Nordic Africa Institute and HSRC Press, 2007).

[13] Peter Albrecht and Finn Stepputat, 'The Rise and Fall of Security Sector Reform in Development', in Paul Jackson (ed.), *Handbook of International Security and Development* (Cheltenham: Edward Elgar Publishing, 2015).

[14] *Ibid.*

was the commitment to a holistic approach:[15] that is, the establishment of a system of institutions, governed by civilians, that can meet the demands of internal and external security. At its heart is the recognition that the provision of technical support to security systems, such as train-and-equip programmes, is not enough; *governance* lies at the core of SSR, thus setting this reform process apart from other approaches.

In addition, from DfID's perspective, it was part of the appeal of SSR that it provided the department with a way of increasing its own political clout and influence within the field of international security. The Africa Conflict Prevention Pool, which was established in 2001 to encourage cross-Whitehall collaboration between the Foreign Office, DfID and the MoD, is a case in point. As Clare Short observed in 2008:[16]

> I don't think the spend out of the Conflict Prevention Pools was ever the significant one, it was a small amount of money, it was peanuts; we could've financed Sierra Leone out of our own pockets. It was the leverage of the Department's engagement. The Foreign Office was obsessed with the money, but we knew what we were doing, we knew it was leverage. So, of course, getting all departments thinking together about an issue isn't always an issue about spending.

Funding SSR programming in Sierra Leone – and the International Military Advisory and Training Team (IMATT), in particular[17] – became one of the

---

[15] Chris Smith, 'Security-Sector Reform: Development Breakthrough or Institutional Engineering?', *Conflict, Security and Development* (Vol. 1, No. 1, 2001), pp. 5–20.

[16] Albrecht interview with Clare Short. The tri-departmental Africa Conflict Prevention Pool, together with the Global Conflict Prevention Pool, was established by the 2000 Spending Review, and commenced operation in 2001. In 2007–08, these were merged to create the Conflict Prevention Pool and a Stabilisation Aid Fund was created to work in 'hot' conflict zones, specifically Iraq and Afghanistan. In turn, in 2009, the Stabilisation Aid Fund and Conflict Prevention Pool were merged under the Conflict Pool. This will be replaced by a new £1 billion Conflict, Stability and Security Fund (CSSF) in April 2015. Independent Commission for Aid Impact, 'Evaluation of the Inter-Departmental Conflict Pool', Report 12, July 2012, <http://icai.independent.gov.uk/wp-content/uploads/2012/07/Evaluation-of-the-Inter-Departmental-Conflict-Pool-ICAI-Report1.pdf>, accessed 17 October 2014; *Hansard*, House of Commons, Col. 121WS (19 December 2013).

[17] Between 2002 and 2008, IMATT cost between £10–16 million, while in 2012–2013, the price was indicated to be £4.6 million. UK Government, 'Sierra Leone: Africa Conflict Prevention Pool Bids for 2003-2004', Freetown, 19 December 2002; IMATT, 'IMATT (SL) Plan 2010 – Report 05', Freetown, 30 September 2005, unpublished; IMATT, 'International Military Advisory and Training Team (Sierra Leone) Transition Study – Terms of Reference', Freetown, 15 December 2011, unpublished. ACPP budget allocations for the years 2002–08 were listed in September 2004 to be between £50 million and £64.5 million. In addition to programme funding, the Africa Conflict Prevention Pool also provided funding for peace support operations. DfID, MoD and Foreign Office, 'The Africa Conflict

primary aims of the Africa Conflict Prevention Pool and through it, the three departments invariably came to play a central role in driving SSR forward, both in practice and in policy terms. Furthermore, as development once again comes to the fore of UK intervention policy, it is clear that some of the fundamental elements of SSR during this period have since been recycled to flesh out the recent policy concept of upstreaming.[18]

In the following sections, various dimensions of upstream conflict prevention are examined in relation to the experience of SSR in Sierra Leone, including context specificity, the importance of taking a holistic and people-centred approach, and the need for commitment over a prolonged period.[19] The 2011 BSOS was criticised for failing to provide adequate guidance as to how upstream conflict prevention should be operationalised;[20] however, this chapter aims to demonstrate that, in fact, many of this new policy's principles are well known within the peacebuilding community,[21] having been discussed and applied at different times during the course of SSR in Sierra Leone.

Sensitivity to Context

The underlying drivers of conflict vary, and so the requirement for in-depth knowledge of the context in which they occur is a cornerstone in development thinking. 'It is essential for international actors to understand the specific context in each country', the OECD notes in its 2007 guidance on engaging in fragile situations, 'and [to] develop a shared view of the strategic response that is required'.[22] Numerous international guidelines and blueprints for interventions exist (such as the UN's Responsibility to Protect,[23]

Prevention Pool – An Information Document: A Joint UK Government Approach to Preventing and Reducing Conflict in Sub-Saharan Africa', London, September 2004.

[18] See Nicole Ball, 'Enhancing Security Sector Governance: A Conceptual Framework for UNDP', UNDP, New York, 9 October 2002.

[19] See, for example, Saferworld, 'Upstream Conflict Prevention: Addressing the Root Causes of Conflict'.

[20] Jeremy Allouche, 'Building Stability Overseas: Shifts in UK Strategy and Suggestions for Implementation', OpenDemocracy.net, 14 April 2012, <http://www.opendemocracy.net/jeremy-allouche/building-stability-overseas-shifts-in-uk-strategy-and-suggestions-for-implementation>, accessed 17 October 2014.

[21] International Alert, Conciliation Resources and Saferworld, 'Investing in Long-Term Peace? The New Conflict, Stability and Security Fund', September 2014.

[22] Organisation for Economic Co-operation and Development (OECD), 'Principles for Good International Engagement in Fragile States and Situations', Paris, April 2007.

[23] Louise Riis Andersen and Peter Emil Engdal, 'Blue Helmets and Grey Zones: Do UN Multidimensional Peace Operations Work?', *DIIS Report* 2013:29, Copenhagen, 2013, p. 29; Gareth Evans, 'The Responsibility to Protect: Ending Mass Atrocity Crimes Once and for All', *Irish Studies in International Affairs* (Vol. 20, No. 1, 2009), pp. 7–13; Richard H Cooper and Juliette Voïnov Kohler (eds), *Responsibility*

for example), but they cannot substitute for a well-grounded understanding of the local cultural, social and political dynamics. It is therefore not surprising that context sensitivity is considered a hallmark of the policy of upstreaming.

Looking to the UK's experience in Sierra Leone, the evolution of the intervention in the early years appears – on the surface, at least – to have been context-sensitive, with DfID, the Foreign Office and the MoD proving both able and willing to react to events as they unfolded. Indeed, benefiting from unique political backing from Whitehall, an initial evacuation mission quickly turned into a military intervention and, ultimately, into a long-term development mission. However, it could be argued that the three departments had little choice but to respond to the changes in circumstance and it is, of course, important not to conflate a willingness to react with context sensitivity. Whitehall's knowledge of Sierra Leone in the late 1990s was relatively poor. Thus, early developments in the UK's intervention were not driven by the government departments, but were the result of advisers reacting to changes on the ground and, suitably empowered, occasionally making decisions that contradicted Whitehall instructions. (This was compounded by the fact that DfID did not have a permanent presence in Sierra Leone until 2005.)

How far the early stages of the Sierra Leone intervention constituted a truly context-sensitive approach is thus a matter for debate. It is certainly clear that the adoption of the liberal-democratic state as the model for the delivery of security and justice in the country reflected the experience of external actors, rather than of Sierra Leoneans, regarding what order means and how it should be constituted.[24] This highlights a fundamental question about the pursuit of context sensitivity: how far, and in what ways, should development efforts be shaped by the context in which they are being implemented? Should political life in the aftermath of conflict be wholly defined by that context and by what is possible politically, economically, socially and culturally? Or should the same broad working

---

to Protect: The Global Moral Compact for the 21st Century (London: Palgrave Macmillan, 2009).

[24] Louise Riis Andersen refers to the 'liberal template for intervention', which reflects two fundamental assumptions: 'Firstly, the idea that *security and development are inextricably linked* and indivisible: One cannot be pursued without the other. Secondly, the idea that *democratization* of war-torn societies will enhance peace, order and stability both at the domestic level and internationally. The first idea is widely referred to as the "security-development nexus", whereas the second idea is known as the "liberal peace thesis".' Louise Riis Andersen, 'Security Sector Reform and the Dilemmas of Liberal Peacebuilding', *DIIS Working Paper* 2011:31, Copenhagen, 2011, p. 5. See also Peter Albrecht and Paul Jackson, 'State-Building through Security Sector Reform', *Peacebuilding* (Vol. 2, No. 1, 2014), pp. 83–99, 95.

definition of how a state operates be applied in all cases, but with adjustment according to the context? It is the latter approach which appears to have dominated state-building efforts in the past 10–15 years.[25]

Settling on the right approach to state-building is also dependent on what can feasibly be achieved by an external state actor, given the inevitable limitations of its knowledge, expertise and power – and the parameters within which it must work. These in turn condition the extent to which such actors can take a context-sensitive approach. For example, and as evident in the case of Sierra Leone, donors are under a number of pressures to promote the liberal-democratic state model. First of all, the international system in which they operate is governed by state-to-state interaction, which in itself limits how much they can pursue an alternative model, regardless of the previous experience of the recipient country. In addition, donors are driven by domestic political agendas and bureaucratic practices, and therefore often try to build other states along similar lines.[26] Moreover, since their funding is derived from taxpayers, donors are relatively risk averse in terms of experimenting with alternative forms of political organisation.[27] From this perspective, the promotion of liberal-democratic ideals and the establishment of a centrally governed state as the primary focus of service provision is a reasonable approach; however, it also seeks to export a particular variety of government to countries where it may not previously have been the norm. As such, considerable modifications must be made to this approach, on a case-by-case basis, if it is to be sensitive to context in its application.

In Sierra Leone, there are a number of examples of model institutional structures being applied in order to serve a particular purpose, even though they had not existed prior to the country's civil war. The Sierra Leonean MoD, Office of National Security (ONS) and Central Intelligence

---

[25] This approach has been debated in a broad range of academic literature. See, for example, Francis Fukuyama, *State Building: Governance and World Order in the Twenty-First Century* (London: Penguin Books, 2004); Pierre Englebert and Denis M Tull, 'Postconflict Reconstruction in Africa: Flawed Ideas about Failed States', *International Security* (Vol. 32, No. 4, 2008), pp. 106–39; Ashraf Ghani and Clare Lockhart, *Fixing Failed States: A Framework for Rebuilding a Fractured World* (Oxford: Oxford University Press, 2009).

[26] Lisa Denney, *Justice and Security Reform: Development Agencies and Informal Institutions in Sierra Leone* (Oxford and New York, NY: Routledge, 2014), p. 134; Michael N Barnett and Martha Finnemore, 'The Politics, Power and Pathologies of International Organizations', *International Organization* (Vol. 53, No. 4, Autumn 1999), pp. 699–732; Peter Albrecht et al., *Perspectives on Involving Non-State and Customary Actors in Justice and Security Reform* (Rome and Copenhagen: International Development Law Organization and Danish Institute for International Studies, 2011).

[27] Peter Albrecht and Helene Maria Kyed, 'Justice and Security: When the State isn't the Main Provider', *DIIS Policy Brief*, Copenhagen, December 2010.

and Security Unit (CISU), for example, were all externally driven solutions to bureaucratic collapse in Sierra Leone and reflected an attempt to recentralise the state. These have met with varying degrees of success. The MoD's integrated civilian-military organisational structure – built around a British model of democratic oversight of the armed forces – was established to oversee and manage RSLAF affairs. Yet this model was never fully accepted in Sierra Leone: whilst the MoD still stands, the number of civilians now working within it is small. This does not mean that creating the MoD in this manner was not the logical thing to do, given the need to exert control over the army, which had been a politically destabilising factor in Sierra Leone throughout the 1990s. From that perspective, its establishment with central civilian involvement served a distinct and vital purpose.

The ONS and CISU, meanwhile, have experienced relative political isolation under both the Sierra Leone People's Party (SLPP) and All People's Congress (APC) governments since their creation. They have had to find their feet in a context that has changed gradually but consistently since the war ended in January 2002. Indeed, economic development has increasingly overtaken security as the priority of the Government of Sierra Leone, while international support has also been significantly reduced in the case of the ONS, and has disappeared entirely in the case of CISU.

What these deliberations show is that a dose of realism is required with regard to context sensitivity, which is integral to the framework of upstream conflict prevention. It remains a question whether sensitivity to context means genuine support for 'local solutions to security challenges' or simply implies 'winning acquiescence for externally generated policies'.[28] Furthermore, it must be carefully considered whether Western states and international organisations have the necessary instruments in their state-building tool boxes to pursue the former rather than the latter.[29]

A Holistic Approach

An inherent weakness of taking a holistic approach is the scope implied and the lack of clarity about what this means in practice for programming upstream conflict prevention. From an SSR perspective, according to the OECD DAC Handbook on Security System Reform, it is SSR's overarching objective to pursue 'holistic and comprehensive reform', which is collated within 'a system-wide approach'.[30] Two primary implications of this

---

[28] Daniel Bendix and Ruth Stanley, 'Deconstructing Local Ownership of Security Sector Reform: A Review of the Literature', *African Security Review* (Vol. 17, No. 2, 2008), pp. 93–104.

[29] Andersen, 'Security Sector Reform and the Dilemmas of Liberal Peacebuilding', pp. 15–16.

[30] OECD, 'The OECD DAC Handbook on Security System Reform: Supporting Security and Justice', Paris, 2007, p. 29.

approach are, first, the ambition to integrate 'all those partial reforms such as defence reform, police reform, intelligence reform and justice reform, which in the past were generally seen and conducted as separate efforts'. Second, underlying the holistic approach is a normative commitment to the 'consolidation of democracy, promotion of human rights and implementation of the principles of good governance such as accountability and transparency'.[31] From this, it is clear that holistic programming, whether in the security sector or beyond, requires the involvement of a wide range of stakeholders, an understanding of how they are connected and an appreciation of the ways in which they affect one another.

There are a number of obvious challenges involved in pursuing holistic programming. First, entry points are uneven, meaning that it may be politically possible to engage with individual security and justice actors, but not to encompass the security and justice system in its entirety. Another challenge is the resources and levels of collaboration needed between programmes and different donor agencies in the pursuit of a 'system-wide approach', which requires different governments or government departments that may have fundamentally different agendas to collaborate. As such, a comment made by Marina Caparina, an SSR expert, in 2004 still holds true today: namely that 'SSR as it aspires to be – holistically conceptualized, planned and implemented – has so far rarely been undertaken or achieved in practice'.[32] At the same time, as discussed throughout this Whitehall Paper, it is also the case that several of the programmes implemented as part of SSR, whether individually or collectively, aspired to be and were labelled as holistic.[33]

For instance, as outlined in Chapters II and III, the Justice and Security Development Programme (JSDP), which began implementation in 2005, was presented as the first holistic justice-sector programme in Sierra Leone (succeeding the Commonwealth Community Safety and Security Project – CCSSP – and the Law Development Programme). As such, it was designed to cut across the Ministry of Internal Affairs, the

---

[31] Heiner Hänggi, 'Conceptualising Security Sector Reform and Reconstruction', in Alan Bryden and Heiner Hänggi (eds), *Reform and Reconstruction of the Security Sector* (Munster: LIT Verlag, 2004), pp. 1–11, 5.

[32] Marina Caparini, 'The Relevance of Civil Society: Response to "Security Sector Reform in Developing and Transitional Countries"', in Clem McCarthy, Martina Fischer and Oliver Wils (eds), 'Security Sector Reform: Potentials and Challenges for Conflict Transformation', *Berghof Handbook for Conflict Transformation* (No. 2, 2004), pp. 53–61.

[33] As Chris Smith noted in 2001: 'What is lacking … are explicit examples of holistic and integrated programmes that meet the now accepted intellectual criteria. In this respect, Sierra Leone is the exception that proves the rule. Arguably this will continue to be the case, primarily due to cost. Smith, 'Security-Sector Reform', p. 14.

police, the judiciary, the prisons service and civil society, and to work at the national and local levels, primarily but not exclusively in Moyamba District, simultaneously. A holistic approach may have been the foundation stone of the JSDP. It was also clear, however, that even though positive changes were made in people's access to justice, there were considerable challenges in making sustainable, systemic change across the justice sector within the timeframe of a six-year programme (2005–11). Unlike preceding programmes, the JSDP manifested an explicit recognition of the fact that systemic changes are needed to enhance overall access to security and justice at the local level. It has also proven that even though a holistic approach is taken, difficult prioritisations and estimates still need to be made about the point of focus.

The JSDP's successor, the Access to Security and Justice Programme (ASJP), is also a sprawling programme, and without due attention there is a risk that it will face challenges similar to its predecessor in terms of limitations on its ability to prioritise. These challenges are accentuated by a variety of circumstances that inevitably delay or slow down implementation, especially the time that it takes for a new programme to build up relations and trust with national partners. In the case of the ASJP, for instance, while working relations with the Sierra Leone Police (SLP) were established relatively quickly, this was not the case with respect to the judiciary, primarily due to interference in judicial affairs by the political elite (see Chapter IV for further discussion). This underscores the argument made above that entry points are uneven and, indeed, that political interests often get in the way of working with one or more key partners. It also means that taking a holistic approach is not a technical matter – it can be built into the programme design, it can be an ambition, but only as implementation is initiated will it become clear what lies within the realm of the possible.

While the JSDP and the ASJP represent DfID's interpretation of what holistic programming implies, and in the process draw on UK and international policy developments, the comprehensive set of programmes that were launched in the late 1990s and early 2000s collectively exhibited characteristics of being holistic. National security, intelligence, civilian-military dimensions of the Sierra Leonean MoD, army, police and judiciary were targeted through a patchwork of programmes: the Sierra Leone Security Sector Reform Programme (SILSEP), IMATT, the CCSSP and the Law Development Programme, which was much smaller in scope than the three others. This conglomerate of several substantial programmes had remarkable range and incorporated resources, human and financial, from all of the three main departments: DfID, MoD and the Foreign Office. The four programmes were not designed to engage directly at the local level and, in particular with respect to the CCSSP, a trickle-down effect was assumed from establishing functioning institutions at the centre. However, their combined foci give a good impression of what being holistic meant as programmes were implemented in the late 1990s and early 2000s.[34]

Processes at the strategic level of the Sierra Leone government were reinforced by the integration of these programmes – which were themselves reinforced by this integration. For instance, the link between security and development was made explicit with the security-sector review carried out between 2003 and 2005 at the behest of and with support from UK advisers in the ONS. In turn, the security-sector review informed Sierra Leone's 2005 Poverty Reduction Strategy Paper (PRSP). This process forced debates on which ministries, departments and agencies to engage in SSR and their reciprocal roles, bringing greater clarity on how the security system as a whole did and should operate. In addition, it played an important role in clarifying the co-ordination function of the ONS, at the time a new and central institution in the Sierra Leone national security architecture.

Of course, one criticism of the UK's efforts in Sierra Leone since the late 1990s was the imbalance of the initial approach, characterised by a focus on the institutional revival of the police and military. This meant that further down the line, the justice sector would have to play 'catch-up' – and it continues to do so to this day. This has caused unnecessary friction within the broader security and justice sector, further emphasising the continued desirability of a holistic approach. The experience has also demonstrated the reality that undertaking reform of entire political systems (including establishing civilian control over the military, intelligence services and justice systems) is not a linear or a predictable process. It is clear that these processes take different amounts of time, develop in different ways and garner differing levels of domestic political buy-in. This constitutes another hurdle to reform efforts: it is important to recognise that being holistic is not an end in itself, if the component parts of that approach are carried out inconsistently and prove unsustainable.

Looking more broadly still it was evident to the UK in the late 1990s that stabilising Sierra Leone and restraining the political ambitions of the armed forces would be a more manageable process than establishing the basis of a thriving national economy and addressing social and economic inequality.[35] Yet economic development and the nurturing of social justice

---

[34] *Ibid.*

[35] Growth in the country's GDP has varied between 4 and 7 per cent since the end of the war in 2002, and it rose dramatically to 15.2 per cent in 2012 due to the commencement of iron ore production.

are also two key elements of the holistic approach to state-building – whether in prevention of or in the aftermath of conflict.[36] Indeed, unemployment and weak economic growth are often significant factors within state fragility. For instance, the distribution of wealth remains notably uneven in Sierra Leone, which is partly driven by the persistence of a consolidated system of patronage.[37] Of concern is that this was considered to be one of the primary drivers of the conflict in the 1990s, with William Reno, for example, explaining that the 'shadow state' collapsed due to the significant accumulation of riches by the powerful few; a minuscule and shrinking formal economy; accelerating mass impoverishment; and a crushing debt burden.[38] Today, therefore, the fear is that this source of tension could once again eventually lead to conflict in Sierra Leone, as it did more than twenty years ago.[39] Thus, the policy of upstream conflict prevention necessarily embraces the development of economic infrastructure and trade relations, measures to address social and economic inequalities, and an examination of international trade restrictions and controls.

The Sierra Leone experience questions the assumption that development follows from security, and on a general level, upstream conflict prevention, with its emphasis on being holistic, also does this. In the same vein, it raises questions about the timing of implementation of programmes aimed at restarting the economy, and the results of such efforts. Ultimately, it is argued, the holistic approach is no panacea, and certainly a systemic approach still requires that difficult prioritisations are made.

Top-Down and Bottom-Up: Meeting in the Middle

The history of external intervention in fragile states shows clearly that success depends on the active support of local populations rather than buy-in at the elite level alone, which in any case may be difficult to achieve to the degree required. It is also clear that for long-term development to occur, the expansion of national ownership to incorporate wider civil-society groups is essential, as is popular participation in decision-making processes. This, therefore, requires reform efforts to go

---

36 Saferworld, 'Upstream Conflict Prevention'.

37 Franck Perrault et al., 'Sierra Leone Country Strategy Paper 2013–2017', African Development Bank Group, August 2013, p. 6.

38 William Reno, *Corruption and State Politics in Sierra Leone* (Cambridge: Cambridge University Press, 1996). See also Paul Jackson and Peter Albrecht, *Reconstructing Security After Conflict: Security Sector Reform in Sierra Leone* (Houndmills: Palgrave Macmillan, 2011), p. 6.

39 Paul Richards, *Fighting for the Rain Forest: War, Youth and Resources in Sierra Leone* (Oxford: International African Institute/James Currey, 1996); Krijn Peters, *War and the Crisis of Youth in Sierra Leone* (Cambridge: Cambridge University Press, 2011).

beyond simply constructing state institutions and expecting them to develop into functioning political entities that serve the public by delivering services.[40] In Sierra Leone in the late 1990s, police reform was concentrated around training the top cadre in order to give the SLP a strong, strategy-focused leadership. The underlying assumption was that improved capacity at the top would then trickle down through the ranks.[41] However, it has become clear over time that this has not occurred. Therefore, a people-centred approach is required, involving direct engagement with communities and those lower down the institutional 'ranks' as an explicit part of programming.

The main purpose of SSR in Sierra Leone in the early years of British engagement was to establish a state-centred security system that would replace the chaos of war and state collapse with a functioning and stabilising security system.[42] While IMATT and its successor, the International Security Advisory Team (ISAT), have consistently focused on the strategic level, working with national-level actors, DfID programming in the justice sector has taken a gradually more people-centred approach since 2005.

This programme reorientation from a state-centric to a people-centred approach – part of a wider reorientation by DfID from strategic-level SSR in the late 1990s and early 2000s to justice-sector reform at the local level in the mid-2000s[43] – opened up engagement with a variety of Sierra Leonean actors who, in one way or another, are involved in providing justice and security at the local level, notably paramount and lesser chiefs. In turn, this shift in focus reflected policy developments at the international level. For instance, in 2006, the OECD published a report calling for what was referred to as a 'multi-layered' approach to reforming security- and justice-sector services.[44] Drawing on a definition of non-state actors presented by DfID in 2004,[45] the report concluded that both

---

[40] Peter Albrecht, 'Local Actors and Service Delivery in Fragile Situations', *DIIS Report* 2013:24, Copenhagen, 2013.

[41] Peter Alexander Albrecht, 'Transforming Internal Security in Sierra Leone: Sierra Leone Police and Broader Justice Sector Reform', *DIIS Report* 2010:07, Copenhagen, 2010, p. 9.

[42] Albrecht and Jackson, 'State-Building through Security Sector Reform'.

[43] For instance, see DfID, 'Poverty and the Security Sector', London, 1999, <http://www.gsdrc.org/docs/open/cc111.pdf>, accessed 17 October 2014; DfID, *Eliminating World Poverty: Building Our Common Future*, Cm 7656 (London: Department for International Development, 2009).

[44] Eric Scheye and Andrew McLean, 'Enhancing the Delivery of Justice and Security in Fragile States', OECD, Paris, 2006.

[45] In 2004, DfID published its first coherent briefing on the issue, 'Non-State Justice and Security Systems'. It suggests that security and justice institutions presided over by non-state actors are 'critically important in the context of DfID's pro-poor approach to security and justice.' These actors, the briefing note

statutory and non-statutory providers should be engaged in reform efforts in order to target 'the multiple points where service occurs and strengthens the linkages between state institutions and local justice and non-state providers'.[46] As argued by Bruce Baker and Eric Scheye in 2007, this approach was developed to remedy the previous 'state-centric bias' in SSR policy, which was seen to contradict the 'development principles of a "people-centred", locally owned' process.[47]

Both the JSDP and the ASJP (initiated in 2005 and 2012, respectively) were built around this reorientation towards local needs and local actors, and were based on a fundamental assumption that there may be neither the will nor the capacity among the political elite within many states in the global South to play this role.[48] Thus, in December 2005, a 'National Policy Framework for the Justice Sector in Sierra Leone' was established as part of the JSDP framework, setting out a 'holistic sector-wide approach to support the development of an effective, efficient, impartial and accountable Justice Sector that is capable of meeting the needs of all people of Sierra Leone'.[49] This would include 'Customary/Traditional Laws and Practices' to 'improve public satisfaction levels with Local Courts, Paramount and Local Chiefs',[50] and a strong emphasis on civil society. Similarly, the ASJP was formally built around 'a local approach to problem solving', emphasising the inclusion of paralegal and mediator organisations, as well as the Local Policing Partnership Boards (LPPBs).[51] The latter were established by the SLP leadership in the early 2000s as 'part of the community policing strategy aimed at involving non-police stakeholders in security and crime prevention',[52] thus serving as a mechanism for 'investigat[ing] and resolv[ing] conflict between

continues, 'deal with the vast majority of disputes' and are 'widely used in rural and poor urban areas, where there is often minimal access to formal state justice'. The briefing recognises that this approach to reform is politicised – being neither neutral nor technical – and that it raises broader governance issues. DfID, 'Non-State Justice and Security Systems', briefing, 2004, <http://www.gsdrc.org/docs/open/ssaj101.pdf>, accessed 17 October 2014.

[46] GFN-SSR, 'Supporting State and Non-State Provision of Security and Justice', 2007.

[47] Bruce Baker and Eric Scheye, 'Multi-Layered Justice and Security Delivery in Post-Conflict and Fragile States', *Conflict, Security and Development* (Vol. 7, No. 4, 2007), pp. 503–28, 503.

[48] Peter Albrecht and Lars Buur, 'An Uneasy Marriage: Non-State Actors and Police Reform', *Policing and Society* (Vol. 19, No. 4, December 2009), pp. 390–405, 397.

[49] British Council, 'National Policy Framework for the Justice Sector in Sierra Leone', Freetown, December 2005, unpublished.

[50] Government of Sierra Leone, 'Justice Sector Reform Strategy and Investment Plan 2008–2010', Freetown, December 2007, p. v.

[51] Libra Advisory Group, 'Interim Program Document for Improved Access to Security and Justice Programme – Sierra Leone', London, unpublished, p. 8.

[52] SLP, 'Sierra Leone Police Strategic Plan (2010–2011)', Freetown, 2009, p. ii.

members of the community', and 'increas[ing] the level of interaction between the police and the local communities'.[53]

This stronger emphasis on work with traditional leaders, local courts and LPPBs was facilitated by a people-centred orientation and was underpinned by the perception that programming should be demand-driven. While based on sound analysis and a conviction that services should be improved at the point where they 'meet' the end-user, this also meant that support to the OSD and CISU, for instance, was phased out and terminated by the mid-2000s, as DfID drew down its strategic-level support. Out of this gap in support, and in response to the need for a successor to IMATT, grew the concept of the International Security Advisory Team (ISAT). Although DfID was consulted, it was not closely involved in ISAT's design. When IMATT's successor was launched, its focus and structure reflected the genuine need (perceived most acutely by the UK MoD and Foreign Office) to engage at the strategic level across the security sector.

In sum, the Sierra Leone experience shows that what is needed is a combination of top-down and bottom-up approaches, working strategically at the national level as well as more closely at the local level with those who are to benefit from support. As SSR expert Louise Riis Andersen observes, this requires the amalgamation of two essentially conflicting models: one that 'focuses on restoring the state's monopoly on the means of violence and a hybrid model that seeks to strengthen local community-based security and justice solutions'.[54] As Andersen further argues, this is ultimately a choice between direct and indirect forms of rule where the former requires the elimination of non-state authority and the creation of uniform standards of governance, while the latter recognises de facto (often local) authorities, such as chiefs, with the 'acceptance of different standards and conditions for different segments of the population'.[55]

The notion of upstreaming does not solve the fundamental dilemma between promoting a liberal-democratic state model top-down and promoting a model that emphasises a people-centred approach that is built from below. Indeed, precisely how to do so has, as indicated above, been a central discussion point in the SSR debate for the past decade, impacting directly on programming in Sierra Leone.[56] For instance, it is reflected practically in DfID's contemporary people-centred approach to security and justice programming and in ISAT's strategic focus at the

[53] SLP, 'Local Policing Partnership Board Constitution', Freetown, 2011, p. 3.

[54] Andersen, 'Security Sector Reform and the Dilemmas of Liberal Peacebuilding', p. 4.

[55] *Ibid.*, p. 15.

[56] One of the key experts in this debate was part of the team that designed the ASJP in 2010.

national level. It will be one of the challenges of upstream conflict prevention to ensure that top-down and bottom-up programming are both pursued.

One step in that direction could be to change Western perceptions of what the state is and should be and to stop making clear-cut distinctions between the 'state' and the 'non-state'. The point is that no local service provider acts independently of the broader system of governance in which it operates. As a rule, local service providers are part of an extensive governance system that incorporates a variety of both centrally and locally embedded organisations and institutions. The systemic nature of public services must be central to any programming endeavour that seeks to enhance service delivery, including the varied nature of the actors that constitute this system.[57]

Upstreaming is a Long-Term Commitment

It is widely understood that building the capacity of legitimate public-service providers takes longer than a three-to-five-year programme cycle; however, programming, particularly in development, continues to be governed by such timeframes. The ten-year Memorandum of Understanding agreed between the UK and Sierra Leone in 2002 was in this respect unusual and has ensured that the former's commitment at the political level has been long term. Indeed, by 2002, IMATT had been providing support to the defence-reform process for two years, while DfID had been supporting police reform and strategic SSR since 1997 and 1999, respectively – elements of which have continued to the present day. However, while long-term commitment to security and justice reform has been a feature of UK support, the consistency of direction that this support has taken is worth exploring in more detail.

With respect to police and broader justice-sector development, for instance, despite long-term commitment, work carried out on the basis of programme cycles has been criticised for abrupt changes of direction, poor management of difficult and sensitive programme transitions, and for underestimating the time required for the service providers – the organisations that implement on behalf of DfID – to get implementation underway. This was evident as the JSDP took over from the Law Development Programme and the Commonwealth Community Safety and Security Project in March 2005, but also when the JSDP transitioned into the ASJP from 2011, and responsibilities for implementation were handed over from the British Council to DAI.

Different agencies have been involved in these three programme cycles, which have come with different internal management structures,

---

[57] Albrecht, 'Local Actors and Service Delivery in Fragile Situations', p. 5.

guided by different policies, aims and objectives. With respect to the SLP specifically, this has manifested 'a distinct lack of co-ordination over the years'.[58] Indeed, DfID support since the late 1990s has developed from being purely reactive – dealing with the immediate results of bureaucratic collapse and war – to the implementation of programmes aimed at conflict prevention, by transforming the underlying causes of conflict, including improving popular access to justice. In essence, this has constituted a move from strategic state-building to demand-driven and people-centred support. What is notable, however, is that while DfID's commitment to supporting the police and justice-sector actors was never fundamentally in question, the way in which its priorities changed and were translated into programming proved disruptive.

These matters are partly a consequence of staff turnover. At a very basic level, staff within DfID – as well as in the implementing agencies such as the British Council (in the case of the JSDP) and DAI (in the case of the ASJP) – have had to spend time building up local knowledge, establishing relationships with partner organisations and consolidating their presence in Sierra Leone. Additional time has been spent on ensuring transparency, justifying spending and other administrative procedures. While necessary, these processes have nevertheless reduced the time available for learning about the local context, which is crucial to supporting and advocating for social and political transformation – thus representing a real problem given the fixed programme cycle. Moreover, when a new implementing agency is brought in, this knowledge and the established processes are lost and the new service provider has to start all over again – a problem experienced by DfID in Sierra Leone at each of the transition points in its programming.

This stands in contrast to the experience of IMATT, for example. Overall, it must be noted that a one-to-one comparison between IMATT and DfID is ultimately misleading, because comparing poverty reduction, broadly speaking, with a targeted focus on defence-sector transformation ignores the fundamental differences between the two processes. However, the fact that IMATT did not change its overall structure, mandate, strategic direction or name – despite changes to its size, approach and direction of activities – yielded stability in the way in which support was provided, and indeed received. IMATT was a 'known entity' to Sierra Leone's executive up until it transitioned into ISAT in April 2013.

A key lesson for upstreaming in this regard is that a timeframe of programming that runs over the course of more than a decade has obvious benefits. It takes seriously the fact that institutional transformation is a

---

[58] Garth Glentworth et al., 'Sierra Leone: Transition Priorities in the Move from the "Justice and Security Development Programme" to the "Access to Security and Justice Programme"', 2011, unpublished, p. vi.

process that can only take place in the medium-to-long term. Furthermore, from a programme-management perspective, it provides stability for institutional relations to build and stabilise over time, which in turn widens the space for positive change to occur. However, while such a long-term commitment has a number of benefits, it is unlikely that it will become the norm. Therefore, the transitions between programmes must be given more careful attention, particularly as new aims, approaches and implementers are involved.

Conclusion

The notion of upstream conflict prevention arose from the UK government's stabilisation efforts in Afghanistan and Iraq. Limitations on the ability to engage in state-building and development interventions simultaneously during conflict were identified as a problem that should be addressed.[59] Out of this grew a stronger focus on conflict prevention as opposed to stabilisation. In short, and as laid out in the UK government's 2011 Building Stability Overseas Strategy, this meant 'helping to build strong, legitimate institutions and robust societies in fragile countries … so there is a lower likelihood of instability and conflict'.[60] At the heart of upstream conflict prevention lays the rationale that international interventions must go beyond military engagement and involve a stronger element of diplomatic efforts and development expertise. This is not a fundamentally new approach, and as this chapter – and the Whitehall Paper – suggests, this tripartite approach lay at the very foundation of the UK's intervention in Sierra Leone, especially in the late 1990s and early 2000s.

Upstreaming articulates a number of principles that have been developed through a decade-long learning process, and which are commonly accepted in the donor community, including the need for context sensitivity, as well as a holistic and a people-centred approach.[61] To take one example, the imperative of understanding the context is an overriding principle when designing external interventions. However, while the UK certainly reacted to the context in Sierra Leone in the late 1990s, it did so by promoting the liberal-democratic bureaucratic state, which was a reflection of its own political system, rather than that which had existed in the recipient nation prior to the war. As the analysis in the

---

59 Allouche, 'Building Stability Overseas'.

60 HM Government, *Securing Britain in an Age of Uncertainty*, p. 18.

61 Laurie Nathan, *No Ownership, No Commitment: A Guide to Local Ownership of Security Sector Reform* (Birmingham: University of Birmingham, 2007); OECD, *Handbook on Security Sector Reform* (Paris: Organisation for Economic Cooperation and Development, 2007); Lisa Denney, 'Overcoming the State/Non-State Divide: An End User Approach to Security and Justice Reform', *International Peacekeeping* (Vol. 21, No. 2, 2014), pp. 251–68.

preceding chapters has shown, the neo-patrimonial system of governance that was a contributing factor to the outbreak of war in 1991 persists. While this does not bring into question Sierra Leone's SSR process as a whole, it should lead to more careful consideration about how such systems – arguably now a driver of potential conflict in Sierra Leone – might be engaged with more effectively in the future through greater context sensitivity.[62]

The bottom line is that all external interventions – whether in prevention of or in the aftermath of conflict – must incorporate flexibility and pragmatism, as well as intelligence and knowledge of the dynamics that drive both conflict and positive change in a particular setting. Conflicts are rarely spontaneous and are usually the result of extant dynamics and long-term tensions within a society, including a lack of access to economic opportunities or the dearth of political representation of some sectors of society, oppressive or incompetent government, or underlying issues of identity that may be linked to unequal and poor access to services. The aim of the policy of upstreaming is to address these issues so that a society is capable of resolving political, economic and social conflicts that arise without resorting to violence. Policy-makers as well as practitioners would benefit from looking back at the Sierra Leone SSR process to learn more about the building blocks of this new policy.

[62] See Denney, *Justice and Security Reform* for an elaborate discussion of this issue, specifically with respect to DfID's security and justice programming in the past decade.

VI. CONCLUSION: LEARNING FROM SSR IN SIERRA LEONE

As this Whitehall Paper was being written, the Ebola crisis in West Africa – notably in Sierra Leone, Guinea and Liberia – was growing, with 8,000 people contracting the disease and 3,800 dying by October 2014.[1] On 10 October, Sierra Leone recorded its highest official number of deaths in one day to date, at 140.[2] Indeed, at this stage, as David Miliband, former British foreign secretary, noted on a recent visit to Sierra Leone: 'We are at an absolute tipping point where either the disease is contained to the low tens of thousands or it becomes an epidemic of a very serious kind'.[3] There is little doubt that the country is experiencing the worst crisis since the conflict officially came to an end in January 2002. It is clear that while the governments of the region are unable to deal with the crisis without external support,[4] the emergency will also be a fundamental test of the region's stability. Certainly, the Ebola epidemic has the potential to undermine the genuine progress that has been made in the security sector – the focus of this Whitehall Paper – as well as in the economic sphere.

In this study, the programmes that have come collectively to constitute security-sector reform (SSR) in Sierra Leone have been the starting point. The Whitehall Paper has reflected upon how they unfolded since the late 1990s and with what outcomes. The central assumption of much of the initial programming was that re-establishing state institutions was vital, whereas later programming, particularly that led by DfID, focused more on the locally oriented, demand-driven needs of the population, particularly in the justice sector. Such changes in

[1] *New York Times*, 'Ebola Facts: How Many Patients Are Being Treated Outside of West Africa?', 12 October 2014.

[2] Stephen Douglas, 'Ebola: Sierra Leone is Fighting a War Against an Unseen, Proliferating Virus', *Guardian*, 12 October 2014.

[3] Sarah Boseley, 'Ebola: "We're at an Absolute Tipping Point", Warns David Miliband', *Guardian*, 9 October 2014.

[4] Adam Nossiter, 'Officials Admit a "Defeat" by Ebola in Sierra Leone', *New York Times*, 10 October 2014.

programming both reflect and combine with the evolving policy environment within the UK and internationally, as well as the shifting political context in Sierra Leone.

The value of taking a long-term view of the Sierra Leonean experience is that it can serve as an example to other countries undergoing similar transitions, exposing the implications over time of specific decisions and the ways in which programming evolved on the basis of those decisions. It is also clear, however, that the genuine achievements of SSR in Sierra Leone cannot be analysed in isolation from the changing context in which they took place. In that respect, there are three main points to take into account.

First, as has been emphasised throughout this study, the pre-9/11 international environment, in which support to Sierra Leone began, enabled the UK to combine diplomatic, defence and development instruments simultaneously and on an equal footing. In the US-led interventions that followed 9/11 in Afghanistan and Iraq, this balance was fundamentally disrupted in favour of an unambiguously militarised approach.

Second, it is worth highlighting the short time it took to stabilise Sierra Leone, occurring between Operation *Palliser* in May 2000 and Operation *Silkman* in November that same year when the build-up of IMATT was initiated. Again, compared to Afghanistan and Iraq, this is a unique feature to consider as lessons are transferred from Sierra Leone to other contexts. While institution-building was initiated during open conflict, the rapid stabilisation of Sierra Leone allowed longer-term planning and development to take place.

Third, when SSR activities began in Sierra Leone in the late 1990s, state institutions had collapsed. The desperate situation faced by the Kabbah government at the time, in comparison with a common colonial history, led to the UK's engagement and the unusual situation in which one country became the largest single donor of support, including to the country's security sector. Combined, these three factors lie at the very heart of the Sierra Leonean experience between 1997 and 2013, and set it apart not only from Afghanistan and Iraq, but also from the ongoing conflicts in Syria, Somalia and Libya.

UK support should be credited with facilitating the stabilisation and emergence of a peaceful Sierra Leone and with laying the foundation of a recognisable centre of government. Exploring this process within a relatively long timeframe, and with the advantage of hindsight, it is also clear that some decisions proved more problematic than others. One example is the limited engagement with the justice sector at an early stage. Similarly, it is worth emphasising that the Sierra Leonean Ministry of Defence (MoD), Office of National Security (ONS) and Central Intelligence and Security Unit (CISU) are today under considerable political pressure from the country's executive, which may undermine these institutions. This is not to be critical of their establishment in the first place, as there are always reasons why particular decisions are made at certain times. Indeed, it has been one of the aims of this Whitehall Paper to elaborate on the context in which decisions were taken, beginning with a dearth of information on which to act, collapsed state institutions, widespread insecurity and an environment characterised by persistent threats to the central government.

Carrying out a long-term review of this nature also makes it possible to obtain a clear picture of the politics behind particular decisions and the exact way in which those politics unfolded and shaped what was possible at a given time. As alluded to above, and as the structure of this Whitehall Paper implies, the most significant recent development within Sierra Leone's security sector was its gradual politicisation following the general election of 2007, and the transition between the Sierra Leone People's Party (SLPP) government and that of the All People's Congress (APC). This is not to say that under continuing SLPP rule some elements of the security services would not have been politicised as UK advisers and funding were gradually withdrawn. It was clear, however, that the APC's view of the SLPP's record, and the former's general mistrust of institutions associated with the latter, affected how security and justice institutions were approached after 2007.

The remainder of the conclusion explores some of the key lessons of the past two decades of support to Sierra Leone's security and justice institutions. First, it analyses the underlying rationale of SSR, driven by the notion of a liberal-democratic state – or more vaguely, a centrally governed state – and the implications of this approach. This constitutes a considerable, and as yet unresolved, weakness of international interventions. Following from this, the chapter delves into one dimension of the SSR process which is inevitably, and fundamentally, a weak point of transformation: the transitions between conflict and long-term development, and between programmes and between governments – and the impact they had on the overall SSR process in Sierra Leone.

What Sierra Leone Tells Us about SSR Interventions

There are a number of broad lessons that can be derived from Sierra Leone's SSR process between 1997 and 2013. They are recognisable in other contexts of stabilisation, post-conflict reconstruction and long-term development, and they represent key stumbling blocks of any externally supported or driven state-building effort to which there are no clear-cut solutions. As such, they are lessons that have been identified, but which must be incorporated into programming and dealt with on a case-by-case basis.

First, it is clear that an exclusive focus on the technical aspects of SSR or the application of a 'one size fits all' (or 'blueprint') approach to international interventions fails to take adequate account of differences in context.[5] In Sierra Leone, the lack of planning that arose from the need for rapid decision-making and intervention in the late 1990s and early 2000s had the unintended advantage that many key decisions were made in Freetown rather than in London. This meant that programme advisers on the ground, with some understanding of the rapidly changing and unpredictable environment, were empowered rather than controlled by strategic planning concerns in Whitehall.

State-building and SSR must be based on a thorough understanding of power relations and dynamics in environments that are transitioning out of conflict (as suggested in Chapter V, a politically informed approach remains one of the pillars of upstream conflict prevention, the UK government's policy approach outlined in the 2010 Strategic Defence and Security Review). In practice, however, there is a gulf between the *aspiration* for a genuine understanding of contextual factors on the one hand and the *implementation* of a programme that is appropriate or tailored to the context on the other. A case in point is the neo-patrimonial logic that remains a guiding principle of governance in Sierra Leone.[6] It may have been momentarily and locally suppressed, for instance within the MoD, but it was never fundamentally tackled within Sierra Leone's state system as a whole. Many advisers were keenly aware of this logic and its practical implications for what they were trying to achieve. However, they were ultimately unable to address it, because it would have led to confrontation and, potentially, the isolation of the individual adviser. Moreover, even if advisers had addressed it consistently, it is unclear whether this would have had a fundamentally transformative impact. The predicament is, of course, that if contextual knowledge is not used to shape programming, this will have a negative impact on the efficacy of institution-building, if not in the present, then in the medium term. As political dynamics change and as international support and presence dwindle, this is likely to be the outcome.

---

[5] Erwin van Veen and Megan Price, 'Securing its Success, Justifying its Relevance: Mapping a Way Forward for Security Sector Reform', CRU Policy Brief, Clingendael, August 2014; Louise Riis Andersen, 'Security Sector Reform and the Dilemmas of Liberal Peacebuilding', *DIIS Working Paper* 2011:31, Copenhagen, 2011.

[6] Peter Albrecht, 'How Power Works in Sierra Leone', in Steen Andersen et al. (eds), *Developing Architecture: Learning From Sierra Leone* (Copenhagen: Arkitekter Uden Grænser and Forlaget PB43, 2013).

An external intervention that builds up potentially powerful national structures increases the power of those who run those structures and, possibly, their successors. This was another point that was very well understood in Sierra Leone. However, precisely how to condition and reorient the political dynamics as an integral part of programming was not or could not be adequately addressed by the UK. Across the security sector, this became apparent in the transition from the SLPP to the APC governments in 2007, when the politicisation of the security sector was fortified. It also transpired forcefully in the transition between the two DfID-funded programmes, the Justice Sector Development Programme (JSDP) and the Access to Security and Justice Programme (ASJP) in 2011–12, when DfID was not able to ensure a smooth transfer, partly because political interests got in the way. This latter case exposed further the reality that the legitimate dispensation of justice remains contested, representing its own source of power for national as well as local actors, a problem to which there was ultimately no response from the international community.

Second, and related to the above point, important questions arise about whether programming is targeted at national (government) or local (popular) ownership.[7] A central issue is how external engagement should incorporate those who might operate outside the boundaries of formal – and, to international advisers, recognisable – state institutions, but who nonetheless play a considerable role as local centres of power *vis-à-vis* the general population. Paramount and lesser chiefs that represent this stratum of Sierra Leonean governance structures were always the weak point or, more accurately, a point of confusion in Sierra Leone's SSR programming that until now has not been adequately addressed.[8] This conundrum raises questions about how far to incorporate local definitions of, and approaches to, security and justice provision into programming. They tend to be far more subjective and, more importantly in the eyes of the donor community, contravene international best practices.[9] These

---

[7] Eirin Mobekk, 'Security Sector Reform and the Challenges of Ownership', in Mark Sedra (ed.), *The Future of Security Sector Reform* (Ontario: Centre for Governance Innovation, 2010), pp. 230–43.

[8] On discussions of paramount and lesser chiefs in Sierra Leone, see Richard Fanthorpe, 'Neither Citizen nor Subject? "Lumpen" Agency and the Legacy of Native Administration in Sierra Leone', *African Affairs* (Vol. 100, No. 400, 2001), pp. 363–86; Paul Jackson, 'Chiefs, Money and Politicians: Rebuilding Local Government in Sierra Leone', *Public Administration and Development* (Vol. 25, 2005), pp. 49–58. Specifically on chiefs' role in security and justice provision, see Lisa Denney, *Justice and Security Reform: Development Agencies and Informal Institutions in Sierra Leone* (Oxford and New York, NY: Routledge, 2014).

[9] Peter Albrecht et al. (eds), *Perspectives on Involving Non-State and Customary Actors in Justice and Security Reform* (Rome and Copenhagen: International Development Law Organization and Danish Institute for International Studies, 2011); Peter Albrecht and Helene Maria Kyed, 'Justice and Security: When the State

discussions relate to the conceptualisation and interpretation of human rights *vis-à-vis* local justice systems, for example, and there may indeed be a fundamental incompatibility between local ideas of justice and international human-rights standards. It is clear from the preceding chapters of this Whitehall Paper that most international resources were invested in reforms of formal state institutions, based on a liberal-democratic, state-centric model of law and bureaucracy. It is by extension also a core argument of the study that this outlook limits donors' ability to engage with diverse sets of organisations and with alternative notions and practices of security and justice. As recently outlined by Lisa Denney in her book on DfID's security and justice programming in Sierra Leone:[10]

> While poor governance and injustice were key features of the breakdown [of Sierra Leone], these failings were not only of the state but also of informal structures such as the chieftaincy system, which was perceived as having held in place many of the injustices that the RUF [Revolutionary United Front] rebelled against. The problem, then, is not the 'failure' aspect of DFID's understanding of the causes of war, but the 'state' component.

Traditional leaders, and their integral role as figures of authority at the local level, were excluded, particularly from the early stages of the SSR process. They were incorporated into the JSDP and have become a central component of its successor, the ASJP, which seeks to clarify the role of chiefs in the provision of security and justice. At the time of writing, the ASJP is in the process of implementation, and it is therefore not possible to assess the programme accurately. Generally speaking, however, there is still a lot to learn about how to accommodate forms of authority that fit uneasily with the centrally governed state model, and as Kellie Conteh, Sierra Leone's former national security co-ordinator noted in 2008: 'I think they [international actors] should help to strengthen chieftaincies because our people, whether you like it or not, for now seem to respect that traditional setting'. Indeed, Conteh continued:[11]

> We should not undermine the authority of the chiefs by trying to introduce several layers of governance within the chiefdoms. At the end of the day it would only hurt government, because we would not have the capacity to do it properly. We simply don't. Let's not make ourselves look stupid on this matter. Let's go back to basics.

---

isn't the Main Provider', *DIIS Policy Brief*, Copenhagen, December 2010; Bruce Baker, 'The Future is Non-State', in Sedra (ed.), *The Future of Security Sector Reform*.

[10] Denney, *Justice and Security Reform*, p. 65. See also Peter Albrecht and Paul Jackson, 'State-Building through Security Sector Reform: The UK Intervention in Sierra Leone', *Peacebuilding* (Vol. 2, No. 1, 2014), pp. 83–99.

[11] Conteh quoted in Peter Albrecht, *Foundational Hybridity and its Reproduction: Security Sector Reform in Sierra Leone*, PhD Series, 33.2012 (Copenhagen: Copenhagen Business School, 2012), p. 127.

Third, the UK took a clear lead in the international intervention in Sierra Leone, which gave it unique access to the higher echelons of the country's government. Initially, the UK benefited from a set of executive powers vested in the inspector-general of police, because between 1999 and 2003 the position was filled by a former UK police officer, while the commander of the International Military Advisory and Training Team (IMATT) for many years served as the primary military adviser to the president. On the basis of this unusual bilateral relationship, the two governments re-established a defence system, internal security and justice providers, a security governance system and an intelligence agency. However, as this Whitehall Paper has also outlined, the challenges have been substantial. This raises two fundamental questions about what can be achieved through state-building, the answers to which require a sense of realism and of humility. The first question is to what extent state-building is feasible in contexts that are equally complex, considerably bigger in scale, and where conflict is entrenched to a greater degree than in Sierra Leone in the late 1990s. Second, is the issue of time required for state-building and the point at which sustainability has been reached. After almost two decades of support by the UK and the international community, this remains an open question in Sierra Leone. This is not necessarily an indictment of the SSR process, but it does confirm the fact that institution-building – and, ultimately, social transformation – only occurs over decades, often unpredictably, never in a linear manner, and always partly if not predominantly outside international control.

Choosing the Appropriate State Model

There is no doubt that the state model upon which Sierra Leone was re-established to defend its borders and provide internal security and justice reflected external actors' experience of how order should be constituted and managed. As discussed in Chapter V, this was driven by ideological convictions regarding the superiority of the liberal-democratic state model,[12] as well as the domestic political agendas and bureaucratic

[12] Roland Paris wrote an article in 1997 outlining an underlying rationale of state-building that is still relevant today: 'A single paradigm – liberal internationalism – appears to guide the work of most international agencies engaged in peacebuilding. The central tenet of this paradigm is the assumption that the surest foundation for peace, both within and between states, is market democracy, that is, a liberal democratic policy and a market-oriented economy. Peacebuilding is in effect an enormous experiment in social engineering – an experiment that involves transplanting Western models of social, political, and economic organization into war-shattered states in order to control civil conflict'. Roland Paris, 'Peacebuilding and the Limits of Liberal Internationalism', *International Security* (Vol. 22, No. 2, 1997), pp. 54–89, 56.

practices in the home countries of those who led the intervention.[13] As such, there is certainly some truth to the basic notion that 'local ownership clearly means "their" ownership of "our" ideas'.[14]

Needless to say, not all within the Sierra Leonean state system at the time accepted the direction of travel pegged out by the UK and other international actors. However, it was also clear that those who did not sign up to it were considered spoilers by UK advisers and were subsequently marginalised, including, most famously, Samuel Hinga Norman, the politician from the Mende tribe who played a key role in bringing an end to the civil war. While he led the mobilisation of the Civil Defence Forces (CDF), a southern-based militia that supported the Sierra Leone government in the fight against the Revolutionary United Front (RUF), and became deputy minister of defence between 1998 and 2002, he was also indicted on 7 March 2003 at Sierra Leone's Special Court for violations committed by the CDF in the 1990s.[15] 'The case has been controversial', the BBC commented in 2007, 'as some saw the Civil Defence Force[s] (CDF) as defending civilians against the rebels during the conflict that ended in 2002'.[16]

There were other, lesser-known individuals who resisted what was put on offer by the UK and the international community, and who were marginalised in more subtle ways – for example, by being sent abroad on study trips. In addition, given that ten years of war had passed, Sierra Leone had inevitably suffered from the fact that many of those who were well-educated had fled the country (a common phenomenon in countries blighted by conflict). It therefore ended up being a relatively small number of individuals who took the lead on SSR within the Sierra Leone government. This did not mean that a broad spectrum of those involved in the reconstruction process were not keen on reconstituting a functioning centre of government – that is, a state in which powers over Sierra Leone's territory were (to some degree) concentrated in State House.[17] However, in hindsight, there is certainly reason to question why

[13] David Mosse, 'Global Governance and the Ethnography of International Aid', in David Moss and David Lewis (eds), *The Aid Effect: Giving and Governing in International Development* (London: Pluto Press, 2005), pp. 1–36; Francis Fukuyama, *State-Building: Governance and World Order in the 21st Century* (Ithaca, NY: Cornell University Press, 2004).

[14] Astri Suhrke, 'Reconstruction as Modernisation: The "Post-Conflict" Project in Afghanistan', *Third World Quarterly* (Vol. 28, No. 7, 2007), pp. 1291–308.

[15] Norman was indicted while he served as minister of internal affairs (2002–04).

[16] *BBC News*, 'S Leone Leaders Convicted', 2 August 2007.

[17] Osman Gbla, 'Security Sector Reform and the Sustainability of Peace and Democracy in Sierra Leone', *Journal of Social Sciences and Management* (Vol. 1, No. 1, 2007); Roland Paris, *At War's End: Building Peace after Civil Conflict* (Cambridge: Cambridge University Press, 2004); Roland Paris, 'Saving Liberal Peacebuilding', *Review of International Studies* (Vol. 36, No. 2, 2010), pp. 337–65; Roland Paris and Timothy D Sisk (eds), *The Dilemmas of Statebuilding:*

centralisation of power in Freetown has been pursued, to what end and with what effect.

These considerations raise the question of national ownership within post-conflict governments.[18] More specifically, they raise questions about who the national owners are as well as the ability of a newly established central government to fundamentally transform popular perceptions of 'the state'. This is particularly pertinent to Sierra Leone given that the state and those representing it in many parts of the country were seen as exploitative before the war, and unable to efficiently protect the population against the RUF during the conflict.[19] Beyond Freetown, among the general population, there certainly was ambivalence towards the chiefs and hostility towards the Sierra Leone Police (SLP), the armed forces and the state more generally.[20]

The degree of responsibility on the part of external actors to move the process forward, local ambiguity and hostility to the central state, and the absence of clear alternatives in turn placed considerable pressure on the reform (or reconstruction) process as a whole. It has been noted above that actors on the ground were given the authority from London to shape responses as events unfolded. However, it was also the case that the advisers who carried out SSR activities had no alternative to the centrally

---

Confronting the Contradictions of Postwar Peace Operations (Abingdon and New York, NY: Routledge, 2009).

[18] National ownership is commonly heralded as a cornerstone of SSR: for instance, in May 2008 the UN Security Council stated that SSR 'should be a nationally owned process that is rooted in the particular needs and conditions of the country in question'. UN Security Council, 'Statement by the President of the Security Council', S/PRST/2008/14, 12 May 2008, p. 1. However, as Luc van de Goor and Erwin van Veen note, '"national ownership" is more likely to take on significance in "regular" developing countries. This does not imply that there cannot be national ownership in post-conflict countries … [but it] is likely that more developed countries have the local capacity to organize supply and demand, an essential step in ensuring that SSR can become sustainable'. Luc van de Goor and Erwin van Veen, 'Less Post-Conflict, Less Whole of Government and More Geopolitics?', in Sedra (ed.), *The Future of Security Sector Reform*, pp. 88–101, 92. See also Timothy Donais (ed.), *Local Ownership and Security Sector Reform* (Zurich: Geneva Centre for the Democratic Control of Armed Forces and LIT Verlag, 2008).

[19] William Reno, *Corruption and State Politics in Sierra Leone* (Cambridge: Cambridge University Press, 1996); Paul Richards, *Fighting for the Rain Forest: War, Youth and Resources in Sierra Leone* (Oxford: International African Institute/ James Currey, 1996).

[20] Paul Jackson, 'Reshuffling an Old Deck of Cards?', *African Affairs* (Vol. 106, No. 422, 2007); Rosalind Hanson-Alp, 'Civil Society's Role in Sierra Leone's Security Sector Reform Process: Experiences from Conciliation Resources West Africa Programme', in Peter Albrecht and Paul Jackson (eds), *Security Sector Reform in Sierra Leone 1997–2007: Views from the Front Line* (Zurich: Geneva Centre for the Democratic Control of Armed Forces and LIT Verlag, 2010), pp. 183–206.

governed liberal-democratic state model. By extension, donors and those who were tasked with implementing their policies became reliant on their own experience and convictions in driving the process forward.

The human factor becomes particularly important in this respect. There is often considerable pressure on advisers operating in an environment that they do not fully understand to create results by implementing institutions and procedures according to headquarters' conceptions of success. Indeed, such is the weight of external expectations that programme implementers can feel pressurised to side-step democratic processes that they themselves are supporting. In turn, this means that even if there is will, there is still very little space for thinking about new types of security and justice arrangements that are not built up around the centralised liberal-democratic state model, and the checks and balances that this model (ideally) entails.[21] This reality can be seen in the UK's efforts to underscore the legitimacy of providing support to a small number of security and justice institutions in Sierra Leone, and notably to those that could be clearly identified with a centrally governed state. This point partly relates to what has been referred to as 'conscious ignorance' by an adviser who served in Sierra Leone in the early 2000s: 'Simply because some options are too difficult, the easier ones are preferred and mistakes are repeated'.[22]

Perhaps the attempt to export a Western understanding of statehood through international intervention is the best that can be hoped for, since one cannot expect advisers to develop and implement models of political order that they are not familiar with. If so, assessments of what can be achieved through state-building need to be improved, and there needs to be a better understanding of what 'less-than-perfect' success entails.[23] In the early stages of the UK intervention advisers had to deal with constant unpredictability. As described in detail in Chapter I and further developed in Chapter II, what had started out as a routine evacuation mission quickly turned into small-scale war-fighting. This was a reaction to circumstances. There was not much time available to plan for a detailed intervention or for post-conflict reconstruction. Even the longer-term involvement that *had* been initiated, such as the work started in 1999 inside the Sierra Leonean MoD and ONS, was overtaken by events as advisers found themselves involved in war-fighting and institution-building simultaneously. It is also worth keeping in mind that the MoD that was

---

[21] Peter Albrecht and Lars Buur, 'An Uneasy Marriage: Non-State Actors and Police Reform', *Policing and Society* (Vol. 19, No. 4, 2009), pp. 390–405, 399.
[22] Quoted in *ibid.*, pp. 399–400.
[23] Louise Riis Andersen and Peter Emil Engedal, 'Blue Helmets and Grey Zones: Do UN Multidimensional Peace Operations Work?', *DIIS Report* 2013:29, Copenhagen, 2013.

envisioned for Sierra Leone was modelled on the UK experience, and the division between national security co-ordination and intelligence collection, for instance, reflected a British experience of best practices.

The reflections in this section challenge state-building as a concept, as policy and as a set of practices. They also provide valuable lessons to be considered and incorporated by other countries negotiating similar transitions. Above all, they urge realism about the time such processes take, and what can be achieved through state-building.

Transitions

The Sierra Leonean experience provides another set of abiding lessons: the importance of transitions and how they are managed. This dimension of any process of change requires careful consideration, in implementation and in policy. The lengthy duration of UK involvement in the security and justice sector in Sierra Leone provides a unique opportunity to examine the evolution of support and, in particular, to explore the way in which different contexts, changeovers of staff and transitions between political leaders have been managed.

From Conflict to Development

The first major transition to be managed in the case of Sierra Leone was that from conflict to post-conflict, and then to a context of development. This is not to say that today there is no chance of relapse into conflict in Sierra Leone, but the UK departments involved have at different times discussed when the country transitioned from a post-conflict phase and the implications of this for programming. In the case of DfID, for instance, this process began immediately after conflict officially ended in January 2002 and the design of the JSDP began. In the case of IMATT the 2012 election, and IMATT's subsequent transition into the International Security Advisory Team (ISAT) in 2013, were seen as clear indications that Sierra Leone had stepped onto the path of long-term development (although it should be noted that the initial discussion about a potential ISAT had begun as early as 2006).

Most of the early interventions in the sector were driven by a context in which there was ongoing conflict or a significant risk of a return to conflict. As such, the emphasis of the support provided was (quite rightly) on hard security. The UK concentrated on reconstructing the armed forces and a police system that could maintain internal security.[24]

[24] Peter Alexander Albrecht, 'Transforming Internal Security in Sierra Leone: Sierra Leone Police and Broader Justice Sector Reform', *DIIS Report* 2010:07, Copenhagen, 2010; Peter Albrecht et al., 'Community Policing in Sierra Leone – Local Policing Partnership Boards', *DIIS Report* 2014:16, Copenhagen, 2014.

Thus the creation or rebuilding of institutions like the army, the police's Operational Support Division (OSD) and the ONS were informed by a particular set of circumstances, above all the need to restrain the army from political involvement and to win a war. The three organisations' transitions to peaceful activity have not been equally smooth. Whereas the Republic of Sierra Leone Armed Forces (RSLAF) have been able to partially reinvent themselves as an international peacekeeping force, making contributions in Darfur and Somalia, the ONS may increasingly be regarded by some within the Sierra Leone government as being better-suited to stabilisation than to a development context. As noted in Chapter IV, this is partly because of personnel changes over this period, as well as financial and political sustainability issues. However, it is also because there is a sense within the wider Sierra Leonean civil service that the security sector reaped disproportionate benefit from the UK's strong focus on supporting security institutions.

Probably the most difficult transition in this area has occurred within the SLP, and specifically within the OSD. The very concept of the OSD was controversial as its legitimacy was drawn from its engagement in combat operations against the RUF, rather than from its effectiveness in policing before the war. Today, the OSD remains a coercive instrument, an armed paramilitary unit based around a pre-war unit with a chequered record. Indeed, in 2014, it was concluded that the relationship between the OSD and the rest of the SLP was that of between two separate organisations. While the official command structure dictates that the OSD is a support unit of the broader SLP, it is the assistant inspector-general – and not the inspector-general of police – who is in charge of the OSD and thus has the final say in its use. As such, the OSD has separate operational priorities, lines of communication, chains of command and recruitment processes.

The OSD remains a key political risk and was shown to be susceptible to pressure with regard to politicised recruitment from the incoming Koroma government in 2007 (it is to the credit of the OSD, and also the SLP more broadly, that it has managed to dispense with some of these recruits from 2010 and to train others correctly, a process that was initiated in early 2014).[25] Such politicisation will remain a risk. If the OSD continues to assume the same combat-based role as it performed under previous regimes and during the war, only with better weapons and training, then the risk is that the government's control of senior officers

[25] It is worth pointing out, however, that following presidential tasking, the SLP withdrew a large proportion of the OSD recruits undergoing general training. They were deployed in Freetown to help address the issue of motorcyclists in the central business district. These recruits had undergone OSD training, and while they were deployed without firearms, they were equipped with batons.

will diminish, weapons will be used when they should not be, and overall standards of policing will drop.

There were good reasons for establishing both the ONS and the OSD during a period when winning a war and stabilising the country were the all-important priorities, and there is no doubt that both continue to have a role to play in a peaceful Sierra Leone. As this section suggests, however, it is also important to plan carefully how the transition of such organisations is made as a country evolves from conflict to a post-conflict state, and ultimately onto a path of development. Long-term strategic planning into peacetime is challenging and may even be impossible while conflict continues. However, it is inevitable that certain institutions, and particularly security-sector institutions, will have less of a role or at least a very different role to play once conflict is over.

From Team to Team: The UK and Sierra Leone

Another critical set of transitions concerned the changeover between individuals and teams engaged in SSR in Sierra Leone. Prior to 2007, the UK deliberately built a team of Sierra Leonean specialists who largely remained in place for well over a decade. This group, which incorporated key individuals like the national security co-ordinator, the inspector-general of police and several other senior SLP officers, as well as a group of senior civil servants and military personnel, were critical in maintaining continuity during a period in which the commander of IMATT changed frequently, as did DfID, UK MoD and Foreign Office staff – all according to different employment cycles within their respective departments. Whilst there was a group of long-serving UK advisers who remained in post for several years, particularly in the police and to a degree within the DfID-led Sierra Leone Security Sector Reform Programme (SILSEP), the institutional memory of SSR in the country was thus in large part held by Sierra Leoneans.

This meant in practice that the network of relationships between the UK advisers and their Sierra Leonean partners was uneven and consisted of a mixture of long-term, committed partnerships alongside short-term efforts undertaken by personnel with only limited institutional memory of reform (and at times limited technical expertise with respect to SSR, but nevertheless with decision-making power over related programming). The most effective of these relationships were valued by Sierra Leoneans and led to deep-seated reform and cultural change in organisations like the ONS. One of the achievements of UK-led SSR throughout this period was that, at any given time, it kept enough people on the ground who were committed to the process and who also knew the local actors and the local context. Where this did not occur – for instance, between the three programme cycles that constituted support to the police and the broader justice sector between 1999 and the present day – it had considerable consequences for the incoming programme in terms of ensuring a smooth transition.

After 2007, this gradually changed in several specific ways, notably in terms of the make-up of the Sierra Leonean team, but also in terms of the UK's management of the process.

Following the change in government in 2007, several of the senior Sierra Leonean staff who had been involved in the SSR process over the long term left their positions. The national security co-ordinator who led the ONS until 2012 was replaced, as was the head of CISU in 2010. Some were promoted, some retired and some became consultants for DfID-funded programmes and the UN elsewhere (several, in fact, contributed to SSR-related programming in South Sudan and Somalia). It was clear that many had stayed in their positions in Sierra Leone with the intention of moving on after a peaceful election had taken place.

One of the lessons drawn from this is that transitions between international advisers and national security professionals were important and notably sensitive points in Sierra Leone's SSR process. With many of those who held the institutional memory of SSR leaving their positions, the pressure was on the UK, a key player in the process, to ease the transition.

However, in this same period, while the UK team continued its support, there was also a breakdown in commitment to the overall aims of SSR as a consequence of the country's changing priorities. This was reflected in DfID's switch of focus from SSR to an approach based around 'security and justice', and more 'traditional' development activities – a decision which was interpreted by the Foreign Office and the UK MoD as unilateral and unexpected. At the same time, there was an internal transition within DfID from implementing reactive and flexible programmes designed to cope with the uncertainties of a post-conflict context (such as SILSEP) to more regular programming, with associated bureaucracy and accountability mechanisms that were entirely divorced from the Sierra Leonean context.

Political Party to Political Party: The SLPP and the APC

One of the main points of this Whitehall Paper is that 2007 marked a watershed for SSR in Sierra Leone. The transition from a SLPP to an APC-led government precipitated a political transition from a political party that had been instrumental in reconstructing the security sector and government to another political party that distrusted much of what its predecessor in government had achieved and some of the key individuals who had been involved. The election was a triumph in that it was a peaceful political transition. However, the actions of the incoming government have inevitably raised a number of questions relating to the politicisation of the security sector.

The issue at stake is risk, particularly with respect to appointments to organisations like the ONS and OSD, which have experienced politicised recruitment at the top as well as among the rank and file. There are therefore wider lessons to be drawn from the change of government in Sierra Leone, including by the UK, on the best way to deal with such transitions. It may be argued that the political dimension of programming should be boosted in the immediate aftermath of elections – and especially when the government ushered in has not been involved in the establishment of security institutions, and which therefore may not trust them or fully understand their purpose. As such, peaceful elections may represent a democratic triumph, but they are also a particularly sensitive moment in time when institutional consolidation should be supported rather than taken for granted.

As such, the failure to invest sufficiently in supporting the transition between two governments or the withdrawal of financial or technical support following a successful election may prove counterproductive. Indeed, it may increase the risk of new political actors attempting to harness the coercive instruments of the state to their own ends. In the case of Sierra Leone, as with a number of other African states, it was the politicisation of actors within the security sector, such as the OSD's predecessor, that contributed to the outbreak of conflict in the first place.

The final point to be emphasised in this conclusion is that the change of government in Sierra Leone in 2007 symbolised a fundamental change in priorities, which had been underway for some time. Security had been a key priority within the SLPP-led 2005 Poverty Reduction Strategy Paper (PRSP), a circumstance that was partly driven by the significant levels of funding that had been channelled into the country's security sector.[26] In the case of the APC-led 'Agenda for Change', the second PRSP for the period 2008–12, security was seen as a precondition for development to take place, but not a strategic priority in itself.[27] Similarly, in the 'Agenda for Prosperity', the third PRSP for the period 2013–18, security was seen as a precondition for continued growth, but

---

[26] Barry J Le Grys, 'British Military Involvement in Sierra Leone, 2001–2006', in Albrecht and Jackson (eds), *Security Sector Reform in Sierra Leone 1997–2007*, pp. 39–58.

[27] The three priorities of Sierra Leone's second PRSP were energy, agriculture and transportation. Government of Sierra Leone, *An Agenda for Change: Second Poverty Reduction Strategy (PRSP II), 2008–2012* (Freetown: Government of Sierra Leone, 2008), <http://unipsil.unmissions.org/portals/unipsil/media/publications/agenda_for_change.pdf>, accessed 8 October 2014.

not an end in itself.[28] The reorientation of the Sierra Leone government away from a strategic focus on the security sector, first by the SLPP and subsequently by the APC, may have been interpreted as a loss of interest in security matters. At the same time, the reorientation also reflected a prioritisation of scarce resources within the government.

On that note, one thing is clear: in the end it will be up to Sierra Leone, and *not* to external actors, to decide the direction of travel for the security sector – and for the country as a whole.

---

[28] Government of Sierra Leone, *The Agenda for Prosperity – Road to Middle Income Status: Sierra Leone's Third Generation Poverty Reduction Strategy Paper (2013–2018)* (Freetown: Government of Sierra Leone, 2013), p. 6, <http://www.undp.org/content/dam/sierraleone/docs/projectdocuments/povreduction/undp_sle_The%20Agenda%20for%20Prosperity%20.pdf>, accessed 8 October 2014.

About Whitehall Papers

The *Whitehall Paper* series provides in-depth studies of specific developments, issues or themes in the field of national and international defence and security. Published occasionally throughout the year, *Whitehall Papers* reflect the highest standards of original research and analysis, and are invaluable background material for specialists and policy-makers alike.

About RUSI

The Royal United Services Institute is the UK's leading independent think-tank on international defence and security. Its mission is to be an analytical research-led global forum for informing, influencing and enhancing public debate on a safer and more stable world.

Since its foundation in 1831, RUSI has relied on its members to support its activities. Annual membership subscriptions and donations are a key source of funding for the Institute; together with the revenue from publications and conferences, RUSI has sustained its political independence for over 180 years.

London | Brussels | Nairobi | Doha | Tokyo | Washington, DC